girls
on the
edge

Also by Leonard Sax

Boys Adrift
Why Gender Matters

girls on the edge

The FOUR FACTORS DRIVING
the NEW CRISIS *for* GIRLS

---

sexual identity, the cyberbubble,
obsessions, environmental toxins

Leonard Sax, M.D., Ph.D.

A Member of the Perseus Books Group
New York

BASIC
BOOKS

Published by Basic Books,
A Member of the Perseus Books Group
387 Park Avenue South
New York, NY 10016

Books published by Basic Books are available at special discounts for bulk purchases in the United States by corporations, institutions, and other organizations. For more information, please contact the Special Markets Department at the Perseus Books Group, 2300 Chestnut Street, Suite 200, Philadelphia, PA 19103, or call (800) 255-1514, or e-mail special.markets@perseusbooks.com.

Every effort has been made to secure required permissions to use all images, art, lyrics, and other original material included in this volume.

Designed by Pauline Brown

Library of Congress Cataloging-in-Publication Data

Sax, Leonard.
  Girls on the edge : the four factors driving the new crisis for girls : sexual identity, the cyberbubble, obsessions, environmental toxins / Leonard Sax.
      p. cm.
  Includes bibliographical references and index.
  ISBN 978-0-465-01561-0 (alk. paper)
  1. Girls—Psychology. 2. Girls—Health and hygiene. 3. Gender identity. I. Title.
  HQ777.S29 2010
  305.23082—dc22

                                                            2010003800

10 9 8 7 6 5 4 3 2 1

For my wife, Katie,
and my daughter, Sarah

Dig into yourself . . .
Go into yourself and find out how deep is the place from which your life springs;
at its source you will find the answer to your question . . .

RAINER MARIA RILKE

contents

three girls

---

emily

When Emily[1] was 5 years old, she brought two lifelike miniature gorilla dolls, one big and one small, to kindergarten for show and tell. She used the dolls to explain dominance hierarchies to the other children using terms like "alpha male" and "dominant." Each succeeding year, she was always anxious the first few weeks of school. "I have to make sure the teacher knows I'm smart. It's hard to change first impressions if you say something dumb the first week," she told her Mom when she was in fifth grade. She need not have worried. Emily seldom said anything dumb. The teachers were quick to recognize that Emily was, indeed, the smart one.

Her dream was to be accepted at an Ivy League school, preferably Princeton. "Everybody talks about Harvard, but Princeton is actually more selective," she told her Mom—in ninth grade. Three years later, she was crushed when she was rejected by both Harvard and Princeton. That's when her sense of self began to crumble.

She was accepted at the University of Pennsylvania. She expected that she would be the smartest kid there. But she wasn't, not even close. She found herself struggling just to pass her courses. And that's when the bottom fell out.

melissa

Melissa and Jessica were best friends from way back in kindergarten. "We were like clones," Melissa told me. The two girls liked to wear the same clothes; they read the same books and went wild over the same movies. "We could read each other's minds."

For eight years—from the spring of their kindergarten year right through eighth grade—the girls shared a unique bond. Then in ninth grade, everything changed. Jessica suddenly turned on Melissa. Jessica invited everyone to a party—but not Melissa. Jessica told all her friends not to sit with Melissa at lunch, and to ignore Melissa if she approached. Jessica managed to get the other girls to deploy the full silent treatment. "All of a sudden, I was invisible," Melissa told me.

It really became nasty when Jessica and her co-conspirators began using instant messaging, texting, and social networking sites to harass Melissa 24/7. "It was awful," Melissa said. "I didn't want to turn on my computer or my cell phone. I didn't want to see what they were saying about me. I seriously wished I could just die."

madison

Madison's dream was to be America's Next Top Model. From her ninth birthday until around 13 years of age, Madison was the prettiest girl, and she knew it.

Then something happened with her hormones and the acne came out. Madison's parents told her to be patient and the acne would go away, but it didn't. It got worse. At Madison's request, they went to their family doctor, who prescribed minocycline, but that didn't help. They went to the dermatologist, who wanted to prescribe Accutane. Madison's parents read about the risks of Accutane causing suicidal depression and birth defects. They told Madison absolutely not. A major battle ensued.

That's also when her weight became a problem. At 5'3" tall, she went from 97 pounds to 124 pounds between her 13th and 14th birthdays. She was no longer the cute slender girl with perfect skin. Who was she? She no longer knew. She struggled with clinical depression. So her parents brought her to see me. I prescribed Lexapro, which helped, but caused even more weight gain, so I switched her to Adderall.

Adderall seemed to be a godsend at first. It not only improved her mood but also helped her to get her weight back down to 107 pounds in about eight weeks. But Adderall sometimes made her heart pound so hard she felt as though it would jump right out of her chest. Nevertheless, she pushed for a higher dose. When I refused, she claimed to have lost her pills and needed more.

Madison defined her value in terms of her appearance. She was worth something only if she were cute, and that meant slender with clear skin. Once she no longer fit that ideal, she no longer knew who she was.

"Go into yourself and find out how deep is the place from which your life springs," wrote the German poet Rainer Maria Rilke. If your daughter can develop a sense of self that is deeply rooted, then she will grow up to be a resilient and self-confident woman. Age itself is not the most important factor. I've met a few 11- and 12-year-old girls who have achieved a secure sense of self and retained it through adolescence and into young adulthood. I know many adult women who have never achieved this.

A sense of self is about who you *are*, not about how you look or what kinds of grades you get or who you're friends with. Emily defined herself as the smart kid. Melissa was Jessica's BFF. Madison was the cute one. Take that away, and each girl's sense of self collapsed.

I began writing prescriptions for children in 1984 during my pediatrics rotation at the Children's Hospital of Philadelphia. After earning my MD at the University of Pennsylvania, I completed a three-year residency in family practice at Lancaster General Hospital in Lancaster, Pennsylvania. Then, beginning in 1990, I spent 18 years practicing family medicine in a suburb of Washington, D.C. For 18 years I had the privilege of being a part of the lives of more than a thousand kids, seeing some of them from infancy right into middle school and high school; others I followed from age 10 or 12 into adulthood.

Some of the girls I saw grew up in a secure home with two loving parents. Others grew up in less fortunate circumstances. But circumstances don't seem to matter much when we're talking about a girl's sense of self. I know girls who have been raised by single parents with no money, and yet some of those girls have grown up to be rock-solid and resilient. I know a girl who was raised by loving parents in a comfortable home, yet she was hopeless and suicidal by the age of 14.

Developing a sense of who you are isn't about how much money your parents have. It's not about how you look, what songs you have on your iPod, or how many friends you have on Facebook. It's about connecting with yourself, developing a sense of your own personhood. During my 18 years in that one community, I saw a growing proportion of girls whose sense of self is defined only in terms of superficials. As a result, those girls are brittle, susceptible to a crack-up with even a mild jolt.

This brittleness in girls' self-concept—and the resultant vulnerability to anxiety and depression—is becoming more common. In one study published in 2004, investigators examined the utilization of mental health services by children and teenagers, both girls and boys, in 1999 compared with 1989. They found a more-than-400-percent increase in the use of these services by girls, compared with a 70 percent increase in the use of mental health services by boys over the same time period.[2] More recent research suggests that this growth in the use of psychiatric services continues— with girls' use growing at a faster rate than boys'.[3] Between 1996 and 2005, the proportion of girls and women in the United States taking antidepressant medications roughly doubled, from 7.5 percent to 13.4 percent; more than one in eight females in the United States now takes antidepressant medication.[4]

Boys and girls are both having problems, but they're having different problems. Many of the boys who are being sent to the psychologist or psychiatrist are being referred for problems such as ADHD and oppositional-defiant disorder. The girls are more likely than the boys to be dealing with problems such as anxiety and depression.

In other words: boys often *act out* their problems. Girls are more likely to turn inward, on themselves. As one research team observed, "The increase in depression and anxiety among girls is especially thought-provoking, as prior studies have shown that adolescent girls have generally reported and exhibited more symptoms of depression and anxiety than adolescent boys, and *this gap seems to be increasing*."[5] These researchers also found that the intensity of the problem, as measured by the frequency of visits to a psychiatrist or psychologist, also seems to be increasing faster for girls than for boys.[6]

Jean Twenge, professor of psychology at San Diego State University, has studied the situation in the United States today compared with 40 or 50 years ago. Psychologists have been asking kids pretty much the same questions since the mid-1960s: "Do you ever feel so anxious that you can't concentrate or focus? Do you ever feel so anxious that you can't get to sleep or stay asleep?"[7] Fifty years ago it was unusual for a teenage girl to answer those questions "yes." Back then, the giggly teenage girl was a common stereotype. That stereotype was familiar because there actually were lots of giggly teenage girls in that era.

Not anymore. Professor Twenge finds a continuous rise in the prevalence of anxiety, with girls consistently and significantly more anxious than boys. Part of the reason, Twenge believes, is a change in our culture, a decline in what she and other psychologists have termed *social connectedness.* "Anxiety increases as social bonds weaken," Twenge writes. "Societies with low levels of social integration produce adults prone to anxiety."[8]

Can you generally trust most of the people you encounter in a typical day? In the 1950s and 1960s, most Americans answered that question "yes." Today, most Americans answer that question "no."[9] Forty years ago it was common for a woman to knock on her neighbor's door to borrow a few eggs or a lemon. Today that's a rare occurrence. Psychotherapist Madeline Levine recalls her own childhood: "I can remember the parade of neighbors who stopped by our house for a cup of sugar, a bit of cream, or an extra potato. The idea of trekking over to a neighbor's house when the pantry is short an item or two seems almost laughable now."[10]

The disruption of those social ties disproportionately affects girls and women.[11] What happens when you feel less connected to your neighborhood, less trusting of the people who live next door or down the street? If you're a guy, then maybe you just stay home and spend a few extra hours playing your video games or put some extra time into your fantasy football league. Girls and women seem to need that network of human connection more, so they miss it more when it's not there. Professor Twenge examined the correlation between 16 different indicators and the likelihood that a woman is feeling anxious. She found that lack of social trust is the highest predictor of anxiety—higher than the divorce rate, higher than the unemployment rate, and more important than economic conditions generally.[12]

By many objective standards, girls today should be happier than their grandmothers were at their age. Girls today have choices and opportunities their great-grandmothers would not have dreamed of. College, medical school, law school—50 years ago, those were mostly for men. When my Mom graduated from medical school in Cleveland in 1953, she was one of only two women in her class. Your grandmother probably did not imagine ever becoming a surgeon or an airline pilot or President. Your daughter knows that all these options are possibilities for her. No door is closed to her merely because she is female.

And yet, many girls today are failing to develop an inner life, that sturdy core of personality that their great-grandmothers (in most cases) had in abundance. I don't think you can blame this change on "modern culture," because their brothers don't have this problem.

Their brothers have other problems. This book began in part because I was interested in lazy boys. Beginning in the early 1990s, I saw more and more families from every economic condition where the daughter is hardworking and motivated while her brother is a goofball: he's more concerned about getting to the next level in his video game than he is about getting a good grade on his Spanish final. In 2001 I began visiting schools and communities around the United States as well as in Canada, Mexico, Australia, New Zealand, England, Scotland, Germany, and Spain to get a sense of what is going on. I have talked with the boys, talked with the girls, and listened to their parents and their teachers. I have found that this phenomenon of lazy boys and hardworking girls is pervasive.[13] The years I spent trying to understand what is going on with the boys led me to write my second book, *Boys Adrift*.

Early on, I began to understand that the girls are not the winners in this story. Both the girls and the boys are disadvantaged, but they're disadvantaged in different ways. More and more boys are developing an epicurean ability to enjoy themselves—to enjoy video games, pornography, food, and sleep—but they often don't have the drive and motivation to succeed in the real world outside their bedroom. More and more of their sisters have that drive and motivation in abundance—but they don't know how to relax, how to have fun and enjoy life. For many of these girls, each accomplishment is only a stepping-stone to the next goal.

About five years ago I recognized that the boys' laziness and the girls' obsessive drive are two facets of the same dysfunction. But many of those unmotivated boys are content in their cocoon, with their video games and their online pornography, reassured in their normalcy by the two other guys who hang with them who are just like they are. The girls are more likely to have some insight into their own situation and to know that something is wrong—but they don't know what to do about it.

Not every girl is struggling. Some girls are turning out fine. They are confident but not narcissistic, self-assertive without being self-centered. They know who they are, they know their own strengths and weaknesses, and they are comfortable in their own skin. So why are some girls doing so well while others are having a tough time? Success isn't random. Parents make a difference. Unfortunately, parents with the best intentions may do their daughter little good if they don't understand their daughter's situation. These parents are sometimes bringing a 1980s solution to a 21st-century problem. That's not going to work. The current era has created some girl-specific issues that didn't exist 30 years ago.

In the first part of this book, I will outline the four factors that I believe are putting our daughters at risk. In Chapter 1 I will talk about how our culture is pushing girls to present themselves sexually at earlier ages than ever before. We will see how the affirmation of the sexuality of women in the 1960s (a good thing) has led to the sexualization of girls (a bad thing). We will figure out what you and I, as parents, must do to help our daughters define themselves by who they *are* rather than by how they *look.*

In Chapter 2 we'll take up the complex questions raised by texting, instant messaging, and the growing proportion of girls who are obsessed with Facebook or other social networking sites. While these girls may be hyper-connected with their peers, they are becoming disconnected from themselves. Again, the focus will be on what you and I as parents need to know, and to do, to help our daughters to use these technologies appropriately, rather than standing by helplessly as our daughters become trapped in the cyberbubble.

There has never before been any culture in which girls have had so many opportunities and yet receive so little structured guidance. As a result, many girls fixate on one activity or one dimension of their lives: Being the top student. Being a star athlete. Being the girl who's really thin. In Chapter 3 we will hear the stories of these girls' obsessions, and we will learn how parents can determine whether their daughter's interest in sports or good grades or fitness is healthy or destructive—and how to intervene before a girl goes over the edge.

In Chapter 4 the focus shifts to toxins in the environment: in the lotions and creams your daughter puts on her skin, or in the food she eats and the beverages she drinks. We will consider evidence that those toxins may be contributing to some of the problems of accelerated girlhood discussed in the earlier chapters.

In the final three chapters, I will share what I have learned over the past decade, meeting with parents and teachers and girls across North America and around the world, about how to nourish and nurture your daughter's mind, body, and spirit while helping her to become part of a larger community.

Parenting is an art, not a science. Although we can learn from happy, well-adjusted girls, the exact strategies that worked for those girls might not work for your daughter. But by sharing the stories of girls who prevailed alongside the stories of girls who struggled, my hope is that we can help our daughters become women who are happy, productive, and at their ease in this new world.

CHAPTER 1: FIRST FACTOR

sexual identity

We are gradually penetrating the highest levels of the work force. We get to go to college and play sports and be secretary of state. But to look around, you'd think all any of us [girls] want to do is rip off our clothes and shake it.

ARIEL LEVY[1]

A teenager who pretends to be an adult is still a teenager. If you imagine that getting high at a party and sleeping around is going to propel you into a state of full adulthood, that's like thinking that dressing up as an Indian is going to make you an Indian. . . . It's a really weird way of looking at life to want to become an adult by imitating everything that is most catastrophic about adulthood.

MURIEL BARBERY[2]

Girls are getting sexier earlier. That's not a good thing.

Kathy has a fond memory of one particular Halloween from her childhood. "My grandmother came to America from Bavaria as a young girl. So one year when I was a little girl myself, trying to decide what I should be for Halloween, she suggested that I should dress up like a Bavarian immigrant girl. She spent a month sewing a genuine Bavarian dirndl for me. She taught me how to wear it. My Mom helped. Looking back, I can see that it was a chance for three generations—me, my Mom, and her Mom—to do something together. Grandma even taught me how to say 'ee be a bairishe maydl'—'I'm a Bavarian girl.' I was so proud.

"When my daughter was 10, I told her that we could have a dirndl made for her Halloween costume, just like the one I had worn. She looked at me like I was crazy. 'I *know* what I'm going as, Mom,' she said in this how-could-you-be-so-stupid tone of voice. She'd already picked out her costume at the party store. It was a French maid outfit, with fishnet pantyhose and a frilly miniskirt. This was an outfit marketed to 10-year-old

11

girls. They even had it in smaller sizes! Unbelievable. I told my daughter, no way. She threw a fit. So we compromised on a cheerleader outfit.

"And here's what's weird," Kathy continued. "The boys' costumes haven't changed that much from what boys wore when I was little. When I was a girl, boys would dress up as Darth Vader or a Jedi knight or a Teenage Mutant Ninja Turtle. And they still do. But so many of the girls today, 9- and 10- and 11-year-old girls, seem to feel as though they have to dress up in something really skanky. How come? I've never heard of a boy who wanted to dress up like a Chippendale's dancer."

It's not just Halloween. In many different ways, our popular culture now pushes *elementary*-school girls to dress and act today in ways that would have been unimaginable for *middle*-school girls 20 or 30 years ago. Hot pants, low-rise jeans, camisoles, and midriff tops are now common apparel for girls in third grade.

Girls who are dressing in camisoles and hot pants prior to the onset of puberty are not expressing their sexuality. They don't have, and should not have, a sexual agenda to express. Dressing sexually in the absence of sexual desire is simply conformism. And it may create long-term problems. As Berkeley professor of psychology Stephen Hinshaw observes, "If girls pretend to be sexual before they really *are* sexual, they're going to find it much, much harder to connect to their own sexual feelings."[3]

There's been a big change in what's expected and what's acceptable. If a girl in 1985 or 1975 came to school wearing fishnet pantyhose with a miniskirt and a midriff-baring top she probably would have been told to go home and change into something decent. But girls today are bombarded with the notion that revealing your body is a valid means of self-expression, even a manifestation of "girl power." As parents, we must reject the notion that girls have to reveal their bodies in order to empower themselves. Boys don't have to take off their clothes to empower themselves. Girls shouldn't either.

Sexuality is good, but *sexualization* is bad. Sexuality is about your identity as a woman or a man, about feeling sexual. That's a healthy part of being human, a healthy part of becoming an adult. But *sexualization* is about being an object for the pleasure of others, about being on display for others. Sexuality is about who you are. Sexualization is about how you look.

The American Psychological Association recently published a monograph about the sexualization of American girls.[4] The authors of the monograph concluded that girls today are being pushed to wear "sexy" clothes at age 9 and 10—well before these girls have any adult sexuality to express. The authors of the monograph observed that in our contemporary culture, "girls are encouraged to *look* sexy, yet they know little about what it *means* to be sexual, to have sexual desires, and to make rational and responsible decisions about pleasure and risk within intimate relationships that acknowledge their own desires."[5]

Pretending to be sexual when you don't feel sexual makes you an object on display for others. It's not who you really are. It's not healthy. As we will see, it sets up girls for depression, anxiety, and an unsatisfying sex life later. "Dare to bare!" is a common exhortation in the spring and summer issues of many girls' fashion magazines. Where did this crazy idea come from, anyhow?

the mixed-up legacy of germaine greer

In 1970, the feminist writer Germaine Greer published her influential book *The Female Eunuch.* Greer's best seller dissected sexual roles from ancient times to the 1960s. She made a good case that throughout most of recorded history, in a wide variety of cultures all around the world, "good girls" have been portrayed as sexually naïve and lacking in sexual desire. In most of these traditional cultures, men are expected to be the experienced agents and initiators of sex, while women are supposed to be inexperienced and reluctant. In almost all of these cultures, girls are sheltered from the sexual attentions of boys until the girls are of marriageable age. Supposed exceptions to this rule, such as Margaret Mead's famous Samoan Islanders, turn out to be not so exceptional after all.[6]

A cultural anthropologist writing on this topic today might well ask, "If we see this pattern in so many cultures, then perhaps it has some adaptive value. Maybe it's there for some good reason. What value might such a cultural paradigm have?" But Greer, writing with the egocentricity and airy self-confidence that characterized so many writers (both female and male) in the 1960s and 1970s, disparages the notion that previous cultures might have anything worthwhile to teach us. Just because most cultures have done it this way doesn't mean that there might be any value in doing things that way. "The new assumption [should be] that everything that we may observe *could be otherwise*," she wrote.[7]

The publication of Greer's book is now four decades past. Her main assertion—that female modesty is a consequence and manifestation of the patriarchy—has achieved the status of established fact in contemporary gender studies. The corollary—that female immodesty is a sign of liberation—is now widely accepted. Girls today are coming of age in a culture in which teenage girls strip off their clothes at the beach or compete in wet T-shirt contests for the amusement of teenage boys. What's especially weird about those competitions is that both the girls and the boys seem to believe that the girls' parading their unveiled bodies is somehow modern, hip, and contemporary.[8]

By chastising feminine modesty as a symptom of patriarchal oppression, Greer provided support to the idea that pole dancers are liberated women. Her argument became so intrinsic to contemporary feminism that many people today don't even know where it came from. If you even hint at an objection to "Girls Gone Wild," you may find yourself labeled as a reactionary who favors a 1950s style patriarchy.

But Greer got this point wrong. There is no contradiction between modesty and sexuality.[9] Two generations ago, a woman could be both modest and sexual. Think of Lauren Bacall telling Humphrey Bogart in *To Have and Have Not*, "You know how to whistle, don't you, Steve? You just put your lips together and blow." Think of Vera-Ellen sashaying with Gene Kelly in *On the Town*, or Leslie Caron in the dream sequence of *An American in Paris*. These movies include some of the sexiest material ever filmed, yet the women never take their clothes off.

Again, I am not suggesting that the 1950s were the good old days. They weren't. A society in which girls don't have the same opportunities as the boys cannot be a model for us. For at least the past 4,000 years, most societies have regarded girls and women as subordinate. The emancipation of women in the developed countries over the past half-century has been a necessary prelude to girls fulfilling their potential, but it's not sufficient. We need to do more.

To be sure, there has always been a seedy fringe culture in which women were semi-clothed. But those were the traditions of the bordello and burlesque. In the past 40 years, the brothel has gone mainstream—so much so that many girls and young women today do not question the idea that baring their skin is a badge of sexual liberation.

I am old enough to remember a particular moment in second-wave feminism, just over 40 years ago, when card-carrying feminists dared to question whether liberated women should wear stiletto heels and short skirts. Gail Collins, a regular columnist for the *New York Times,* remembers that moment too: "There was one minute back in the late 1960s when the women's movement tried to convince everyone that being liberated involved wearing sensible shoes. It was not a success," she writes.[10] Germaine Greer's vision of feminism triumphed.

The fortunes of pornography over the past 40 years illustrate how far off the mark Germaine Greer was. Three years after the publication of *The Female Eunuch,* the porn magazine *Playgirl* was launched, featuring full-frontal male nudity. After all, if Greer was right in her belief that female modesty was a creation of the patriarchy, then liberated women should enjoy photos of nude men as much as men enjoy photos of nude women, right?

Wrong. *Playgirl* never achieved a market anywhere approaching the leading porn magazines for men, such as *Playboy.* Even at its peak, the fortunes of *Playgirl* were heavily dependent on a gay male readership. With the advent of explicit pornography for gay men (featuring men having sex with other men, which was never *Playgirl's* style), *Playgirl's* meager circulation dwindled further. It published its last print edition in November 2008.[11]

Women's sexuality is simply different from men's. Many teenage boys can be sexually aroused just by looking at a picture of a naked woman whom they have never met. A photograph of a woman's genitals or breasts, omitting the face, can be exciting for some teenage boys. But very few teenage girls will be sexually aroused by a picture of a naked man whom they will never meet. A photograph of an erect penis is actually a turnoff for some girls.[12]

For boys and young men, sexuality is often the driving force behind a relationship. But for most girls and young women, it's usually the other way around: the relationship has to drive the sex—otherwise the sex won't be any good. The most fulfilling sexual experience for most teenage girls, and for most young women, is physical intimacy with someone with whom they have a meaningful and ongoing relationship. Those differences were not constructed by the patriarchy. The origins go much deeper than that.[13]

what do girls really want?

Ask a typical 21st-century American girl wearing a midriff-baring top with a short skirt whether she really wants to dress like that. "Dress like what?" is the most common answer I have received. That's just how the cool girls dress. After dozens of conversations like this, I realized that no other perspective seems real to them, or possible. Choosing to wear an ankle-length skirt with matching blouse and sweater, for example, is simply inconceivable.

Azar Nafisi's *Reading Lolita in Tehran* offers a reverse perspective on this question. Women in Tehran today are required to veil their hair when in public. In one passage, Professor Nafisi asks one of her students, a young woman, how she feels about being compelled to wear the veil. Because Nafisi herself recalls the freedom that Iranian women enjoyed before the revolution in 1979, she herself feels frustrated and exasperated every time she must put on the veil. But her student, born after the revolution, is puzzled by the question. "She had always worn the veil. . . . She said she could not imagine [herself] without a veil. What would she look like? Would it affect the way she walked or how she moved her hands? How would others look at her?"

It struck me that Professor Nafisi's student, although she has no choice in the matter, is analogous to today's American girl, who does have a choice. Both girls have been raised in cultures that expect young women to dress in the way dictated by the prevailing culture. But the American girls may not be expressing themselves any more than Nafisi's student is expressing herself.

The same "everybody's doing it" mentality applies to sexual intimacy itself. After a 16-year-old girl told me that she has provided oral sex for "maybe a dozen" guys, I asked her whether she enjoyed doing it.

"I don't know, it's OK, I guess. It's really no big deal," she said.

I'm not the only person who's heard girls talk like this. Dr. Stephen Hinshaw, chair of the department of psychology at the University of California–Berkeley, describes a similar experience interviewing a young woman. He kept asking a girl named Randi whether she enjoys this kind of impersonal sexual activity, specifically providing oral sex to boys she doesn't know very well. "Randi seems more and more puzzled. It's almost as though I were asking her whether she enjoyed any of the individual drinks she had at the party. It's fun to drink, it's fun to get drunk, it's fun to hook up—or if it isn't . . . [if there is] a sense of, well, boredom, so what? Hooking up is what you do." Dr. Hinshaw concludes that many young women today are "likely to view sex as relatively joyless and impersonal, something that's part of frantic, drunken social activity rather than a source of pleasure, intimacy, or fulfillment."[14]

"it's no big deal"

Remember Madison, the girl I mentioned in the Introduction, the girl who was obsessed with being slender and hot? Many girls like Madison are faking it. They don't even know that they're faking it, because they started faking it before they were old enough ever to have experienced from the inside the sexuality they are pretending to manifest. They are dressing to look hot, but most of the tween and teen girls who are wearing the short skirts are not actually trying to lure boys into sex. Like most young people, they want attention. They want to feel special. They have figured out that one sure way to accomplish that is to look good in the eyes of the boys. The boys rush to compete for the favors of the pretty girl. The other girls notice that, so the status of the pretty girl goes up in the eyes of the other girls.

As a result, the girl wearing the short skirt can easily confuse her desire for attention with her desire for sex. She wears the sexy outfit and enjoys the attention she gets from the boys. Or she wears a T-shirt that says "yes but not w u."[15] That's precisely the image many tween and teen girls want to present: I'm sexy, I'm sexually experienced and *potentially* sexually available, but I'm not a slut.

The mixed message here can create problems. Girls who dress in sexy outfits may eventually have to perform sexually, or risk being labeled a "tease" or, worse, a prude. But they often don't feel the desire for intercourse. Hence the popularity of oral sex, with the girl servicing the boy. I have been stunned by the detached tone in which some girls describe oral sex. "It's no big deal," is the recurring refrain. A girl who knows how to give "good" oral sex can raise her status in the eyes of the boys, without risking pregnancy or even making eye contact.

I have talked with many girls and young women whose main sexual experience, from age 14 onward, has been providing oral sex, with the girl on her knees servicing the boy. One woman, age 20, told me, "To be honest, I wouldn't mind if I never see another [penis] as long as I live." Many of these girls seem to believe that sex is a commodity that girls provide to boys.

As I described in my book *Why Gender Matters,* girls and boys approach sexual activity with different motivations. For teenage boys and young men, sex is often about obtaining relief from an urge that can be overwhelming. "It's just something I have to do sometimes. When I need sex, I can't think about anything else until I get it," one boy told me. Only a few teenage girls feel that kind of overwhelming need for a sexual outlet. Instead, providing a boy with a sexual outlet may give a girl the feeling of being wanted, desired, and somehow in control. Even girls who insist that they enjoy sexual intimacy for its own sake often want the intimacy more than the sex. In a classic paper entitled "The Need or Wish to Be Held," Dr. Marc Hollender described how even young women who had labeled themselves as sexually voracious actually craved the closeness — being held, being hugged. The sexual act was their way of getting that closeness.[16]

This is a fundamental difference between female sexuality and male sexuality. For many boys and young men, sex is primarily about achieving a sexual climax and release. For most girls and women, satisfying sex is about intimacy, being desired by someone you like, feeling loved. Orgasm is great, but for most girls and women, it's best when it comes in the context of closeness with a caring person. "Second-wave feminism accomplished sweeping, grand social change," writes Courtney Martin. Nevertheless, she observes, "we still can't be authentically sexual — only raunchy like our brothers or asexual like our mothers."[17] Forty years after Germaine Greer, young women are still struggling to figure out what it means to be female and sexual in their own frame of reference.

Ignoring these gender differences doesn't help girls; it disadvantages them. I discussed this problem with Dr. Laura Irwin, professor of obstetrics and gynecology at the Medical College of Georgia. She told me about a number of young women in their mid- to late 20s who have come to see her, all with the same kind of question: "I'm 27 years old," one woman said. "I've had sex with lots of different guys. But I've never had an orgasm. Is there something wrong with me? Could you please, um, check me out down there, and see whether I'm normal?"

Dr. Irwin then proceeds to do a thorough evaluation. In each case, Dr. Irwin told me, she found nothing unusual with the woman's anatomy. "There's nothing wrong with you," she told this particular woman. "It's the men you've been with. They have no idea that 'sexual intercourse' is supposed to be intercourse *between* two individuals. These young men are basically using your body as an aid to masturbation. They do their business and then they're done. They don't have a clue about what you or other young women want or need."

beauty products for tweens

In ancient times, say a decade ago, it was unusual for 10-year-old girls to go to a beauty spa for a full facial, manicure, and pedicure. Not anymore. As Jessica Bennett wrote for *Newsweek* magazine, "This, my friends, is the new normal: a generation that primps and dyes and pulls and shapes, younger and with more vigor. [Some] girls today are salon vets before they enter elementary school."[18] As recently as 2005, Bennett found, young women began using beauty products, on average, at age 17. That's now down to age 13, and dropping rapidly. She also cites data from the market research firm Experian showing that 43 percent of 6- to 9-year-old girls are using lipstick or lip gloss and that 38 percent are using hairstyling products. Anna Solomon, a social worker, told Bennett that her 8-year-old daughter is "so into this stuff it's unbelievable. From the clothes to the hair to the nails, school is like number 10 on [her] list of priorities."

Bennett rightly observes that this phenomenon is different in emphasis from girls wearing short skirts and revealing tops. Bennett calls this process "diva-ization," which is a bit clumsy. I would say it's another aspect of self-objectification, the process whereby our culture pushes girls to define themselves in terms of how they look instead of helping them to develop a sense of who they are.

twilight and other conservatives

He caught my face securely between his iron hands, ignoring my struggles when I tried to turn my head away.

"Please don't," I whispered . . .

His mouth was on mine then, and I couldn't fight him. Not because he was so many thousand times stronger than me, but because my will crumbled into dust the second our lips met . . .

So I kissed him back, my heart pounding out a jagged, disjointed rhythm while my breathing turned to panting.

That's a passage from *New Moon*, the second book in the four-book *Twilight* saga by Stephenie Meyer. The popularity of these books is staggering. For many months in 2008 and 2009, the four books occupied four of the top ten slots on the amazon.com best-seller list. More than 85 million copies of the *Twilight* books have been sold.[19] At the end of 2008, the four books had occupied four of the top five slots on the *USA Today*'s best-seller list for the entire year, an accomplishment never previously achieved by any author.[20] Yet many Americans had never heard of these books until the movies came out. Unlike most other hugely successful best-selling books, these books do not appeal to a wide swath of the market. The *Twilight* books have been purchased primarily by girls and young women.

J. K. Rowling still leads Stephenie Meyer in the total number of books sold, but the Harry Potter books were read by a broad audience of children, teenagers, and adults, an audience that included boys as well as girls. The books of the *Twilight* saga target a much narrower demographic. *Breaking Dawn* is the final book in the *Twilight* saga. When I picked up my copy of *Breaking Dawn* at the midnight launch party at a Barnes & Noble store in Philadelphia, the salesperson gave me (and everybody else who bought a book) a complimentary sheet of stickers. These stickers are not for boys. A typical sticker reads "My ♥ belongs to Edward." I saw only one other man there, accompanying his teenage daughter. Many of the girls were wearing costumes, dressed up to look like one of the female characters in the novels. As a middle-aged man, I felt as out of place as if I had stumbled into the girls' powder room at the high school prom.

So what is the secret behind the success of these books? I have met with hundreds of teenage girls all across North America, as well as hundreds more in England, Australia, and New Zealand, and I have asked them why they love these books. One part of the appeal of the *Twilight* saga derives, I believe, from the fact that it combines a modern ambience with traditional ideas about gender. In the *Twilight* books, the central character, Bella, likes watching reruns of *The Simpsons* while she nibbles on Pop-Tarts; but Bella and most of the other girls adhere to gender roles that are straight out of the 1940s. The girls are girls, and the boys are men. More specifically, the male leads, Edward Cullen and Jacob Black, are muscular and unwaveringly brave, whereas Bella and the other girls make supper for the men and hold all-girl slumber parties. Carmen Siering, who teaches women's studies at Ball State University, has expressed concern about the gender stereotypes perpetuated in the series: "testosterone-driven male aggression, females who pine away over lost loves, boys who fix motorcycles and the girls who watch them."[21] It may not be politically correct, but it's popular.

Another reason for *Twilight*'s success, I think, is the relative dearth of traditional romance in contemporary teen culture. In a culture that regards oral sex as a casual encounter, Bella remains chaste; she never has sex, nor any intimacy beyond kissing, with either of her beaus until she marries Edward in book four. In a culture that eschews dating and long-term commitments in favor of the carefree hookup, Bella's two suitors pursue her with elaborate zeal.

Girls love this stuff. Maybe they shouldn't, but they do. At least, many girls do—enough to drive these books to the top of the best-seller lists and keep them there for years. And remember, we're not talking about the "most popular books for teen girls" best-seller list; we're talking about the "most popular books for everybody" best-seller list.

Imagine going back to the 1940s, when the Nancy Drew books enjoyed huge popularity. In *The Hidden Staircase*, Nancy's father is kidnapped by three bad guys. Nancy tracks down the bad guys, has each of them arrested, and rescues her father from the dungeon where the men have kept him prisoner. Nancy's boyfriend is a minor character who plays no role in the rescue of Nancy's father. In the *Twilight* books, Bella's boyfriends Jacob Black and Edward Cullen are always the central focus of the story, from start to finish. It is ironic that in our supposedly enlightened and hyper-modern 21st century, girls are flocking to books that are arguably less "enlightened," in some ways, than the Nancy Drew books of two generations past.

In the Nancy Drew era, there was no lack of traditional romantic stories in which a young man courts a young woman. The Nancy Drew series was refreshing, for its time, in that it portrayed a young woman as an independent agent. It may be no coincidence that all three women who have served as justices on the United States Supreme Court—Sandra Day O'Connor, Ruth Bader Ginsberg, and Sonia Sotomayor—are themselves fans of the Nancy Drew books.[22] Today, when popular culture is continually bombarding girls with messages about how liberated and independent they are and should be, it's remarkable that so many girls seem to be so hungry for a more traditional alternative.

When she began writing the *Twilight* books, author Stephenie Meyer was a 30-something stay-at-home mother of three sons. But the same longing for romance is expressed by teenage girls themselves. Taylor Swift was the best-selling vocal artist of 2008, with combined sales of more than four million albums that year. She was then 18 years old. Her song "Love Story" was the most successful track on her second album *Fearless,* which became the second-best-selling album of 2009. (Michael Jackson, after his death, gained the number-one spot.) "Love Story" is romantic fantasy, pure and simple. In the song, Swift imagines a traditional romance with a young man who will be the "prince" while she is the "princess." She even imagines the young man seeking her father's permission to marry her.

How politically incorrect can you get? Doesn't Taylor Swift know that the idea of a young man asking a father's permission to marry the daughter is an absolute no-no? Any feminist can tell you how that ritual endorsed the Original Sin of the patriarchy, the idea that a young woman should be subservient first to her father, then to her husband. The central message of Swift's song is a longing for romantic gender roles that no longer exist; yet girls are buying this song and downloading the accompanying video by the millions.

"i figured you'd think less of me"

Fifty years ago, the lines were clearly drawn. "Good girls" didn't have sex before marriage—well, not until just a few months before marriage, perhaps. In the 1950s, the average age at first intercourse for young women was 19 years, and the average age of marriage for young women was 20.[23] Today a girl may commonly have her first sexual experience (including oral sex), at 13, 14, or 15 years of age,[24] but she may not marry until her late 20s, if she marries at all. That means she may have a decade or more where she is a sexual agent outside of the context of a lifelong commitment. "Getting married to a guy without having sex with him first would be like buying a dress without trying it on first," a college woman told me. There has never previously been a culture in which young women have had so many years of unconstrained sexuality. In the long perspective of the past 4,000 years of recorded human history, this is unprecedented.[25] Whether you view this development as good or bad depends on your personal values; what's clear is that girls today have more freedom and more choices, but less guidance from adults, than any generation of girls in history. Most girls are not getting the guidance they need to navigate this uncharted territory. Many don't have any applicable moral compass.

It's no longer clear to girls today what it means to be a "good girl" or even whether a girl would want to be "good." Consider the most basic question of teenage behavior: have you ever had sex?

Figure 1 shows how teenage girls and boys have answered that question, from 1950 through 1999. Back in 1950, nearly two-thirds of boys reported having had sex, but fewer than one girl in six had sex. The teenage boys were having sex either with the few "bad girls" their age or with older women, some of whom may have been professional prostitutes. The proportion of boys getting some action actually declined slightly between 1950 and 1999. The proportion of girls roughly quadrupled.[26]

But the changes go even deeper than these numbers might suggest. Fifty years ago, girls were the gatekeepers for sexual activity. The boys had at least to pretend they liked the girl in order to get physical. Today, girls often engage in sexual activity with boys, particularly oral sex, with-

Figure 1

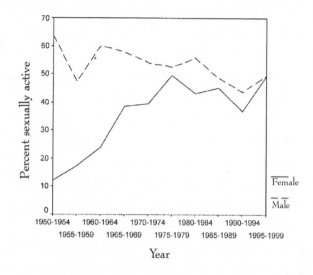

Year

out any promise of relationship.[27] Being hip, being cool, means not insisting on a romantic commitment prior to sexual intimacy. Being hip means being a guy as far as sex is concerned: sex with no strings attached. As Ariel Levy puts it, with regard to female sexuality, "We are all Tarzan now, or at least we are all pretending to be."[28]

Fifty years ago, the dividing line between good girls and bad girls was clear. Good girls didn't have sex before marriage. Bad girls did. In that era, it was good to be a good girl, and bad to be a bad girl. Today, Bad is the new Good. A recent issue of *Cosmopolitan* magazine had a banner on the cover, in large type: "Bad Girl Issue—For Sexy Bitches Only."[29]

The culture of 50 years ago encouraged romance without sex. Today's culture encourages sex without romance. For many girls, the result is profoundly depressing, literally. Pediatrician Meg Meeker has suggested that girls who engage in sex in their early teenage years are at higher risk for depression compared with girls in their peer group who don't. Dr. Meeker has gone so far as to assert that depression in teenage girls may often be a "sexually transmitted disease," by which she means that having sex *causes* some girls to become depressed.[30] Researchers at the University of North Carolina–Chapel Hill have reported evidence that supports her idea. They found that girls who engage in sex are indeed more likely subsequently to become depressed. That's not true for boys.[31] Most boys aren't wracked with regret if they lose their virginity to the wrong person. But your daughter may be.

As journalist and author Laura Sessions Stepp observed, for girls, "Losing your virginity is closing the door on childhood and stepping into adulthood. If you're not ready for it and do it anyway, it can feel 'like death,' as one young woman put it. You just want to put it behind you, except that you can't."[32] Stepp has also observed that today's hookup culture, free of commitment, is "gravy for guys." So, she asks, How much have women really won?[33]

There's the irony. In an era that preaches gender equity, the guys have been awarded a windfall prize without lifting a finger. They can have sex not merely without marriage, but without any sort of romantic relationship. Most cultures in most times and most places have frowned on pre-marital intercourse. Our culture now expects it. Indeed, teenage girls today are often ashamed to admit that they are virgins, in much the same way that girls 50 years ago would have been ashamed to admit that they were NOT virgins.

I recall watching an episode of *The OC,* an evening TV drama about high-school kids that was very popular with teenagers in 2004 and 2005. In this particular episode, Summer, one of the two leading female characters, confesses to her boyfriend, Seth, that she had been a virgin when they had sex a few days earlier. She lost her virginity that night, but she hadn't told him (or anybody). "Why didn't you tell me?" he asks. She answers: "I guess I felt like I had this reputation to uphold, and I figured you'd think less of me or something."[34] Her reputation is that she's a cool popular girl, and cool high-school girls have had sex. Seth has to reassure her that he doesn't like her any less because she was a virgin and not the experienced vixen she had pretended to be.

This change has taken place with remarkable speed. When I was a teenager myself, 30-some years ago, Meat Loaf had a popular song called "Paradise by the Dashboard Light." The song describes a teenage girl and boy getting hot and heavy in the front seat of a car. They are on the verge of sexual intercourse, when the girl interrupts the action, saying:

Stop right there!
I gotta know right now!
Before we go any further!
Do you love me?
Will you love me forever?
Do you need me?
Will you never leave me?
Will you make me so happy for the rest of my life?
Will you take me away, will you make me your wife?

I have played this song for today's teenagers all across the United States and Canada. They giggle when they hear the questions being asked in the song. But their giggles hide their underlying confusion. "It's obviously just a hook-up," one girl said. "Why is she making such a big deal about it? If she doesn't want to have sex, fine, no big deal. Why would she want the guy to marry her, I mean, that's really weird."

I explain that in ancient times—back in 1977 when this song was a hit—girls often wouldn't agree to go all the way without a promise of marriage.

"But why?" the girl insists. "Didn't they have birth control back then?"

Yes, they had birth control back then (and running water and television too), I explain. It wasn't about birth control. It was the idea that sex was something precious that even cool girls, like the girl in the song, wouldn't give away without a promise of a lifelong commitment.

"Lifelong," the girl mutters. "Weird."

I wrote an op-ed for the *Washington Post* about the surprising popularity of the *Twilight* books. One blogger objected to my article. She insisted that she saw no tension between wearing sexy clothes and being an excellent student. "We can be hot and still come out on top in the class-room," she wrote.[35]

Is she right? Does wearing sexy clothes not affect a girl's ability to be a top student?

"that swimsuit becomes you"

Barbara Fredrickson and her colleagues had a wacky idea for an experiment. They recruited college women and men, then randomly assigned each volunteer to wear either a bulky sweater or a swimsuit. The men wore swim trunks, and the women wore one-piece bathing suits. Each volunteer was sitting in a dressing room: no windows, no observers. Each volunteer was then asked to take a math quiz while sitting in the dressing room. Fredrickson and her team then compared how women wearing swimsuits performed on the quiz compared with women who were wearing bulky sweaters, and likewise for the men.

The results are shown in Figure 2. The men who were wearing swim trunks did slightly better than the men who were wearing bulky sweaters. The women who were wearing swimsuits did significantly worse than the women who were wearing bulky sweaters.[36] And remember, the women in this study were in a closed room with no windows and no observers. It's a good bet that this effect would have been even greater if the young women were in a classroom with young men.

"Self-objectification." That's the term Dr. Fredrickson and her colleagues used. They found that these women were objectifying themselves. Just wearing a swimsuit made these young women focus on their own bodies as objects to be evaluated and rated. That's distracting, not to mention degrading and dehumanizing. If your daughter goes to school wearing a midriff top and a short skirt, she's putting herself in a situation similar to the swimsuit condition in Fredrickson's study. At some level, she's going to be thinking about, analyzing, and judging her own body when she ought to be thinking about geometry or Spanish grammar.

Figure 2

This is where you come in. Parents have to be willing to assert their authority. Parents have to be willing to overrule their daughter's decision regarding what she is wearing to school.

"But all the other girls are wearing it! And you should have seen what Ashley wore yesterday: I mean it was *totally* skin tight," your daughter says.

"I'm sorry. I'm your parent, and I'm telling you that you can't wear that to school."

"What is *wrong* with you, you are so clueless, you are going to like totally *ruin* my whole *life*! I hate you!" your daughter screams.

You have to stand your ground. When your daughter goes to school wearing an outfit that is not as revealing as what some of the other girls are wearing, you can't expect her to say "I chose to wear this outfit so that I can focus on my schoolwork rather than worrying about my appearance." It's not reasonable to expect any girl to say that in the 21st century. But she *can* say, "My evil witch of a mother made me wear this ridiculous outfit."

You have to be willing to be the evil witch (or the evil wizard, if you're Dad).

Of course it's hard to ask your daughter to wear a modest outfit when the other girls are wearing midriff tops and short skirts. A better solution is to find a school where all the girls are expected to dress appropriately, or to work with other parents at your school to ensure that your school's dress code is sensible and that it is enforced. School uniforms can be helpful in this regard. We'll talk more about working with your school leaders in Chapter 5.

lesbian chic

In the summer of 2008, the American singer Katy Perry released a single entitled "I Kissed a Girl."

> *I kissed a girl and I liked it*
> *The taste of her cherry chap stick*
> *I kissed a girl just to try it*
> *I hope my boyfriend don't mind it*
> *It felt so wrong*
> *It felt so right*

The song quickly shot to number one on the Billboard national charts, where it stayed for seven straight weeks. The video was nominated for five MTV Video Music Awards and became the number-one most-viewed music video of 2008 on MySpace.[37]

Imagine a song sung by a young man with the title "I Kissed a Boy and I Liked It." Would such a song be equally successful? I don't think so.

Lesbian is cool. Bisexual is cool, but only for girls. MTV has now run three seasons of a reality show in which an attractive bisexual woman plays the role of "bachelorette," with a dozen handsome men *and* a dozen gorgeous women competing for her affections. The 2009 installment boasted not one but two beautiful bisexual women, identical twins Rikki and Vikki, serving as the bachelorettes. The two women winnowed down two dozen great-looking contestants—half women, half men—until finally, both women chose the same man, and he had to decide between the two sisters.[38]

Can you imagine a show in which an attractive bisexual *man* offered young women and young men the chance to be physically intimate with him—a show in which we would watch the "bachelor" French-kissing another man, complete with moans of pleasure?

Me neither.

Forty years ago, the gay rights movement was mostly about men. Male homosexuality was in the news, for example with the Stonewall riot in 1969 and the film *Boys in the Band* in 1970. There were no similar iconic cultural events for lesbian or bisexual women in that era. Girl-girl action was almost invisible in the 1960s. Lesbian women themselves tended to be politically conservative and socially cautious.[39]

What a difference a generation makes. Today, girl-girl sexual intimacy is everywhere: on TV shows (remember *The L Word* on Showtime?), in popular music, and online. When actress Megan Fox asserted in 2009 that "everyone is born bisexual" and she claimed to be bisexual herself, nothing she said was controversial; on the contrary, her interview had a politically correct tone to it.[40] According to one recent nationwide survey conducted by researchers at Cornell University, the proportion of girls and women who have engaged in lesbian sex or had lesbian fantasies is now 14.5 percent. That's slightly more than one girl in seven. For boys and men, the proportion who have engaged in homosexual sex or had homosexual fantasies is 5.6 percent, less than half the proportion for females. Other surveys suggest that the proportion of girls and young women who identify as bisexual or lesbian today may range from 15 percent to 23 percent.[41]

What's going on?

And what does all this have to do with your daughter?

Point #1 is that even straight girls are comfortable being physically intimate with other girls in ways that straight boys today are not comfortable with other boys. Two girls might snuggle under a blanket to watch a movie, or give each other hugs and kisses, but they'd think you're being silly if you interpreted that behavior as evidence of lesbian attraction. It is much less common in North America today to find two straight boys snuggling under a blanket to watch a movie.

Point #2 is that sexual orientation is more fluid for girls than it is for guys. Let's suppose a 17-year-old male he tells you he's 100 percent gay; he has no interest in sex with females. If you return ten years later and interview the same guy, chances are very high that he will still identify himself as a gay man. But that's not as true for females, whether they are lesbian, straight, or bisexual. Whatever her sexual orientation at age 17, there's a good chance that it may be different ten years later. If she's lesbian at age 17, she may be bisexual or straight ten years later. If she's straight or bisexual at age 17, she may be lesbian or bisexual ten years later. Psychologists call this "erotic plasticity."[42]

According to one of the leading investigators of sexual orientation in women, Professor Lisa Diamond, a straight woman may in some cases just be a woman who hasn't yet met the right woman.[43] When a woman finds her "soul mate" and her soul mate happens to be another woman—someone she can really open up to, share secrets with, be comfortable with—it's not too difficult for that emotionally intimate relationship to become physically intimate as well.

Now we're getting close to understanding the relevance of all this to your daughter. Forty years ago, girl-girl sexual intimacy was taboo. Now it's the stuff of reality shows and number-one pop songs. Lifting the taboo may have opened the door to girls discovering a different sexual orientation they would never have discovered in an earlier, more repressive era.

But here's the problem: what is genuine and what is fake? I have already mentioned how today's girls often confuse their desire for attention with their desire for sex. I spoke recently to parents from several private schools. One of the parents told me how some of the sixth-grade girls will kiss other sixth-grade girls in front of the boys. The boys hoot and holler their approval, so the girls do it again, this time with some deep tongue action, to even louder applause. This mother was worried because she believes that if a girl pretends to be lesbian, she is more likely to explore lesbian sexuality. And Professor Diamond's research provides some support for that view.

I'm concerned that some girls might be pretending to be lesbian when they don't really feel lesbian sexual attraction. They're putting on a show for the boys. Ariel Levy heard similar stories in her interviews with teenage girls. "Definitely girls hook up with other girls because they know the guys will like it," according to one of the girls she interviewed. These girls think, "'Then the guys are going to want to hook up with me and give me a lot of attention' . . . definitely. If they think a guy's going to like it, they'll do it."[44]

I am not suggesting that lesbian girls or bisexual girls should pretend to be straight. I am suggesting that *our popular culture is pushing girls to put on a girl-girl show for the boys—a show that may not be in synch with who they really are.* The girls themselves may not understand what's happening because the girls aren't in touch with their own sexuality.

"maybe men just don't satisfy"

One possible explanation for the increase in the visibility of bisexual or lesbian women may be that our culture now encourages bisexual and lesbian behavior for girls and young women—behaviors that were out-of-bounds two generations ago. But there's another possibility. I asked Mary June, a young woman, why she thought that the visibility of lesbian and bisexual women has increased so much in recent years. She immediately answered, "Guys today just don't know how to satisfy a woman. The guys just want 'wham, bam, thank-you ma'am.' They don't care about building a relationship. Maybe girls who love other girls are more careful to nurture a relationship. Maybe the girls are less focused on the physical aspects."

I think Mary June may be on to something. I have already mentioned how many young women describe their sexual encounters with young men as being joyless chores. Because both girls and boys are having sex several years earlier today than was the case 40 years ago, the boys are less mature themselves, and more egocentric. In addition, there has been a cultural shift with boys today feeling less of an obligation to care about the girls. As I said earlier in this chapter, we have moved from a culture of dating to the culture of the hook-up. Popular music, particularly hip-hop and rap, often depicts sex as something that girls provide for boys, for the pleasure of boys, with girls subordinate to boys. This music affects the attitudes of both girls and boys. Girls and boys who listen to this music are more likely to agree with statements such as "sex is for guys."[45] Even in country music videos, girls are usually on display for the guys, rarely vice versa.[46]

The growing influence of the porn culture plays some role here as well. Most young men today will tell you that they visit online porn sites. Some of them will even enthusiastically describe to you the features of their favorite sites.[47] Given the choice between masturbating over online pornography and going out on a date with a real girl—that is to say, a girl who doesn't look like a porn star and who isn't wearing lingerie—more and more young men tell me that they prefer online porn. "Real girls cost too much money. Besides, the girls on the online porn sites are way better-looking," one young man said to me, with no apology or embarrassment. More than a few young women have told me how their "boyfriends" have suggested that they shave their pubic hair so that they look more like porn stars. The lesbian subculture may seem like a welcome oasis of connection and caring in comparison with impersonal heterosexual sex. In other words, a growing proportion of girls may be choosing a bisexual or lesbian identity in large part because the guys are such losers. At least that was Mary June's theory.

We are *not* debating whether your daughter "should" or "should not" become a lesbian. The problem I see is that our culture is pushing girls into adopting a sexual identity—and to becoming sexual agents and sexual objects—too soon. And that's unhealthy, regardless of whether your daughter will ultimately be straight, bisexual, or lesbian.

I rarely cite passages from the Bible. But if you have never read the Song of Songs, you should read it. The Song of Songs is a love story—quite passionate and unbelievably explicit in the original Hebrew. Toward the end of the story, the woman at the heart of the narrative gives a command to the other women in her circle: "I charge you, daughters of Jerusalem: *do not awaken love before its time.*"[48]

That's the key lesson to be learned from everything we have discussed, from Halloween costumes to bisexuality. *Do not awaken love before its time.* Girls today are being pushed to present a sexy façade, to put on a show for the boys, before they are ready to decide whether that's even something they want to do. The result too often is sexual confusion: they are alienated from their own sexuality.

Let girls have a chance to be girls. Don't push them to be women and sexual agents before they have had a chance to be girls for as long as they need to be. In Chapter 7, we will consider a few examples of how other parents, and other communities, have accomplished this.

the cyberbubble

. . . the way we live now, where we're forever sending off e-mail and texts, field-ing cell phone calls: where we're no longer any one place but everywhere—and nowhere—at once.

JEFFREY EUGENIDES[1]

The most precious gift we can offer others is our presence.

THICH NHAT HANH[2]

Describe yourself in two words.

"Party animal" is how Caitlin answers that question. Fifteen years old, just starting tenth grade, Caitlin plans her life around parties. Getting invited to the cool parties. Then hopping from one party to the next. And most important of all, uploading photos to her Facebook page, illustrating her exploits at the various parties.

I spoke with Caitlin and her Mom, Karen, together. Karen says she doesn't mind her daughter's passion for parties. "As long as she's not drinking or doing drugs, and I know where she is, I really don't have a problem with all the parties," Karen says. "When I was in tenth grade, that was all I wanted to do. What bugs me is how obsessive she is about putting it all on her Facebook page. It's like the whole point of the party for her is to upload a photo. She spends at least an hour every day, and more on weekends, editing photos for her Facebook page."

"But you kept a diary too when you were my age," Caitlin interrupts. "You told me you used to spend hours writing in your diary."

"But that was private," Karen says. "I wasn't putting it on display."

"So how does that make it better than what I do?" Caitlin answers. "If you're going to spend so much time on yourself, why not share it with other people? It seems kind of weird to spend all that time writing about yourself, just for yourself."

"But you spend so much time on the pictures," Karen replies. "You're not even writing."

Caitlin gives an ineffable shrug of her shoulder and shakes her head with her eyes almost closed. It's a perfect *I-don't-expect-you-to-understand* gesture. "They didn't *have* Facebook when you were growing up, remember? They didn't even have the *Internet*," Caitlin says, with a mix of disdain and disbelief. "You didn't share photos online because you *couldn't*, not because you didn't want to."

When I refereed this conversation between mother and daughter, it seemed to me that Caitlin had a point. After all, isn't sharing with one's friends online a more social activity than scribbling in a diary in one's bedroom?

It wasn't until much later, after discussing this issue with many other parents and their daughters, that I saw the problem with Caitlin's argument. When tweens and teenagers write and post photos online, they are seeking to please/entertain/amuse their friends. When you are writing in your bedroom in a diary no one else will ever see, you can write whatever you want, at whatever length you want. You can explore your own thoughts and feelings through your writing.

One danger of online blogs and social networking sites is that your daughter may not be expressing what she really feels. She may instead be writing what she thinks will entertain or impress her peers who read it. She might not even be aware of the difference. She may not realize that what she *says* she is feeling isn't what she actually *is* feeling. She subtly adjusts what she is writing to suit what she thinks her friends want to read. After a while, she may gradually become the girl she is pretending to be.

Xiyin Tang was a student at Columbia University when she was interviewed about her online blog, which she began posting online when she was in fifth grade. "When I first started out with my Livejournal, I was very honest," she told reporter Emily Nussbaum. "I basically wrote as if there was no one reading it. And if people wanted to read it, then great." But she soon changed her style to fit the prevailing style of Internet blogs and social networking. "I tried to make my posts highly stylized and short," Xiyin said, instead of the long digressive essays she might have wanted to write.[3]

"Highly stylized and short" with lots of photos. Don't forget the photos. A recent report from Harvard Business School found that the number-one reason why teens and young adults go to social networking sites is to look at photos. That's especially true for boys and young men; they are looking for photos of girls and women, some whom they know, and some they don't.[4]

Girls know this. Girls know that if they want their social networking site to be popular, then that site needs to include lots of photos. Funny photos are good; sexy photos are better, as long as the photos aren't skanky. It's all about projecting the right image: cool, hip, ironic.

I spoke recently with parents of a girl, let's call her Julia, who was spending hours a day working on her MySpace page and/or instant messaging ("IM'ing") or texting her friends. Some nights Julia was staying up well past midnight, tweaking photos for her MySpace page, texting and instant messaging her friends. I suggested to her parents that they should restrict her time online.

"But kids need to be comfortable in the digital world," her father said. "This is the 21st century. This is the technology they will use at college and in the workplace. Why shouldn't she develop her proficiency?"

For many parents, this Dad's comment seems reasonable. But this Dad is mistaken. Posting blog entries and uploading photos is not the best way to develop skills that will be useful in the workplace. Emory University professor Mark Bauerlein has reviewed the available research on this point, and he concludes that "teen blog writing sticks to the lingo of teens—simple syntax, phonetic spelling, low diction—and actually grooves bad habits."[5]

The girl who spends hours in her bedroom on a social networking site may not do better at school, either now or subsequently, compared with the girl next door who never goes online at home. That's what the research seems to show. It's important to control for socioeconomic variables when you do these studies: that's why some early reports, in the late 1990s and early 2000s, led parents to think that there might be some advantage to kids spending lots of free time online. If you simply compare the academic performance of kids who spend many hours online with kids who don't, you might well find that the kids spending time online do better, on average, than kids who never spend any free time online. Maybe you read a report of such a study ten years ago. But kids who had access to the Internet ten years ago often came from homes and communities that were significantly more affluent than kids who didn't have access to the Internet. One of the most enduring facts about Western society is that kids who come from affluent neighborhoods do better in school than kids who come from low-income neighborhoods. So if investigators don't control for socioeconomic status, the use of the Internet may just be a proxy for household income. As one team of investigators recently reported, "Once other features of student, family, and school background are held constant, computer availability at home shows a strong statistically *negative* relationship to math and reading performance."[6]

Professor Bauerlein has found that spending time on social networking sites, or updating a blog, "doesn't impart adult information; it crowds it out. . . . To prosper in the hard-and-fast cliques in the schoolyard, the fraternities, and the food court, teens and 20-year-olds must track the latest films, fads, gadgets, YouTube videos, and television shows. They judge one another relentlessly on how they wear clothes, recite rap lyrics, and flirt."[7] That doesn't leave much time for reading actual books.

The real world of the adult workplace is very different from the tween/teen blogosphere. The skills honed on the social networking sites may actually impair performance in the adult world. Bauerlein concludes that "success in popular online youthworlds breeds incompetence in school and in the workplace."[8]

Take a look at Facebook or MySpace and browse pages by girls who are (or are claiming to be) 18 years old. This is especially easy to do on MySpace. Go to www.myspace.com, click on "browse people" (under "Friends"), and specify women 18 years of age. (MySpace does not do any kind of age verification: it's immediately clear that a significant number of those girls are under 18.) You will quickly find pages from girls in locations thousands of miles apart, but there's a certain sameness to the posts and photos. Far from enhancing the individuality of the girls, the format seems to homogenize them, so that the girl from Perth, Australia, presents herself in a manner very similar to the girl from the Upper East Side of Manhattan. It's all superficial, cute, trying to be funny in an adolescent sort of way, with lots of references to the latest minutiae of popular teen culture—and the most popular sites offer lots of photos.

The kids themselves sometimes show acute insight into how the cyberbubble can warp a young person, making him or her less able to interact in the real world. One high school girl told me about a crush she'd had on a boy at her school. She was a junior, he was a senior. He would glance at her, smile, and raise an eyebrow. She was intrigued. They began texting each other. His texts were short and funny. One day in AP Latin, during a particularly tedious lecture, she felt her phone vibrating. She glanced down at the phone, which she was holding casually under her purse so the teacher wouldn't see. He was texting her: "R we having fun?" She glanced over at him. He winked.

"At that moment, I actually felt my heart skip a beat," she told me. "I thought I was falling in love."

The next day, she noticed him sitting alone in the cafeteria, so she went over and sat at his table. "Mind if I join you for lunch?" she asked. He shrugged. She tried to make small talk. Nothing. "It was the weirdest thing," she said. "I suddenly realized at that moment that we had never had an actual, face-to-face conversation lasting more than about twenty seconds. He didn't know how to make eye contact. He just kept looking down at his plate, or he'd look out the window, or up at the ceiling. He didn't seem to be able to say anything except 'yes' and 'no.' I felt like I was interrogating him, just trying to get a conversation started. Maybe he didn't like me after all, that's fine, but he couldn't even *talk*. I couldn't decide whether he was autistic or if he was just being rude." This boy had honed his skill at texting, while his ability to converse had atrophied. It's an extreme case, but the basic story is becoming common: girls and boys who have developed great skill at texting and IM'ing, but who have not even begun to learn the art of face-to-face conversation.

The cyberculture gives rise to a relentless focus on the presentation of self in images and sound bites before the self has had a chance to fully form. Girls who pretend to be obsessed with *Gossip Girl* and *Twilight* because it's cute and amusing to portray such a persona may find themselves turning into girls who actually are obsessed with *Gossip Girl* and *Twilight*. "Instead of opening adolescents and young adults to worldly realities, acquainting them with the global village," Bauerlein writes, "digital communications have opened them to one another—which is to say, have enclosed them in a parochial cosmos of youth matters and concerns."[9] God forbid that you post something on your blog about *Gossip Girl* if nobody's watching it anymore. The Jonas Brothers are the hot group for many teen girls right now, but those three young men could be out of fashion in a month or a week. If you mention the Jonas Brothers to a teen girl by the time this book comes out, she may roll her eyes and say, "The Jonas Brothers are *so* last year." Staying hip, staying on top of the latest whim of adolescent fashion, requires constant vigilance. But it achieves nothing lasting.

Spending so much time in social networking sites is "like a meal of cotton candy," according to University of Richmond neuroscientist Craig Kinsley, who has studied people who are addicted to Facebook and Twitter: "When you come right down to it, there is not much substance."[10] And like cotton candy, too much can make you sick.

better living through chemistry

Mariah should have known better. She's a smart girl. She had been a nearly straight-A student from elementary school through middle school. That's why her parents were puzzled and concerned when her grades began to tumble in ninth grade. She seemed to have the motivation to do well. She worked hard on her homework: Mom and Dad would knock on her door late at night, and she'd be typing away on the keyboard, working on her Spanish assignment or creative writing for her English class. She spent hours every night at the computer. But even so, she was having trouble finishing some assignments. She was getting mostly Bs now, even the occasional C. When she scored a 72 on the Spanish test—and Spanish had always been her best subject—her Mom, Linda, decided it was time to take action.

"Is it the teacher?" Linda asked. "Do you have a problem with the teacher?"

"No, Mom, the teacher's fine," Mariah said, mildly exasperated.

"Then what is it? You've never struggled with Spanish before."

"I don't know. I just seem to be having trouble concentrating," Mariah said.

"You mean it's hard for you to pay attention?" Linda asked.

"Yeah."

Aha. A problem with attention. Linda had been reading a popular book about attention-deficit hyperactivity disorder (ADHD). It all fit. Mariah had also been forgetting simple things like where she put her favorite sweater. She had even lost her house keys, something that had never happened before. Had Mariah developed attention-deficit disorder?

Linda made an appointment for Mariah to see the pediatrician. The pediatrician asked Linda to fill out a questionnaire called the Conners' Parents Rating Scale. The questionnaire includes a checklist of items such as "has trouble finishing assignments" and "is often forgetful" and "loses things." For each of these items, the parent is supposed to indicate whether the item applies to their child often, or seldom, or never. As she was filling out the questionnaire, Linda felt sure that she had discovered her daughter's problem. Linda had checked the "very often" column for most of the items listed. Linda was convinced that Mariah must have ADHD.

Dr. Shapiro, the pediatrician, was running behind schedule. She listened to Linda explain her concerns, then asked Mariah a few questions.

"Is it hard for you to pay attention in class?" Dr. Shapiro asked.

Mariah nodded.

"Do you find yourself forgetting things a lot? Leaving things at home that you meant to bring to school, for example?"

Mariah nodded.

Dr. Shapiro glanced over the Conners' Scale that Linda had filled out. "Let's try Concerta, 18 mg every morning. You should see at least some improvement right away. Call my office and let me know how you're doing. If things don't get better, we can increase the dose to 36 mg or even 54 mg. But a dose of 18 or 36 mg every morning should do the trick." Dr. Shapiro wrote the prescription, handed it to Linda, and left the room.

After the prescription had been filled, Linda and Mariah both looked at the little oblong beige tablets with fascination.

"Do you really think this will make a difference?" Mariah asked.

"I hope so," Linda answered.

Linda's prayers were answered, or so it seemed. The first day Mariah took the medication, she reported that it was definitely easier to pay attention in school. Over the next few weeks, she still stayed up past midnight to finish her homework, but at least she was finishing it instead of turning it in half-undone. On the next Spanish test, she earned an 88. That was a big improvement over her previous performance, though still not an A.

Linda called Dr. Shapiro after Mariah had been on the medication for three weeks and gave her a progress report. Mariah was better but still not back to where she had been a year or two before.

"Has she had any problems, any side effects?" Dr. Shapiro asked.

"Like what?"

"Difficulty sleeping, tremor, loss of appetite?" Dr. Shapiro said.

"Well, she certainly doesn't have any trouble sleeping," Linda answered. "She falls asleep at the drop of a hat. And I haven't seen any tremor. She doesn't seem to be eating a whole lot, but I can't say whether that's a big change."

"Let's try upping the dose to 36 mg each morning," Dr. Shapiro said.

The stronger dose seemed to do the trick. Mariah noticed a further improvement in her ability to concentrate the first day on the 36 mg dose. Her grades on her homework and her quizzes soon improved as well. Mariah seemed on her way to being a straight-A student again.

Then one day Linda noticed that Mariah didn't look right. She seemed short of breath, though she was sitting still. "Are you OK?" Linda asked.

Mariah didn't answer the question directly. Instead, she asked her Mom, "Is it normal for your heart to go *thump thumpity thump* a lot?"

Linda knew how to check a pulse at the wrist. Thump thump *thumpity* thump thump *thumpity.* Linda called Dr. Shapiro's office and spoke with the nurse. The nurse explained that the palpitations might be a side effect of the medication and that they were probably not dangerous.

"Should I bring Mariah in to see the doctor?" Linda asked.

"Only if the palpitations are bothering her," the nurse said.

Linda brought Mariah to me for a second opinion.

For many girls today, life is out of balance. Imagine a girl growing up 40 years ago or 100 years ago. She had a home life, usually with siblings and one or two parents, so she had to deal with the challenge of getting along with her parents and brothers and/or sisters. She may have had extended family in the neighborhood—grandparents, aunts and uncles, cousins. She certainly knew other girls and boys in her age group at school, and perhaps a somewhat different group at her church or synagogue. She very likely knew other kids outside her age group, younger and older. Her social life had different dimensions and characteristics depending on whether she was interacting with her household family, extended family, same-age peers, or different-age peers. It varied depending on whether she was in her own home or a friend's home or at school or at church or synagogue.

As recently as 50 years ago, most girls cared more about their parents' opinion than about the opinions of their friends. In one classic study, published in 1961, researchers asked girls whether they would join a school club if their parents disapproved. Then they asked the girls whether they would join the same club if their best friend disapproved. The majority of girls said that they would not join the club if their parents disapproved, but the approval or disapproval of their best friend carried less weight.[11]

What a difference five decades make. For the past 50 years, the importance of same-age peers has been increasing while other social frames of reference—parents, siblings, extended family, and different-age peers—have been dissolving into irrelevance. The modern girl's attitude is nicely summarized in the memorable title of Anthony Wolf's 1991 best seller for parents, *Get Out of My Life—But First Could You Drive Me and Cheryl to the Mall?*

Today, "social life" for children and teenagers means "social life with kids the same age." Everything else has become trivial by comparison. Tweens and teens now have their own culture, a culture their parents may barely understand.

This may seem obvious today, but as recently as the 1950s scholars disputed whether teens even had their own culture.[12] Going back 80 years or more, before 1930, children and teenagers truly did not have their own culture, their own music, their own movies. Though there has always been a small market for books specifically for children, the cultural life of the family was not sharply segregated by age. In the 1920s, the family might have had a single phonograph player, and family members usually listened to whatever the parents wanted to listen to. The family listened to radio programs together on the family's one radio. Radios were expensive in that era. Going back to the era before radio, in the 1800s, most events and attractions in the cultural life of the community—musical events, theatrical performances, church revivals—were attended by the family as a unit. The circus was one notable exception, as a form of entertainment in the 1800s that targeted children, although it did not exclude adults. But going to the circus was a rare treat, not a daily routine.

James Coleman, professor of sociology at Johns Hopkins University, was among the first to call attention to the phenomenon of the adolescent culture, with a language all its own and a value system that differs from adult value systems. "To put it simply, these young people speak a different language. What is more relevant, the language they speak is becoming more and more different," he wrote in 1961. "We think of high school in our society as having been in existence for a long time. But in 1900, only 11 percent of this country's high-school-age youth were *in* high school; as late as 1930, the proportion was only 51 percent."[13] Before 1900, many societies, including North American and Western European society, were delineated by sex. By the time they reached their teen years, most boys in that era were already working with men; likewise, most of the teenage girls were working with the women. Education beyond roughly age 12 was the exception rather than the rule until the 20th century.

Even in the second half of the 20th century, when most teenagers were in high school and therefore participating in the new adolescent culture, they were not completely submerged in it. Certainly before 1995 — before the explosion in the availability of cell phones, e-mail, instant messaging, and the technology of 24/7 connectedness — girls had a private life and private time. Girls spent time with their peers, either face to face or on the telephone, but they also had time by themselves, whether they wanted it or not.

Today, a girl can be connected to other girls her own age almost every waking moment, via cell phone, texting, instant messaging, and so on. This technology can put girls at risk, because it deprives the girls of any break, any breather, any alternate perspective. According to one recent report, American teenagers now send an average of 2,272 text messages each month.[14] That works out to an average of more than 70 messages every day. And that's just the *average*.

But as these girls become hyperconnected to their peers, they are disconnecting from themselves. Professor Sherry Turkle, director of the Initiative on Technology and Self at the Massachusetts Institute of Technology, believes that all this texting is likely to disrupt adolescent development. Tweens and teenagers need time to reflect on who they are and who they want to become: time to "just chill," as they themselves say. But "if something next to you is vibrating every couple of minutes, it makes it very difficult to be in that state of mind," Professor Turkle observes.[15]

Mariah's resting EKG in my office showed a heart rate of 110 beats per minute with occasional ventricular and supraventricular contractions. That's a fancy way of saying that her heart was beating in a fast and irregular rhythm, nothing immediately life-threatening, but definitely not healthy. We had to find out what was causing the problem and fix it.

I ordered all the usual tests that should be ordered when evaluating a teenager with irregular heartbeat: thyroid hormone levels, complete blood count, blood mineral levels, and the like. But the fact that the palpitations only began after Mariah's dose of Concerta had been increased made me suspect that the medication was to blame. I asked how the diagnosis of ADHD had been established in Mariah's case.

There are five criteria that must be satisfied in order to make the diagnosis of ADHD.* Of those five, difficulty paying attention is the *least* important—that is to say, it is the least useful in distinguishing ADHD from other problems that cause inattention. One of the five criteria is that the physician must exclude other causes for the attention deficit, such as sleep deprivation.

"How much sleep are you getting?" I asked.

"Enough," Mariah answered curtly.

"Mariah, please, be polite," Linda said.

"What time do you usually go to sleep?" I asked.

Mariah glanced at her Mom. She realized she couldn't cheat on this question, because her Mom knew perfectly well what time Mariah actually turned off her lights. "Sometimes I'm in bed by midnight," she said.

"But most nights?" I asked.

"Most nights I'm asleep by 1 A.M."

---

* For more information on the five criteria for diagnosing ADHD, please see pp. 193–199 of my second book, *Boys Adrift*.

"And when do you get up in the morning?" I asked.

"Usually 6 A.M.," Mariah said.

"So that's about five hours a night," I said. Most teens need nine hours a night to function at their full potential. "What keeps you up so late?"

"Homework," Mariah said. "I have tons of homework."

"You're doing homework until one in the morning?" I asked.

"Yeah," Mariah said. When I looked unconvinced, she said, "Ask my Mom. She can tell you. I'm doing my homework."

Before Linda could confirm what Mariah was saying, I said: "Wait. Your computer is in your bedroom, isn't it?"

"*Obviously,*" Mariah said, rolling her eyes. "Where else would it be, in the bathtub?"

"Mariah, please," Linda said.

"And your Mom respects your privacy, right? So she knocks before she comes into your bedroom?"

Linda and Mariah both nodded.

I turned to Linda. "I don't think Mariah is working on her homework nonstop, 10 P.M. till 1 A.M. I think she is spending a good chunk of that time on her Facebook page or texting or instant messaging her friends. You don't know that, because you very politely knock on Mariah's door. It only takes one mouse click for Mariah to switch screens, so that when you come in the room, you see her homework on the screen instead of her cell phone or her Facebook page."

Linda shook her head in disbelief. "How can you be so sure of that?"

"Mariah?" I asked.

I waited for Mariah to speak next. A long pause followed.

"OK, so maybe I'm spending *some* of that time working on my Face-book page," she conceded with a shrug. "When else am I supposed to do it? By the time I get home from soccer practice, it's supper time, then I do my homework and then bam, it's 11:00."

I glanced at Linda. She understood.

I explained to Mariah and her Mom how sleep deprivation can mimic ADHD almost perfectly. The sleep-deprived teenager will have trouble focusing and concentrating. She will have trouble finishing tasks. She will be absent-minded. She will lose her house keys. She will look exactly like a teenager who has ADHD. But the appropriate remedy for sleep deprivation is to get more sleep, not to start taking stimulant medications. (Nor is the solution to drink lots of coffee. I am seeing more and more teenage girls, especially in affluent communities, who start their day at the coffee shop with a double-shot espresso latte. They're caffeine addicts by the age of 15, sometimes even younger.)

The problem with medications such as Adderall, Ritalin, Concerta, Metadate, Focalin, Daytrana, and many of the other medications that are most often prescribed for ADHD is that they work. They are powerful stimulants in the same chemical family as amphetamine, a.k.a. "speed."* College students know this. Go to any American university and you can find students who admit to using these medications to stay up all night to write a paper or study, then ace the examination the next day. If you take 60 mg of Adderall in the evening, it's easy to stay up all night. If you take another 60 mg the next morning, it's not hard to concentrate on the examination and even do well on it.

But it's dangerous to abuse these medications in this way. There's a high risk of cardiovascular complications, beginning with the palpitations that Mariah experienced and extending up to more serious irregularities of heart rhythm, and even stroke. The Canadian government briefly pulled Adderall off the market precisely because of its concern about these risks.[16] There's also a much greater risk of psychological dependence when the medications are abused this way.

I explained to Mariah and Linda that Mariah's difficulties at school might be due at least in part to her sleep deprivation. The only way to find out for sure would be for Mariah to cut back on her dose of Concerta—preferably eliminating it altogether—and at the same time for Mariah to get more sleep.

---

* Adderall—the most commonly prescribed medication for ADHD in the United States—is a mixture of four different types of amphetamines.

"How am I supposed to do that?" Mariah asked. "It's not like I waste a lot of time watching TV. I barely even watch TV. Either I'm at practice or I'm doing my homework."

"Or you're working on your Facebook page," I added.

Mariah shrugged.

"Mariah, I think you're going to have to cut back on your Facebook time. No more than 30 minutes per day on Facebook or texting or instant message, at least for the time being," I said. Linda nodded, but Mariah was seething. "And we need to get your computer out of your bedroom. It needs to be out in the open, where your Mom and Dad can see you. I respect your right to privacy, but your parents have to know what you're doing on your computer. Your computer has to move to the family room or the kitchen or the living room. It can't be in your bedroom."

Mariah threw a major fit. She absolutely did not want to give up her unrestricted Facebook time. But Linda supported my recommendations and agreed to enforce them. The computer was moved to the family room. Mom and Dad installed software that timed Mariah's access to Facebook and recorded every website she visited, as well as logging how she spent her time on the computer—browsing the Web, instant messaging, or working on her homework. Linda also agreed to enforce a bedtime of 11 P.M.

Mariah left the office speechless with anger. I learned later that she complained bitterly to her friends about me and her Mom, and also about her Dad when he sided with Linda on this issue. We didn't *understand*. We were totally *clueless*. But Mom and Dad stuck to their guns.

We immediately cut back the Concerta to 18 mg. Mariah started sleeping at least seven hours a night. Then we were able to stop the Concerta altogether. The palpitations went away and did not come back.

Mariah didn't have ADHD. The previous doctor had failed to do a careful evaluation and had made the wrong diagnosis. The Concerta helped not because Mariah had ADHD but because Concerta—like most medications prescribed for ADHD—is a powerful stimulant that compensated for her sleep deprivation.

Mariah never agreed with the intervention suggested by me and implemented by her parents, but after a few weeks, according to Linda, she wasn't complaining about it quite as much. Nevertheless, it's clear that Mariah would never have regulated her Facebook time on her own. Mariah was fortunate that her parents were confident enough of their authority as parents to do what was best for Mariah.

too hard, too soft, just right

Diana Baumrind has spent most of her adult life studying what makes for good parenting. For more than 30 years, she and her colleagues interviewed families, getting to know the parents and the children, so that they understood how those parents were raising their kids. Then they watched to see how those kids turned out.

Dr. Baumrind identified three basic parenting styles, which she calls "authoritarian," "permissive," and "authoritative." I've always found it confusing that she uses two similar words, *authoritarian* and *authoritative,* to describe two very different parenting styles. Author Judith Rich Harris shares my confusion, so she refers to Baumrind's styles as "Too Hard," "Too Soft," and "Just Right."[17] I will borrow Harris' nicknames here.

Authoritarian (Too Hard): This is the ultra-strict parent. Any deviation from the rules is penalized, sometimes with corporal punishment, regardless of any mitigating circumstances. This parent seldom shows love or affection to the child and is not reliably responsive to the child's needs. He or she may be hypercritical of the child's behavior and may make excessive and unrealistic demands. If you saw the movie *Dead Poets Society,* the character of Mr. Perry played by Kurtwood Smith is a classic authoritarian parent. He is a demanding father who dictates which activities his son may or may not participate in and what career he must choose. The father's harshness and lack of responsiveness ultimately pushes the boy to commit suicide. That's the nightmare scenario.

Permissive (Too Soft): These are the laid-back parents, very good at expressing love and affection for their child, and not so good at enforcing the rules. If you've watched episodes of the TV series *The Gilmore Girls*, the mother, Lorelai Gilmore, played by Lauren Graham, is a classic permissive parent, taking advice and instruction *from* her daughter more often than she provides it. That role reversal makes for entertaining television, but it's not a good model for parents to follow.

Authoritative (Just Right): This parent is firm but not excessively rigid. Rules can bend to accommodate special circumstances. Though these parents communicate their love for their child, they also enforce the rules in a fair and consistent manner. The characters of Dr. and Mrs. Huxtable on *The Cosby Show* exemplify authoritative parents. Over Dr. Baumrind's three decades of research, she accumulated overwhelming evidence that the healthiest parenting style is the *authoritative* style: firm but not rigid, loving but not permissive. Most of us are striving to get it "just right": not too hard, not too soft.

In dealing with Mariah's excessive use of Facebook and other online sites, Mariah's parents were authoritative: they were "Just Right." Linda and her husband were willing to accommodate Mariah when possible, but they were also willing to be "tough" when they had to restrict Mariah's access to Facebook for the sake of her health.

Parenting is an art, not a science. You can't type the details of your situation into a computer and get a printout of what the "Just Right" parent should do. Reasonable parents with good intentions may differ about what's "Just Right" in a particular situation. I find many parents who are striving to be "Just Right" parents in most areas, but who make no effort to exercise parental authority over their child's use of 21st-century technology. These parents may not understand social networking sites very well. Their children don't want them looking over their shoulders in any case. Some parents feel that they are violating their daughter's privacy by watching what she's doing online. Some parents seem to feel that "she's in her room, by herself, tapping away at the keyboard—it can't be that bad." If you think about what you have just said, you will immediately realize that a girl tapping away at a computer keyboard alone in her room could be getting herself into all kinds of trouble.

You wouldn't let your 15-year-old daughter, much less your 10-year-old daughter, go to a college fraternity party by herself. By the same token, although for different reasons, you should not allow your daughter to engage in online social networking without your supervision. If you let your daughter post anything she wants on her social networking page without your knowledge, then you are engaging in permissive parenting as per Dr. Baumrind's categories. And we know that permissive parents are more likely to have kids who get into trouble, kids who get in over their heads, kids who don't understand boundaries.

For your daughter's sake, you must be aware of what she's doing on her social networking page. But how can a parent who doesn't fully understand MySpace or Facebook really be aware of how her 11- or 14-year-old daughter is using those sites? Don't worry: you are not the only 21st-century parent who wants to understand what her daughter is doing online. There are two devices you need to oversee: your daughter's computer, and her cell phone. Here's how to do it.

you the parent, a.k.a. computer cop

Let's begin with a few basics regarding your daughter's use of the computer.

First: the computer should be in a public space within your home, such as the living room. Your daughter has a right to her physical privacy. You should always knock before entering her bedroom, for instance. But that means that the computer can't be in the bedroom. It has to be in a common space.

Second: your daughter must understand that her access to the computer and to the Internet is a privilege, not a right. She may lose that privilege if she abuses it. These rules should ideally be explained to her before you ever plug in the Internet connection, but if you haven't explained this reality to her before, do so now. Better late than never.

Third: make sure your daughter understands that it is your responsibility to be aware of what she's doing on the computer. She needs to know that you are looking over her shoulder. That knowledge may provide her with the excuse she needs not to go along with the crowd. "I *can't* do that because my Dad checks everything I do online" is way easier for your daughter to say than "I *won't* do that because I don't think it's right."

Once you've decided to be the "Just Right" parent with regard to your daughter's use of social networking—firm but not harsh, reasonable without being permissive—how do you follow through? Not to worry. Many good computer programs have been developed with your needs in mind.

NetNanny is one such program.* It can track every site your daughter visits and can block access to sites you specify. NetNanny also allows you to create a day-by-day schedule, in half-hour increments, so you can specify exactly when your daughter is allowed to be online. You can also specify a weekly cap on the total amount of time online per week. Other programs such as WebRoot and CyberPatrol allow you to specify how much time your daughter spends at particular sites (NetNanny only monitors total time online).

As the tracking software gets more sophisticated, kids try to come up with ways to get around it. Proxy sites and secure prefixes are among the strategies kids use to outwit the software. Say that you don't want your child to visit www.leonardsax.com. Kids have discovered that if they use the secure prefix "https," most software will allow them through. But the latest version of NetNanny will block access both to the regular URL, http://www.leonardsax.com, and to the secure URL, https://www.leonardsax.com. This technology is constantly evolving, so make sure that you keep current. Remember to check for updates for whatever monitoring software you decide to install.

Instant messaging is another area where you need to give careful thought to what degree of monitoring is appropriate for your daughter. NetNanny and similar programs offer you a range of options. You can

---

* I'm not endorsing any one program. By the time you read this book, there may be better software programs available. I mention a specific brand here just to make it easier for you to start your search.

block all access to instant messaging, or you can allow access and record every word of the conversation, or you can allow access but flag only dangerous content. This is a judgment call that depends on your daughter's maturity. The younger the girl, the more monitoring I recommend. The program alerts your daughter that her conversation is being recorded, as it should.

It's not enough to monitor your daughter's use of the computer; you must also be aware of what's going on with her cell phone, if she has one. Because many of today's cell phones can access the Internet, sending and receiving instant messages, photos, and so on, you should be aware of what your daughter is doing with her cell phone for the same reasons you should be aware of what she's doing on the computer.

Let me emphasize that monitoring your daughter's use of the cell phone and the computer should never be done surreptitiously. You must explain to your daughter why you need to be looking over her shoulder. Make sure that the software also reminds her that you are watching.* That's good not only for your daughter but also for her friends. Your daughter can show her friends the message on her cell phone screen reminding her that Mom and Dad are looking at everything she does.

Not all parents agree with me on this point. What one parent considers intrusive or authoritarian may be "Just Right" parenting for another. Some parents are uneasy with any sort of monitoring. As one parent said to me, "In a few years, she'll be away at college and I won't have any control at all, so it doesn't make sense to me to try to be Big Brother now." As I tried to explain to that mother, girls become more mature and develop better judgment as they get older. An 18-year-old young woman probably has a better understanding of risks and benefits than a 15-year-old girl has. We know a lot about brain development in teenagers. We know that the areas of the brain involved in balancing risk and benefits, such as the dorsolateral prefrontal cortex, mature significantly in girls between 15

---

* "My Mobile Watchdog," www.mymobilewatchdog.com, is one program that allows parents to monitor all aspects of their child's cell phone usage while reminding the child that Mom and Dad are watching.

and 18 years of age.[18] So what's appropriate for an 18-year-old may not be appropriate for a 15-year-old.

Here's a tip from one Mom and Dad: keep the cell phone charger in the parents' room. Every evening at 10 P.M. your daughter's cell phone goes into the charger in your room. Next morning, your daughter gets her phone back. I've heard of too many girls who are receiving text messages on their cell phone past midnight.

You have to practice what you preach. Declare the family dinner table to be an electronics-free zone: no texting and no cell phone use allowed at the dinner table. That means you too, Dad. Although teenage girls are more likely than teenage boys to be addicted to texting and instant messaging, there seems to be a gender reversal in the over-30 crowd, with Dad more likely than Mom to be surreptitiously checking messages on his Blackberry at the dinner table.[19] All electronic devices should be prohibited at mealtime.

I recommend that you monitor your daughter's cell phone use and Internet use right up until her eighteenth birthday. By keeping close tabs on her during her teen years—and by your daughter knowing that you're keeping tabs on her—you help her to develop good habits. She's also had plenty of opportunities to see how much time other kids can waste with this stuff.

There are no guarantees in parenting, but if you give your daughter years of practice doing it the right way, the odds that she will do it the right way at college are better than if she never had that practice.

mean-girl cyberbully

Mariah's experience was relatively benign. Nobody was bullying her online. Nobody was posting cruel messages on her Facebook page.

Other girls have a different experience.

Recall Melissa and Jessica from the Introduction. They were best friends starting in kindergarten. They were both friendly, athletic, and above average intelligence. Melissa was brunette and Jessica was blonde. Aside from that, they might have been clones. They liked to wear the same clothes, read the same books, and listen to the same music. "We were inseparable," Melissa told me. "We were more than best friends. We were way better than most sisters. We were like those identical twins you read about. We could read each other's minds. We didn't even need to talk. If somebody said something silly, we could just look at each other and then laugh hysterically for an hour."

It was a unique bond. Both girls agree that it lasted for an amazingly long time: from the end of kindergarten right through eighth grade.

Then in ninth grade, in a matter of days, it was over. Jessica suddenly developed an insatiable need to make new friends. Because Jessica and Melissa were so alike in so many ways, they occupied the same social niche. At some not-quite-conscious level, Jessica seems to have decided that there wasn't room for two athletic/smart/pretty white girls in the same niche. Jessica turned on Melissa. It started with the usual sort of nastiness. Jessica hosted a huge party. She invited practically the whole class—but not Melissa. Next, Melissa found that she no longer had anyone to sit with at lunch. If she tried to sit with Jessica or any of Jessica's friends—which now seemed to include most of the girls—they ignored her. None of the girls would speak to her. "It was like I wasn't even there," Melissa told me.

Then Jessica and her collaborators went online. Girls posted mysterious comments on Melissa's MySpace page like "we know what you did with Justin on Saturday." Justin was a boy Melissa barely even knew, and she hadn't even seen Justin that Saturday. Another comment read, "Melissa—please get help for your drinking problem. We care about you!" Melissa didn't have a drinking problem. She didn't drink. Jessica sent her an instant message late one evening that read, "I can't believe how nasty you are. I don't want to be friends with you anymore." Melissa immediately sent a message back: "What did I do? Why can't we talk?" She received no reply.

"It was relentless," Melissa recalls. Girls would text her on her cell phone, inviting her to nonexistent parties, or send her messages like "y r u so mean?" She would try to send a text message in reply, but she would receive only cursory responses such as DIKU—Do I Know You?—or no message at all.

"By the middle of tenth grade, not a single girl at school would even talk to me," Melissa told me.

"How did you survive?" I asked.

"I started making friends with the boys," Melissa said. She had previously been shy around boys, preferring to hang with the girls. But "the boys were totally oblivious to what the girls were doing," she said. "They had no idea that the girls were boycotting me. They had no clue that they were rescuing me, but they rescued me." She started hanging out with the boys, even watching ESPN with them.

This made the girls even more malicious. The MySpace posts grew more hateful. Melissa closed her MySpace page. Someone else, claiming to be her, opened a new page. The cruel comments and photos proliferated— only now Melissa could no longer delete them. "It made me physically sick just to look at that page and see all the horrible things they were saying about me. I couldn't stand to go to school. I couldn't make eye contact. I could only wonder, 'Is this girl one of the girls who's been saying those awful things about me?'" There was no safe place.

Melissa and her parents spoke with the school's guidance counselor and the assistant principal. They said there was nothing they could do. There was no way to determine who was behind the cyberbullying, even though Melissa is sure to this day that Jessica was the ringleader. So Melissa arranged to take all her senior-year courses at the community college. "I just had to stop caring," she said.

One thing Melissa really needed, and didn't have, was an alternative community of girls and women who could have given her a hug and told her not to care what those mean girls were saying about her. Boys can't provide that. The boys Melissa had befriended were fine, but when a teenage boy hugs a teenage girl, the subtext is different, and a girl needs to stay on her guard. What Melissa needed was another place where she could feel at home. (I will have more to say about alternative all-female communities in Chapter 7.)

There is nothing new about girls being mean to other girls. What's new is the technology that allows cyberbullies to inflict their pain 24/7. Bullying in the cyberbubble differs from the bullying of previous generations in two important respects: first, it's nonstop with no escape. Even when your daughter is alone at home, she is still being victimized online, and she knows it. Her cell phone is vibrating with nasty texts. Who's sending them?

That brings us to the second difference from bullying in the olden days (that is, the 1990s and earlier): cyberbullying can be completely anonymous. Twenty years ago, if a girl wanted to spread rumors about another girl, everybody would know who was doing it. That knowledge constrained what the bully might say. If you got too nasty, your nastiness could reflect badly on you. But now you can pretend to be a boy who's just received sexual services from Leeanne, then post something about Leeanne online, and nobody will ever know that you are actually a girl who invented the whole story to make Leeanne look bad.

* Facebook and MySpace are the best-known of the social networking sites. Many lesser-known sites are more toxic. The *Washington Post* recently reported on one of them, www.peoplesdirt.com, which was developed specifically to enable high-school kids to say awful things about other high-school kids with complete anonymity. The reporters for the *Post* noted that this site is "a hive of anonymous slander where girls are listed by name as promiscuous." The principal of Walt Whitman High School in Bethesda, Maryland, Alan Goodwin, said that he is particularly vexed by the complete anonymity the site provides. "Some of these things are causing certain students great distress," he said. According to Debra Munk, principal at another Maryland high school, one girl was so upset by comments posted about her on the website that she refused to go to school. "There is no limit to what is said," Munk observed. "People can say it's free speech, but it's very toxic for our kids and their culture."

There's nothing illegal about one girl posting an anonymous note, allegedly from Jason, saying that another girl tried to give Jason a blow job but Jason laughed at her. Montgomery County detective John Reinikka investigated the site described in the *Washington Post* article but found no illegal activity. Calling other girls names is not against the law. "It's so frustrating," he said. "There's nothing positive about the site at all. Young girls are coming home crying."[20]

That's why you *must* know what is going on when your daughter is online. You have to know whether she is being bullied. You have to know whether she is a bully. Remember, even nice girls can be bullies. Jessica is — to everybody besides Melissa — a very sweet girl, truly, and now a successful student at a top university.

the invention of alcohol — in 2005?

Imagine that alcohol had just been discovered. Imagine that the human race had existed for all these millennia, and then suddenly in 2005 somebody discovered how to ferment grapes to make wine. Within just a few years, let's imagine, beer and whiskey and gin were developed as well. It wouldn't take long to understand the risks of drunkenness. But it might not be immediately obvious that these beverages should generally be prohibited to 15-year-olds.

That's the situation we are in with regard to these new technologies. As reporter Emily Nussbaum observed after interviewing teenagers and young adults on these topics, "We are in the sticky center of a vast psychological experiment, one that's only just begun to show results. . . . We're living in frontier country right now. We can take guesses at the future, but it's hard to gauge the effects of a drug while you're still taking it."[21] We are going to learn the hard way what happens when kids are allowed to immerse themselves in this technology before their sense of self has had a chance to form.

Adult guidance is essential. To continue the analogy: some countries allow teenagers to drink alcoholic beverages, but most countries that allow 16-year-olds to drink permit this drinking only in the company of a parent or other responsible adult, and they usually don't allow 16-year-olds to buy alcohol, only to drink alcohol that has been purchased by an adult. Maybe that tradition can provide a rough template for us. Maybe young teenagers who want to use these sites should do so only under the auspices of an adult who takes responsibility for them. This is a discussion that we, as parents, need to have. We haven't even begun.

sexting

Greensburg, Pennsylvania, is a small town about 30 miles east of Pittsburgh. Three girls there—14 and 15 years old—thought it would be fun to take pictures of each other, semi-clothed or unclothed, with their cell phones, and then send the photos to their boyfriends. One of the girls brought her cell phone to school, where it was confiscated by a school administrator. No cell phones are allowed in the school. The administrator discovered the pictures on the phone and alerted police. The police arrested the three girls and charged them with distribution of child pornography. If convicted, the girls will have to register as sex offenders and will have to report to local police authorities as sex offenders, wherever they live in the United States, for the next 20 years. The fact that they were distributing pictures of themselves doesn't change the law. If you distribute a photo of an unclothed juvenile, you're distributing child pornography, even if *you* are the juvenile and it was "just for fun."[22]

One issue here, of course, is that the child pornography laws were conceived and written mostly in the prehistoric era—that is to say, before 2005. In that era, only the privileged few possessed cell phones that could easily take photos and upload them to the Internet. Ten years earlier, before 1995 say, such technology was practically unknown, the stuff of science fiction and Dick Tracy. But the child porn laws do not contain exceptions for kids taking photos of themselves.

In case you haven't heard the term, *sexting* refers to sending sexy pictures via your cell phone. The latest surveys indicate that at least one in five teens engage in sexting, and it's almost always photos of girls, not boys, that are being sent.[23] If your daughter takes a picture of herself semi-clothed, even if she never sends it to anyone, she could be prosecuted for production of child pornography. If she sends the photo to her boyfriend, she could be charged with distribution of child pornography.

Certainly it would be appropriate to update the laws so that girls doing silly things don't get labeled as "sex offenders" for the next 20 years of their life. Dante Bertani is the chief public defender in West-moreland County, Pennsylvania. That's the jurisdiction where those girls from Greensburg had to face charges of child pornography. He said that the prosecutor's decision to bring child porn charges against these kids was "horrendous." Such treatment should be reserved for sex offenders, he said, not for some silly teenagers. "It should be an issue between the school, the parents, and the kids — and primarily the parents and the kids," Bertani said. "It's not something that should be going through the criminal system."[24]

Meanwhile, you must be on your guard. Legal expert Lisa Bloom recommends that parents should not give their kids cell phones or Internet access "without educating them about the consequences of misuse. Monitor their online behavior. Check their phones." If you find that your daughter has sent or received "one blurry boob picture [then as a consequence,] they lose the phone and computer for a week. . . . They will HATE you, Mom, you are so mean! What-ever. Beats trying to sneak snacks to them at the Big House."[25]

The larger issue for us as parents is how this new technology interacts with the first factor we considered: sexual identity. As we discussed in Chapter 1, more girls today are self-objectifying, focusing on how they look instead of on who they are. This phenomenon of sexting — and the associated phenomenon of girls posting suggestive photos of themselves on their social networking pages — makes the cyberbubble a really toxic place, even without regard to the risk of criminal charges. As Dr. Hinshaw observes, the cyberculture exacerbates the "culture of self-objectification; girls turn themselves instantly into images, meant to be viewed from the outside in, actively inviting viewers to watch, judge, admire. Experience itself becomes an object to display."[26]

your daughter the (micro-)celebrity

Columnist Clive Thompson, writing for *Wired* magazine, recently observed that we have entered the age of "microcelebrity." When real celebrities like Angelina Jolie or Reese Witherspoon go to a party, they know that somebody may take their photograph. They know that the photograph may appear within a matter of hours or minutes in the blogosphere before finding its way into the print media. They know that if they say something dumb, someone at the party might quote them on a social networking page or a blog or on Wikipedia. These celebrities know they have to be careful about what they say and about how they look. They know that they must be always on their guard.

Girls in the cyberbubble nowadays learn that they must exercise much the same caution. As Nussbaum wrote in her interview with some of these blogger girls, the girls have "to be constantly aware that anything you say can and will be used against you." Nussbaum observes that these girls, just like real celebrities and like politicians, are learning that they must "learn to parse each sentence they form, unsure whether it will be ignored or redound into sudden notoriety. In essence, every young person [in the cyberbubble] has become, in the literal sense, a public figure. And so they have adopted the skills that celebrities learn in order not to go crazy."[27] Watch what you say. Be witty—but don't offend your friends. Be cute—but not skanky. Be spontaneous—but not stupid. And if you make a single mistake, it could go online and stay there . . . forever.

In his essay for *Wired*, Thompson writes that "we're learning to live in front of a crowd." That's precisely the problem. The strain of living in front of a crowd, 24/7, 365 days a year, is what causes real celebrities to fall apart. Remember Britney Spears shaving her head and attacking that car with an umbrella? Spears was 25 years old at the time. She wasn't a teenager. She was (or was supposed to be) a mature adult. She was the mother of two young children.

How much harder is it for teenagers? When today's teenage girls go to a party, Thompson says, "they make sure they're dressed for their close-up—because there *will* be photos, and those photos *will* end up online. In managing their Web presence, they understand the impact of logos, images, and fonts."[28] But do they? Is the average teenage girl better able to manage her Web "brand" than, say, Britney Spears at age 25? *Should* she be? Should we be expecting teenage girls to manage their "brand" with the slick sophistication of a public relations professional?

Many girls are trying their best. That's part of the problem. Theresa Senft teaches media studies and was one of the first to identify this phenomenon of microcelebrity. "People are using the same techniques employed on Madison Avenue to manage their personal lives," says Senft. "Humans are getting corporatized."[29]

That's what concerns me. It's one thing for an adult woman who has chosen the life of a celebrity to use slick Madison Avenue techniques to present herself to those watching, but we are talking about tween girls and teenage girls. These girls are not yet adults. They are packaging a product—their own self—that has not yet had a chance to develop.

In the previous chapter we discussed how girls are being pushed to present a sexual identity before their sexual identity has been formed. As a result, many girls are confused about who they are sexually. The cyberbubble is driving a similar process, but with respect to the sense of self, the very notion of who you are as a person.

Every child and every teenager needs to have a "sense of place."[30] They need to know where they came from, where they are, and where they want to go. Tweens and teens who get trapped in the cyberbubble will find it harder to acquire that sense of place. Instead of feeling at home with who they are, they will try to corporatize their image, to make their brand slick and cool. Even adult celebrities have trouble keeping themselves straight in their own heads, distinguishing who they really are from who their publicity people say they are. And those are the grown-ups.

It's all happening way too early in the lives of these girls. The end result of both these factors—confused sexual identity, and the claustrophobic world inside the cyberbubble—is girls who don't know who they are. Because they don't know who they are, they are all too ready to seize on anything real to define themselves: something tangible and solid and sharp. Even if it's a razor blade they use to cut themselves. Or a bottle of gin. Or a finger down the throat. Or a straight-A report card combined with an incredible list of extracurriculars.

Obsessions.

obsessions

One of the trademark perfect-girl talents is this ability to ignore and overcome the body's weakness in pursuit of a goal. We quickly condition ourselves to tune out our own internal signals, our aches and pains, our hungers, and tune up our plans, our determination, our control. What works in the short term, however, eventually leads to burnout.

COURTNEY MARTIN[1]

thinspiration

I first met Lauren while I was doing a medical consultation on the psychiatric ward. She was 14 years old. She looked as though she were made out of translucent porcelain. She spoke softly, as though she might crack into pieces if she raised her voice. Lauren, who was 5'5" tall, had been hospitalized when her weight dropped to 87 pounds.

Lauren and I shared an interest in Japanese language and history, so it was easy for us to talk, at least at the beginning. "The Japanese are so disciplined," she said. "I really admire that." When I asked about her other interests—friends? hobbies?—she smiled a Mona Lisa smile, as though she had a secret no one else could ever know. "I guess I don't really need them," she said. "I used to, but I'm way past that now."

Lauren explained that she and the other girls used to compare to see who was thinner. But soon after her twelfth birthday, something had kicked in. "I just—I discovered that I could turn on this tremendous willpower, like pushing a button."

"Like pushing a button?" I asked.

She nodded. "All of a sudden it felt good not to eat," she said.

"I don't understand," I said. "When I'm hungry, I want to eat."

Lauren gave me that smile again, and a little shrug. "When I haven't eaten for a while, my mind gets really clear. I stop caring about what the other girls think or what the boys say. I just feel calm and relaxed and at peace."

Calm and relaxed and at peace. What can I say to that? Who wouldn't want to be calm and relaxed and at peace?

There have been many useful books written about eating disorders. What's missing from many of those books is an awareness that eating disorders are just one manifestation of a larger problem affecting girls and young women today. As Courtney Martin observes in her book *Perfect Girls, Starving Daughters,* "Eating disorders are more extreme versions of what nearly every girl and woman faces on a daily basis—a preoccupation with what they put in their mouths and how it affects the shape and size of their bodies. . . . Almost every girl I know lives as if how she feels about her body is representative of how she feels about everything else. It doesn't matter how successful or in love or at peace she is in the rest of her life, if she feels overweight, she is unhappy."[2] If you conquer that fear by becoming thin, really thin, then maybe at least that part of the anxiety might go away.

For some girls, like Lauren, the anxiety really does go away. The popular notion that most anorexics are unhappy is false, in my experience. I have met a number of anorexic girls who seemed genuinely happy—in an odd, ghostly sort of way—when they were concentration-camp skinny. After those girls were put on medications and/or force-fed in order to gain weight, they seemed less happy. Healthier, certainly, but not happier. Part of that might have to do with loss of control: nobody likes to be force-fed. Nobody likes to be compelled to take medication. But another part of the loss of happiness I have seen some anorexics experience as they go through treatment is that they are losing their sense of self. The anorexic girl may have come to define herself as the thin girl, the girl who has actually accomplished what the other girls talk about but never achieve. Take that accomplishment away from her, and she doesn't know who she is.

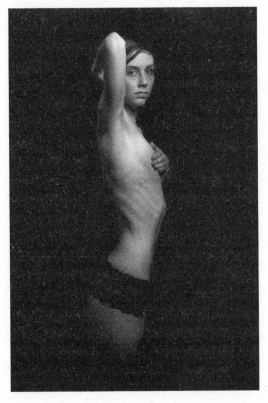

This image is typical of those you will see on pro-ana websites, glorifying and glamorizing anorexia and the cult of the ultra-thin.

Photo by James Carver-Grenside, www.flickr.com/photos/jamescg/. Used by permission.

There has been an explosion in the number of websites that are collectively termed "pro-ana"—sites that unapologetically promote anorexia.[3] According to the creators of these websites, anorexia is a lifestyle choice, not a psychiatric disorder. The photograph above is typical of images you will see at these sites, glamorizing anorexia and the cult of the ultra-thin.[4] In addition to photos, these girls share motivating quotes that they call "thinspiration." Here's a sample:

- "Other girls will want to look like me and look up to me." [5]
- "I can run on sheer mind power alone."[6]
- "Self-denial shows strong willpower."[7]
- "Thin people look good in ANY kind of clothes."[8]

How can you tell whether your daughter might be at risk for developing an eating disorder? Here are some clues:

- Your daughter is obsessed with dieting even though she's not overweight.
- She is preoccupied with food and cooking: for example, she makes a batch of chocolate brownies from scratch but won't eat any.
- She insists that she's not hungry, even when she hasn't eaten all day.
- Her hair is falling out.
- Her resting heartbeat is less than 60 beats per minute, although she's not an athlete.
- Her menstrual periods stop.
- She complains that the room is cold when it's not.

This last clue merits some additional comment. If your daughter complains that she feels cold when nobody else feels cold, then she should be evaluated by a physician. That symptom can be a sign of a low thyroid condition as well as anorexia. Anyone who has worked with anorexic girls knows that they like to wear layers of clothes: a sweater on top of a vest on top of a T-shirt. Though some counselors claim that these girls do this in order to hide how skinny they are, in my experience these girls are wearing layers of clothing mainly because they feel cold. As humans, we rely on our subcutaneous fat to help keep us warm. Once that fat is gone, the world's a cold place.

How different is anorexia from bulimia? Twenty years ago, it was common to pigeon-hole anorexic girls in one category and bulimic girls in another. Anorexic girls were supposedly hyperachieving skinny loners whereas bulimic girls were gregarious normal-weight girls who were terrified of gaining weight. Although some girls do fit these stereotypes, there is growing awareness that many girls who are obsessed about their weight and have unhealthy eating habits may not fit neatly into either category. And girls can shift categories over time. Girls who are anorexic this year may become bulimic next year. When researchers followed one group of 216 girls and young women for seven years, they found that more than half the anorexic girls subsequently went on to have problems with bulimia or binge eating.[9]

If you think your daughter may be struggling with an eating disorder, by all means consult the experts in your community, but realize that successful treatment of anorexia has to include much more than just gaining some weight. Likewise, treating bulimia involves more than stopping the purging. The key to lasting success in treating eating disorders is for your daughter to develop an authentic sense of self that doesn't depend on how she looks or how much she weighs.

I have found that anorexia is a paradigm for many other problems that I see and hear about so often now in girls and young women. In each case, the girl seizes on one aspect of her identity—her weight, or her grades, or her sports—and she focuses on it to the exclusion of everything else. Her life is out of balance, but she doesn't care as long as she achieves her goal in that one realm: her obsession.

"running helps me relax"

Chloe always enjoyed sports. Even as a little girl, she loved to chase the other kids around the playground or to be chased. She was on MSI, the Montgomery County (Maryland) after-school soccer program, beginning in second grade. She quit soccer three years later, at age 10, when the coach yelled at her to stop hogging the ball. She tried softball but never really cared for it.

Her private school offered competitive track beginning in seventh grade. Chloe signed up. Almost immediately, something connected. Chloe wasn't the fastest member of the team, but she was the most motivated. She soon discovered that her motivation paid off for the long-distance events. "I'll never be the fastest in the sprints, because I wasn't born to be a sprinter," she explained to me. "But the long-distance events are all about training and hard work. The girl who trains the hardest can win in the long-distance events."

Chloe soon proved how true that was. Even as a seventh grader, she was competitive in the 800-meter race. At her first meet as an eighth grader, she came in third. At the next meet, she won the event. "That was such a high," she told me later. "It was the first time I won. My first victory. I felt like I was queen of the world. My parents told me how great I was. Even Coach said something nice, which doesn't happen very often. But I didn't need it. I *knew* how great I was. After that, I got serious about running."

Chloe was soon running almost every day, between 15 and 20 miles a week, while she was still in eighth grade. Her parents brought Chloe to see me when she started complaining of shin splints. I explained to Chloe how and why shin splints develop. "You're accelerating your training faster than your legs can handle," I said. "It's great to be serious about your running, but you need to build up more slowly. Take two weeks off, then start back up at 1 mile a day, and no more than 5 miles per week. From that point on you want to build up gradually."

"Five miles per *week*?" Chloe said. "Can't you just give me something for the pain?"

"Pain is your body's way of telling you that you're overdoing it," I replied. "You don't want to cover up the pain. You want to listen to it. Get rid of the *cause* of the pain."

"But I'll get out of shape. I'll turn into a blob!" Chloe protested.

"Go swimming," I said. (Chloe's school has an indoor swimming pool.) "You can swim as much as you want to. Swimming will keep your fitness level up, and it's great cross-training for runners. It's December. Take two weeks off from your running, then start your 5-mile-a-week program in January, add 1 mile per week, and you'll be all set when track season starts in the spring."

Chloe agreed to do as I suggested. She threw herself into swimming. I learned later that she briefly considered becoming a long-distance swimmer. But when the weather warmed up she was back outside running, following the program I had set out for her. By April she was running 15 miles a week.

In ninth grade, she started to lose her edge in the 800-meter. Her times were still good, but the other girls had caught up to her. So she switched to cross-country and much longer distances. That way her edge in motivation could still translate into victory.

The high school required yearly doctor visits for all athletes. When I met with Chloe the summer before tenth grade, she admitted to lots of pain: in her feet, her legs, her knees, and her lower back.

"Do you remember what I said to you, about how pain is your body's way of telling you that something is wrong?" I asked.

She remembered, but she didn't agree. "Working through the pain is what this sport is all about," she said. "That's what Coach says. Besides, running helps me relax."

I tried to talk to her about balance. It's great to be disciplined, to push yourself hard, to test your limits, I said. But when that drive squeezes everything else out of your life, it's not healthy. It's become an obsession. Many of Chloe's friendships had withered due to neglect. Her only friends now, she acknowledged, were the other kids on the track team. She had invested all her resources, both physical and emotional, in running.

For a teenager, that's life out of balance.

I'm not against girls competing in sports. In Chapter 6 I will discuss some of the benefits associated with competitive sports for girls. Girls' sports, done right, can really help girls to focus on who they *are* rather than on how they *look*. But sports can become an obsession for some girls, and when that happens you have to intervene—just as the parent of an anorexic girl has to intervene. You can't wait for your daughter to decide that she's too obsessed with sports, just as the parents of an anorexic girl shouldn't wait for their daughter to decide that she's too skinny. As Martin points out, there are many characteristics shared by the girl who's anorexic and the girl who is obsessed with her sport: "overexercising, undereating, a reluctance to listen to the body's signals that it's tired, hurt, hungry. And the destination—the thin, muscular, perfect body—of the parade of scantily clad athletes also looks strangely similar. Athleticism was supposed to empower us, and in so many cases it has; but in others, it has created another giant cover-up."[10]

My patient Chloe had a good relationship with both her parents. Her father often accompanied her jogging, although by the time she was in tenth grade he had to run as hard as he could in order to keep up with her. Dr. Margo Maine has seen many girls who are trying too hard to please their fathers through their sports. She finds that these girls are "exercising excessively, with their dads or independently, pushing their bodies to the point of exhaustion. They strive for a hard, lean body, believing that their dads will accept them if they achieve this. Often they pursue sports hoping to please their father rather than to fulfill any personal desires of their own."[11]

Courtney Martin shares the story of a young woman she knew named Heather, who had built her life around her competitive cross-country running. Things were going fine until Heather literally started to fall apart. "Slowly but undeniably, Heather's body started to break down. She suffered from stress fractures, from fatigue, from a pulled hamstring. . . . Running was her entire identity, so when her coach recommended she take a couple of days off, it felt like a death sentence. Who was she if she wasn't maniacally circling the track or pounding through the woods around campus?"[12]

Female athletes are famously prone to the "athletic triad": (1) loss of the menstrual period associated with (2) disordered eating and (3) brittle bones. Teenage girls who exercise too much may throw their endocrine systems out of whack. Excessive exercise can lead to lower estrogen levels, which in turn can cause brittle bones and irregular or absent menstrual periods.[13]

The physical consequences for girls who exercise too much are important, but in my firsthand experience with teenage girls, trying to frighten them about the risks isn't an effective strategy. Instead, you have to understand your daughter's motivations. Where exactly is the hole in her soul that she is trying to fill?

In eleventh grade, Chloe came to see me again. This time the pain in her shin was much more severe and persistent than her shin splints had ever been. The diagnosis was easy: a tibial stress fracture. The MRI scan showed it clearly. Chloe's brittle bones, weakened by years of over-exercise and undereating, had taken their revenge. The prescription was intolerably difficult: crutches. I told her that she would have to be off her feet for at least four weeks. Chloe was furious with me. Her parents were skeptical.

"We want to see an orthopedic surgeon," they said.

I gave them the names of several good orthopedic surgeons. I even made a phone call to arrange for the specialist they chose to see Chloe the very next day. He concurred with my diagnosis, but he didn't agree with my recommendation of four weeks off her feet. He insisted that she would have to be off her feet for *eight* weeks.

Chloe wanted to get still another opinion, but at this point her parents had begun to understand the situation. Chloe's career as a long-distance runner was in jeopardy. More important, her sense of self was on the verge of a major crack-up. She had defined herself as a runner. If she wasn't able to run anymore, then who was she?

anorexia of the soul

Emily was the smart girl. She wasn't the pretty girl, but that didn't bother her. Even in elementary school, she would shake her head in disgust when other girls would talk excitedly about the elaborate outfits they wanted to wear. When she turned 12, she was seriously offended when a cousin gave her a subscription to *CosmoGirl* as a birthday present.

She wasn't the popular girl, but that didn't bother her either. She had a few close friends, most of whom happened to be the children of recent immigrants: Emiko from Kyoto, Jaswinder (a boy) from Bangalore, and Xiu Li from Shanghai. Beginning in eighth grade, the four of them would meet at one another's homes to study and to share their dreams of attending elite universities. Xiu Li wanted to go to Stanford. Jaswinder wanted to attend Harvard. Emiko wanted to go to either Oxford or Cambridge. Emily's sights were set on Princeton.

"Everybody talks about Harvard, but Princeton is actually more selective," Emily told her Mom, Annette. A few weeks later, Annette asked me whether it was normal for a girl in ninth grade to know or care so much about college admissions. I told her I didn't think there was necessarily anything wrong with Emily being so interested in college admissions, as long as she was engaged in a healthy mix of different activities.

Annette answered, "She's a reporter for the school newspaper. She's also on the school yearbook, the debate team, and she's in the Spanish club."

"That's great, but what does she do for *fun?*" I asked again.

Annette shrugged. "She's really busy with all her activities," she said.

Emily and her little clique—Emiko, Jaswinder, and Xiu Li—dominated the top academic ranks in their grade. All of them were nearly straight-A students. Their friendship was closest when they were in ninth and tenth grades. In eleventh grade, they each became more competitive as college admissions became dominant in their minds. Although they remained friends, there could be only one valedictorian (Xiu Li eventually won that slot) and one editor of the school newspaper (Jaswinder). Their friendship rekindled briefly when Emily, Jaswinder, and Xiu Li began attending the same SAT prep class together and would go out to a restaurant for a snack afterward. Emiko, who was being privately tutored for the SAT, joined them once or twice.

I was vaguely concerned about Emily throughout her high school years, although I didn't see her often. Her mother wasn't concerned in the slightest. On the contrary, she was proud. "I hear all these horror stories about other girls who are obsessed about their weight, or spending a zillion hours online, or demanding the most expensive clothes—and I'm just so thankful that Emily has turned out so well, and so sensible," Annette said to me.

I nodded, but I was thinking of the old proverb, *Do not praise a day until it is over, or a sword until it has been tested, or a man until he is dead.* A girl at age 17 still has a long way to go.

Emily came in for her yearly physical at the beginning of her senior year. "So tell me, what do you do for fun?" I asked her.

She gave a snort. "I don't have *time* for fun," she said. "Between volunteering at the soup kitchen and taking four AP courses and writing for the newspaper and doing most of the layout and formatting for the yearbook, I'm lucky if I have time to sleep at night."

Jaswinder was accepted at Harvard, but each of the three girls in their group had to make do with a respectable second choice. Xiu Li was accepted at UCLA. Emiko was accepted at the University of Sheffield.

Emily's Mom called me the evening that Emily got her letter from Princeton. "When she saw that it was a thin envelope, she burst into tears," Annette said. Annette sounded as though she were on the verge of tears herself. "Emily opened the letter and it was a rejection, not even a deferral or a waitlist. She kept saying to me, 'But I did *everything!* What more do they want?'" It was past midnight and Emily was still crying, Annette said. "She's shaking and shivering like she's cold."

I called in a prescription for Xanax (a mild nerve pill) to the 24-hour pharmacy near their home. Emily could take one pill immediately and another in the morning. It was a Saturday, so Emily could stay home and grieve. Xanax can be addictive, so I called in just seven pills to tide her over the next few days. I told Annette that if Emily wanted a refill, she would need to come in and talk with me first.

At least in the academic realm, Emily appeared to be the perfect girl. But trying to be the perfect girl can be dangerous. As Anna Quindlen writes in her essay about trying to be perfect, the danger is likely to strike when you fail "at something at which you badly wanted to succeed. And sitting there, you will fall into the center of yourself. You will look for some core to sustain you. And if you have been perfect all your life . . . chances are excellent that there will be a black hole where that core ought to be."[14] Emily didn't fall apart when she got the rejection letter from Princeton, but the black hole was lying in wait for her a few months down the road.

Emily had her friends and her parents fooled. She even had herself fooled. She had no idea how close she was to the edge. Her minor breakdown when she received the rejection letter from Princeton, and her major disintegration the following fall, came as a surprise not only to her family and friends but also to herself.

These girls "can present as models of competence and still lack a fundamental sense of who they are," writes psychotherapist Madeline Levine. "Psychologists call this the 'false self,' and it is highly correlated with a number of emotional problems" including depression and anxiety.[15] Emily had created a false sense of self. She had built her life around being "the smart girl"—but as she was to discover over the next seven months, that wasn't who she truly was. It wasn't even who she *wanted* to be.

The *New York Times* devoted front-page coverage to this topic in an article entitled "For Girls, It's Be Yourself, and Be Perfect Too." As the reporter, Sara Rimer, observes, these girls' "quest for the perfect résumé" is conflicting with their search for a sense of who they really are. Rimer found:

> Girls by the dozen who are high achieving, ambitious, and confident. . . . Girls who do everything: Varsity sports. Student government. Theater. Community service. . . . But being an amazing girl often doesn't feel like enough these days when you're competing with all the other amazing girls around the country who are applying to the same elite colleges that you have been encouraged to aspire to practically all your life. . . . There is something about the lives these girls lead—their jam-packed schedules, the amped-up multitasking, the focus on a narrow group of the nation's most selective colleges—that speaks of a profound anxiety.[16]

Rimer interviewed many of these "amazing girls" along with their parents. One mother expressed concern that the obsession with achievement could give rise to "anorexia of the soul." I think that's a powerful metaphor.

The problem isn't ambition or even perfectionism per se. Dr. Levine makes a useful distinction between healthy perfectionism—the drive to do better and be your best—and what she calls *maladaptive* perfectionism. "Maladaptive perfectionism is driven by an intense need to avoid failure and to appear flawless," Levine writes. "Maladaptive perfectionism hides deep-seated feelings of insecurity and vulnerability."[17] Levine believes that maladaptive perfectionism has its roots "in a demanding, critical, and conditional relationship with one's parents."

I'm not sure that the parents are always to blame. I have seen girls who are prototypes of the maladaptive perfectionism Levine describes whose parents are not at all demanding or critical. Instead, I think that the pressure often comes from the larger society — or more precisely, from the niche the girl has made for herself within the larger society, the niche of being "the amazing girl."

In any case, the notion of "perfectionism" doesn't get to the core of the issue. "Anorexia of the soul" comes closer. There is good reason to believe that a similar dynamic underlies the growing number of girls who are abusing alcohol, and the growing proportion of girls who deliberately cut themselves. It's a search for an authentic sense of self. In some girls, like Emily, that search can morph into a frantic and ultimately self-destructive perfectionism. In other girls it can become a relentless focus on sports, or on thinness.

Emily came to see me on Tuesday morning, a little more than 72 hours after her mother called me. Emily had told the receptionist she just needed a quick visit for a prescription refill. "Thanks for the Xanax. It was a life-saver," she said. "I felt like I couldn't breathe. But half an hour after I took that pill, I was able to take a deep breath."

"I'm sorry to hear about Princeton," I said. "What's your plan now?"

Emily explained that she had been accepted to the University of Penn-sylvania. "It wasn't my first choice, but it's an Ivy League school and it's got a strong pre-med program."

"You still want to be a doctor?" I asked.

"A trauma surgeon," she said. "Absolutely. I'm not going to give that up just because I didn't get into Princeton. You know, maybe it's not so bad that I didn't get into Princeton. I've heard that lots of snobby rich kids go to Princeton. Penn sounds more normal. And I'll probably be the smartest kid there."

I nodded.

The following November, Emily's Mom called again. "Emily's used up all the Xanax you prescribed for her. Could you please call in a refill?"

I explained that I would need to speak with Emily directly. After all, she was 18 now and away at college. Mom was happy to give me her number.

Emily was polite when she answered her cell phone. "I'm sorry to bother you, Dr. Sax, I just need a refill on the Xanax."

"What's going on?" I asked.

Emily at first sounded composed as she explained how she had worked hard on an assignment in her philosophy class. "Compare and contrast Nietzsche and Kierkegaard" was the assignment. She read the textbook entries for each philosopher carefully, skimmed their Wikipedia entries, and looked up related essays at www.sparknotes.com. She then wrote what she thought was a thorough 12-page essay answering the question, being careful not to plagiarize the essays she had read online. She got a C. "I looked around to see what other kids got," Emily said. "I saw one A, mostly Bs. But I didn't see anybody else who got a C. I was totally freaking out, thinking, *What did I do wrong?* I went to meet with the instructor. He said that there was nothing original in my essay. He said I had just 'regurgitated' what was in the textbook. He seemed to enjoy telling me how awful my paper was.

"If it was only him, I could probably have blown it off, but I actually expected philosophy to be my easy class. Organic chemistry has been a total disaster. I don't understand it at all. I got a 5 on my AP exam in high school chemistry. How come I can't understand organic chemistry?"

"Organic chemistry is really tough," I said. "The concepts are so different from high school chemistry."

"Right now I barely have a passing grade in organic," she said, "a C– or a D+"—then suddenly her voice broke. "What am I going to do?" she sobbed.

The crisis was about more than organic chemistry. It was existential. Emily was discovering that she wasn't as smart as she thought she was.

Her sense of self, which was so dependent on being the smart girl, was collapsing.

I spent half an hour listening to her and talking with her. I asked her to promise me that she would see a counselor on campus, which she did. Just once.

Two weeks later, Emily dropped out of school and came home.

Emily's parents at first wanted to blame Penn, but the university was not at fault. Emily didn't belong at an elite, highly competitive university—but Emily didn't understand that until she got there. Emily's sense of self was based too narrowly on academic achievement—just as Lauren's was based on how much she weighed, and Chloe's was based on her speed in the 800-meter.

You have to help your daughter to connect with who she is in a way that doesn't depend on what grades she gets, or how well she does in a track meet, or how much she weighs. I think Emily's parents might have had more of a clue what was happening if they had shown interest in something other than her academic achievement and her extracurricular activities. Ask your daughter questions like, "What do you like to do for fun?" If a girl answers that question, as Emily did, by saying that she doesn't have time for fun, that's a red flag.

Ask your daughter, "What three words describe you?" If those words include "hyper" or "anxious" or "wired" or "sleepless" or something similar, dig deeper. Try to understand the source of your daughter's anxiety. Is she worried about something she thinks the other girls are saying about her? Is she worried about her grades? Is she worried about her weight? You need to know what keeps your daughter awake at night.

Be a good listener. Don't be in a hurry to make recommendations. Just nod and keep your mouth shut until your daughter has had her say. As Levine observes, "When we listen to our friends it is usually with the purpose of understanding their dilemmas, of helping them clarify how they feel, and of letting them know that we care. We listen long enough to know what it feels like to be in their shoes. Too often with our children, we rush in and offer suggestions, propose alternatives, or solve problems."[18]

Emily's parents were astonished and horrified when she returned home that November without even completing her first semester. "How could you do that?" Annette asked.

"I'm not as smart as I thought I was," Emily answered.

"How can you say that?" her Mom replied. "Maybe if you had a tutor . . ."

"I don't want a tutor, Mom," Emily answered.* "What's the point? Why should I go on pretending to be something I'm not? Why should I kill myself trying to learn this stuff if I'm going to be at the bottom of the class? Why should I waste $100,000 getting a degree in subjects I hate?"

Defining yourself in terms of how you rank is always dangerous—and ultimately immature. It doesn't matter whether the rank has to do with your grades, your weight, or where you finished in the 800-meter race. Becoming a mature adult means, among other things, that you define yourself relative to your own potential, not relative to somebody else's standard. The well-meaning praise and encouragement from her parents to "pursue the dream" of getting into Princeton all throughout middle school and high school actually helped to set her up for a fall.

Instead of encouraging Emily to put all her emotional investment into the dream of getting into Princeton, Emily's parents might have tried to help her broaden her horizons. Emily was focused on one dream, a dream based not on her own likes and dislikes but on impressing *other* people: getting into Princeton. Emily's parents might have tried to help her discover something she really enjoyed for its own sake. All through middle school and high school, Emily never really gave much thought to questions such as "what do I love to do?" without regard to whether that activity might be prestigious in the eyes of others.

---

* This conversation is Emily's version. I never heard her parents' take on this conversation. Emily's parents were angry with me after Emily decided to drop out, because I would not cooperate with them in pushing Emily to return to her university.

Emily's parents wanted her to return to Penn, but Emily refused. Instead, she became a full-time volunteer at a sanctuary for abused farm animals. Working with the sheep and goats, a few cows, and a retired race horse, she began to find a new way back to herself.

Emily soon became friends with Carol, a middle-aged woman at the sanctuary. Carol took Emily under her wing and taught her how to work with the animals. "It's all about patience," Carol said. "These animals expect the worst of people, because that's what they've experienced. You have to show them that people can be gentle and loving. You have to move slowly. Take one step toward the animal and then wait five minutes if you must. If you approach them too quickly, they may panic. You have to wait for them to be ready."

Emily was fascinated by Carol's calmness and focus. She wanted to find out Carol's secret. Eventually, Carol shared it with her: Carol had spent seven years as a Catholic nun, and she still meditated and prayed for an hour or more almost every day.

"I thought meditation was just something Buddhists did," Emily said.

The next week, Carol lent Emily two books by Thomas Merton: *The Seven Storey Mountain* and *The Seeds of Contemplation.* This was a completely new world for Emily. She devoured those books. The following week, Carol lent Emily her copy of Omer Englebert's biography of St. Francis of Assisi. Emily had never heard of St. Francis of Assisi, but she was so inspired by his life that she started talking with Carol about possibly becoming Catholic herself.

Another 40-something woman at the barn, Rachel, overheard Carol and Emily talking one afternoon and joined in their conversation. Rachel is a great fan of books about "mindfulness" and she began sharing these books with Emily. Rachel suggested that the three of them meet for lunch one Friday at the Corner Café, a coffeehouse right next to my office in Montgomery County, Maryland, where patrons are welcome to linger around tables and chat for hours. The Friday lunch soon became a regular feature for the three women.

At this point, Emily told me, her parents were getting seriously annoyed. "The Catholic thing was amusing to them, because they never took that seriously. But when I started talking about mindfulness, especially Friday afternoons when I came home after coffee with Rachel, my Dad would get really steamed. 'You dropped out of college in order to become some kind of New Age hippie?' was the sort of thing he would say. He was really riled."

Her parents still didn't get it. They couldn't see any other standard of value besides earning a degree from a prestigious university and then going into the professions or landing a high-paying job. But Emily continued, and continues, to resist her parents' pressure. "I'm trying to figure out who I want to be rather than what would impress other people."

Will Emily ever earn a four-year college degree? I think she probably will, eventually. Emily would say that's not the most important thing. Meanwhile, she is taking courses at the local community college, one or two at a time, trying to figure out what she really enjoys.

She laughed when I asked her whether she still wants to be a trauma surgeon some day. "I don't think I ever really wanted to be one," she said. "That is just *so* not who I am. I don't like blood. I don't like cutting things. And I don't like to do anything in a hurry. I'd be a pretty pathetic trauma surgeon. I'll figure it out," she added. "I'm not in a rush anymore."

Emily was fortunate that she did finally connect with herself after less than one semester at the wrong university. Author Liz Funk shares the stories of many girls like Emily in her book, *Supergirls Speak Out: Inside the Secret Crisis of Overachieving Girls*: girls who don't discover until well into their college experience that they don't want to be the supergirl scholar they have previously tried to be. As one young woman told Funk, "I didn't get into Yale, [so] now I'm a little bit like, 'screw it.' I wasted high school studying to try to achieve something that clearly wasn't possible, and I'm not going to do that again for college."[19]

Other women don't make the connection until their mid-20s. The years after college graduation, when the woman has landed her first job, are often the time when the existential crisis finally occurs. Psychologist Robin Stern says, "Sometimes there is just so much disparity between what young women are told to expect and what actually happens that they get disillusioned. The ones who blame themselves tend to get depressed."[20]

As I said a moment ago, it's helpful periodically to ask your daughter some open-ended questions about herself: "Describe yourself in four sentences or less," that sort of thing. These questions don't have right or wrong answers. The point is to explore what the answers might mean. For example, if you ask your daughter to describe herself, she might give very concrete answers: "I'm tall. I'm thin. I'm really smart. And I hate sushi." Those answers are fine as far as they go, but they are superficial. They are great answers if your daughter is 8 years old, not so great if she is 17. By age 17 your daughter should have a sense of herself that is multidimensional. When I asked Emily that question after she started working at the animal refuge, she answered: "I really care a lot about animals, so I've thought about being a veterinarian. But veterinarians have to put animals to sleep, and I couldn't do that. And I really don't care for the blood and guts aspect of being a vet. So I think I might prefer to run an animal shelter. But it would have to be a shelter like this one, where they never kill any of the animals." That's a good answer. It's substantive. It tells me something about who this girl is, not just her surface. As girls move from childhood through adolescence, the answer to "Tell me about yourself" should evolve from concrete descriptors to more abstract ideas about what they want, and how they see themselves now compared with their past and their future.

smashed

Alicia was 13 years old when she took her first illicit drink. That's not unusual for girls in the United States today.

In the 1960s, only 7 percent of American girls reported having their first alcoholic drink between the ages of 10 and 14. Today, nearly one-quarter of all American girls report beginning to drink before age 13.[21] Over the past 40 years, the rate at which boys abuse alcohol has remained roughly constant. Over the same time period, the rate at which girls abuse alcohol has roughly quadrupled. Today, about 40 percent of girls in ninth grade drink alcohol, compared with about 42 percent of ninth-grade boys.[22] More than one in four high-school girls engage in binge drinking.[23] Among college students who meet clinical criteria for alcohol abuse, young women now slightly outnumber young men, 5 to 4.[24] Between 1999 and 2008, the number of males arrested for driving while intoxicated (DWI) dropped by 7 percent; the number of females arrested for DWI *rose* by 35 percent over the same period.[25] Statistics like these give the phrase "gender equity" a whole new meaning.

Like her parents, I was astonished when we learned about Alicia's drinking problem. Nobody saw it coming: certainly not her parents, nor me. She was doing well in school, she was on the cheer squad, she had lots of friends. When I asked her about cheer squad and other school activities, though, she was dismissive. "Those are just things I *do*," she said. "That's not who I *am*." We soon learned that Alicia had come to define herself through her drinking. Being a drinker became a core feature of her identity in her own mind. That made it much more difficult for her to stop. To paraphrase her earlier comment, with a twist: drinking wasn't just something she *did*, it became part of who she *was*. Giving up drinking would mean giving up her sense of self.

Koren Zailckas began drinking at age 14, just one year later than Alicia. In her memoir, *Smashed*, Zailckas describes how a teacher told her class about the rites, the *sacra*, in different cultures, to mark a girl's transition to adulthood. Koren wondered what would be her sacred rite, her *sacra*. "I have been waiting for something sacred to present itself," she wrote. "Even though I haven't had sex yet, I know it can't be the sacred thing I am waiting for, either. For girls sex is seen as a fall, not a triumph. When word got out that Sara Dohart messed around with Trent Cooper in the athletics closet, he rose to the status of teen heartthrob, and she was called 'Sara Blows Hard' so often her parents had to put her in private school. . . . It only makes sense for the *sacra* to be the bottle."[26]

Unlike Alicia, who was always outgoing and gregarious, Koren Zailckas was shy. She initially hoped that alcohol might help her to be more comfortable in groups, might help her true personality shine through. But she soon realized that drinking alcohol actually makes me act *less* like myself. For all intents and purposes, it should make me more comfortable being regular old Koren . . . but instead I, too, conform to a beer-ad version of myself. I kick off my shoes and pirouette in the sand. I agree to drink beer from a funnel, even though I know the boy channeling it through will pour too fast, and I will end up wearing the thick tar of beer and wet sand. When Natalie and the other girls strip down to their underwear, I do too. . . . I concede to shifting my personality, just a hair, to observe the standards I think the situation calls for. From now on, every time I drink, I'll enhance various aspects of myself, willing myself into a state where I am a little bit brighter, funnier, more outgoing, or vibrant. The process will be so incremental that I'll have no gauge of how much it will change me. I will wake up one day in my twenties like a skewed TV screen on which the hues are all wrong. My subtleties will be exaggerated and my overtones will be subdued. My entire personality will be off-color.[27]

Alcohol doesn't give teenage girls personality; more often, alcohol takes it away. Just as the cyberbubble pushes girls to conform to the conventions of Facebook and MySpace, so Zailckas discovered that alcohol pushes girls to conform to the conventions of beer commercials and television sitcoms. "That's the thing about social drinking," she writes: "In the end, it's the drinking that creates the scene, not the other way around. You grow to relish the buzz, regardless of the situation. Once you're there, really there inside that moment, with its neighborly warmth and conversation, it's hard to tell what's responsible for producing emotion. What's responsible for the light-headed feeling? Is it the Molson, or the boy [Greg] who is running his fingers through the ends of your hair? . . . When you're fifteen and female, when you experience these feelings . . . only when you are drinking, it becomes a question of which came first, the liquor or the Greg?"[28]

Koren was searching not only for a *sacra* but for a sense of self, something to combat the nihilistic urge. "Other girls my age steered into that urge with starvation diets or razor blades, but I chose alcohol because it seemed far less fanatical. On nights when I felt sad, particularly, I could feel my drinking accelerate. . . . Drinking is a visible sign to the world that you're hurting, in the same way that starving and cutting are for some girls."[29]

Many parents misunderstand the reasons why girls begin drinking. It's generally not peer pressure, in my experience, but rather the sort of mixed motives that Zailckas describes: the desire to do something associated with adulthood, mixed in with the desire to find the true self. As mature adults, we know that there is no surrogate, no shortcut to discovering your true self. You can't find it in a bottle or a razor blade. But your daughter doesn't know that yet.

Gender matters. Throughout the 1970s, 1980s, and 1990s, most research on alcohol use and abuse by children and teenagers was not gender-specific. In that era, gender was regarded primarily as a mere "social construct." Nobody guessed that the determinants and consequences of alcohol use might be fundamentally different for girls than boys.

Fortunately, those days are past. As the National Center on Addiction and Substance Abuse emphasizes on its website, girls and young women use alcohol "for reasons different from boys, their signals and situations of higher risk differ, and they are more vulnerable to substance abuse and addiction and its consequences."[30]

Drink per drink, alcohol is more dangerous to young women than it is to young men, even after adjusting for differences in height and weight.[31] Alcohol abuse appears to damage girls' brains differently and more severely than the same degree of alcohol abuse affects same-age boys.[32] These facts are well-established among researchers who study alcoholism, but they are not as well known as they ought to be—maybe in part because gender differences are so politically sensitive. For some people, suggesting that alcohol is more toxic to women than to men seems sexist. But we now understand that ignoring gender differences, pretending that girls are no different from boys, puts girls at risk. Nowhere is that clearer than when we are talking about alcohol abuse.

For some girls and young women, alcohol becomes a way of defining themselves, a kind of obsession, even a kind of salvation (or so they hope).

They may believe that getting buzzed will help to alleviate their anxiety. As Zailckas writes, "People with substance-abuse issues like to think that changing physical states [getting buzzed] is the equivalent of changing emotional states [feeling less anxious]."[33] I find that same confusion is also common among anorexic girls and among girls who are obsessed with fitness.

Interestingly, researchers have found that girls and young women who drink coffee regularly are much more likely to drink alcohol. Among girls and young women who drink coffee regularly, 70 percent also drink alcohol; among girls and young women who don't drink coffee, only 29 percent drink alcohol.[34] Why is this? I think that many girls and young women who drink coffee regularly may have learned to fix one problem, namely fatigue due to sleep deprivation, by drinking a certain beverage, namely coffee. Once you have the mindset that you can fix a problem by taking a drink of something, it's not a big jump to the notion that you might fix a different problem—such as anxiety or insomnia or depression—by taking a drink of a different beverage, maybe two shots of vodka.

Do girls drink because they're depressed? Or are girls depressed because they drink? A study from the Harvard School of Public Health suggests that the arrow may point in both directions. Depressed teens are more likely to drink, and teens who abuse alcohol are more likely to become depressed.[35] Other researchers have found that for young women in particular, the likelihood that drinking will lead to depression is especially strong—much stronger than it is for young men.[36]

Community matters—especially for girls. That's the finding of a recent survey in which researchers compared the likelihood of binge drinking in permissive communities, where there was little or no stigma attached to bingeing, with the likelihood of binge drinking in communities with strong norms, where binge drinking was severely frowned upon.

Figure 3 shows the results. For men, community standards had a barely significant effect. But for women, the effect was large. Women in communities with weak norms were more than twice as likely to engage

Figure 3

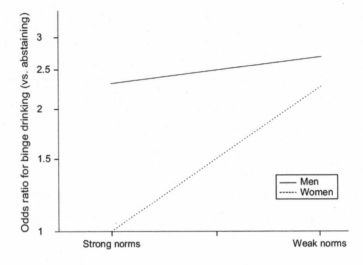

in binge drinking, compared with comparable women living in communities with strong norms.[37] Asian American girls are significantly less likely than black, Latina, or white girls to drink alcohol and to binge drink, perhaps in part because Asian American communities appear more likely to teach their girls that drinking can be very risky.[38]

So it helps to tell girls in no uncertain terms that teens shouldn't drink. And you have to start very early to educate your daughter about the dangers of drinking. Girls have one great advantage over boys: as a rule, girls don't want to fry their brains just for the sake of frying their brains. That's not true for some boys. I've seen more than a few boys and young men who take pride in getting totally wasted. It's their twisted idea of macho. But there's nothing feminine about throwing up all over the front lawn. As Zailckas observes, "drinking confirms men's gender role, whereas it diminishes women's. We are meant to believe that men who drink heavily are men's men. Beer ads play strongly to the idea that men drink because they like shooting pool, watching ESPN, and bonding with other men. . . . By contrast, a girl's drinking makes her less feminine."[39] Let your daughter know how disgusting it can be for a girl to be drunk; teach her this by the time she is age 11, or even earlier.

The perils of drinking include sexual risks. A boy who is drunk may do stupid things—things he wouldn't do when he is sober. And if you're drunk, you will be less able to stop him. Alcohol is involved in the majority of all rapes, including date rape.[40] As Zailckas wrote after a semi-consensual sexual act that occurred while both she and the young man were drunk, "I can't let myself feel abused. He was drunk, which makes him less blameworthy; and I was drunk, which makes me more so. I don't need anyone to explain this equation to me."[41]

The perils of drinking include the risk of being in a car with a drunk teen driver. This risk is especially high for "nice" girls. Nice girls don't like to make trouble, so if a boy is a little bit drunk, a nice girl is less likely to take his car keys away, less likely to refuse to get in his car. Nice girls don't make a fuss. I know a nice girl in my own practice who ended up in the hospital for three weeks with broken ribs and a punctured lung after being out with a young man who had been drinking. She warned him that he shouldn't drive; she offered to drive for him. He insisted on driving. A sensible girl would have refused; a sensible girl would have called her parents for a ride home. But nice girls aren't sensible girls. She got in the car. A few minutes later, they were in a head-on collision.

But you have to use your judgment as a parent. Don't lay on the warnings too thick. If you do, and your daughter has a drink, she may be terrified to tell you about it. If your daughter is 16 years old and has a glass of beer at a friend's house, she has to be able to call you and tell you to come pick her up and drive her home. If you've been authoritarian ("Too Hard") rather than authoritative ("Just Right"),* then she won't make that call, because she's afraid you'll be angry. She'll try to drive home even when she knows she shouldn't.

---

* See the previous chapter for my discussion of Diana Baumrind's parenting styles.

Here's a tip: have a code word or phrase that you and your daughter agree upon in advance. I recommend this for any occasion when your daughter will be separated from you, even if she's only 9 years old. The code word might be "brownie," or it could be a phrase, such as "bake some brownies." If your daughter calls you and asks, "Mom, are you going to bake some brownies?" that means, *Come get me right away*. You don't want your daughter to have to explain, with her friends listening, why she needs you to come pick her up. All you have to say is, "Are you still at Courtney's house?" When she says, "Yes, I'd love some," you say, "I'm on my way."

Don't be reassured just because your daughter is a good student or is involved in lots of extracurricular activities. I can't tell you how many parents of "good girls" have told me, "I never thought this would happen to my daughter." Their daughter was earning good grades; how could she possibly have a drinking problem?

Koren Zailckas herself struggled with a drinking problem for years, but nobody understood how bad it was, not even her parents, who were as loving and caring as any daughter could ask. As Zailckas observes, "Too many people rely on outward signs of aggression to indicate their daughters or girlfriends or sisters have problems with alcohol. They wait for fights, or DUI charges, or destruction of property, when girls who drink are far less apt to break rules in [such] overt ways. As a gender, we are far more likely to turn our drunken destructiveness inward, to wage private wars against ourselves."[42] Girls can be subtle.

The core intervention you have to undertake as a parent is to ensure that your daughter develops a strong sense of self. If there's anything I have learned from my conversations with girls who struggle with alcohol, it's that girls begin using alcohol to compensate for something that's missing in their lives. If they have a strong sense of self, then they don't need to drink.

girls on the edge

On the table there was a roll of batting, a glue gun, a doily, a 1997 Krafty Kitchens catalogue. Next to the catalogue was a special craft knife. . . . It was sleek, like a fountain pen, with a thin triangular blade at the tip. I picked it up and laid the blade against the doily. The little knots came undone, just like that. I touched the blade to a piece of ribbon draped across the table and pressed, ever so slightly. The ribbon unfurled into two pieces and slipped to the floor without a sound. Then I placed the blade next to the skin on my palm.

A tingle arced across my scalp. The floor tipped up at me and my body spiraled away. Then I was on the ceiling looking down, waiting to see what would happen next. What happened next was that a perfect, straight line of blood bloomed from under the edge of the blade. The line grew into a long, fat bubble, a lush crimson bubble that got bigger and bigger. I watched from above, waiting to see how big it would get before it burst. When it did, I felt awesome. Satisfied, finally. Then exhausted.

That's a passage from the opening chapter of Patty McCormick's *Cut*, about a young girl named Callie. Callie was doing very poorly after 4 miles in a cross-country race. She was in last place and couldn't even see the runners in front of her. Instead of finishing the race, she ran home—where she found the knife.

McCormick's description of Callie's first cut rings true for me, based on my own conversations with girls who have cut themselves. In particular, the dissociation—the sense of being detached from her body, watching herself from up above—has been a central feature of the experience for many of the girls with whom I've spoken. "I knew the pain was there, but I didn't really feel it, because I was like not really *there*, I was *high*—literally I felt like I was up in the sky." That's how one girl explained it to me.

Cutting used to be rare. In the early 1980s, psychiatrists announced the emergence of a new clinical syndrome, the "deliberate self-harm syndrome."[43] At that time, estimates of the prevalence of this "syndrome" were well under 1 percent of the population. Today it's so common that some researchers have argued we should no longer consider girls who cut themselves to have a psychiatric problem at all; rather, these girls are basically normal girls engaging in a "voluntarily chosen deviant behavior."[44] For these researchers, deliberately cutting your skin with a razor blade is not so different from dying your hair purple. After all, these researchers point out, many of these girls "feel positive about their self-injury" and don't seek treatment, so who are we to say that they have a psychiatric disorder?[45]

I respectfully disagree. These girls are struggling. A girl who dyes her hair purple may be indulging a playful whim. But every girl I have met who is deliberately taking a blade to her own skin has major issues, and cutting herself is one way of dealing with these issues.

I concede that these researchers are correct in their observation that most girls who cut themselves don't see their cutting as pathological or even peculiar. Most research on this topic conducted before the year 2000 involved girls who were in treatment for a psychiatric disorder, either inpatient or outpatient. The new direction in research on girls who cut themselves is on girls who have never sought treatment.

Estimates of the prevalence among teenage girls have been rising steadily over the past decade, with most estimates now at or above 20 percent; some of the most recent surveys are reporting even higher numbers.[46] In a recent survey of girls who read *Seventeen* magazine, 51 percent of girls reported cutting themselves or inflicting other forms of deliberate self-injury.[47] The rates are rising so fast that studies published even five years ago are now out of date. And girls are at much higher risk than boys. Most recent studies have found that the average teenage girl is at least three times more likely to cut herself compared with a teenage boy in the same community.[48] It's important to keep that in mind when you read scholarly articles on this topic. For example, if researchers interview kids at a high school that has a roughly 50/50 mix of girls and boys, the researchers may report an overall prevalence of cutting as, say, 12 percent. But that number may be misleading if only 4 percent of the boys are cutting themselves compared with 20 percent of the girls.[49]

Furthermore, the significance of cutting appears to be different depending on whether you're talking about girls or boys. When you find a boy who is cutting himself, he is often the outcast, the loner. But you will find girls who cut themselves among almost every demographic at the school, including the popular girls, the star students, and the athletes.

When I was doing my first psychiatry rotation, more than a quarter-century ago in the 1980s, the attending psychiatrist told us that girls who cut themselves do so as a "cry for help." In some cases, that may be true. If a girl cuts herself on her hand, or she cuts herself on her wrist and then wears short sleeves so that everyone can see the wounds, then I would agree: this girl is expressing a cry for help.

But those girls are a small minority among the millions of girls in this country today who are cutting themselves. *Most girls who are cutting themselves do NOT want you or any other adult to know about it.* If they cut themselves on their arms, then they wear long sleeves or baggy sweaters. Psychotherapist Madeline Levine is always on the lookout for these girls. When she sees a girl wearing "a long-sleeve T-shirt pulled halfway over her hand," she has found that "such T-shirts are almost always worn to camouflage an array of self-mutilating behaviors: cutting with sharp instruments, piercing with safety pins, or burning with matches."[50] I myself saw several girls who cut themselves on the upper inner part of their thighs, because that was a place nobody else was likely to see.

In the 1990s, child abuse emerged as the most popular explanation for why girls cut themselves. Certainly that's true in some cases: a girl who is sexually abused early in childhood is more likely to start cutting herself as a teenager, compared to a girl with the same demographics who was never abused.[51] But it's not the case that *most* girls who cut themselves do so as a consequence of childhood sexual abuse. The 1990s notion that every girl who cuts herself does so because she was a victim of sexual abuse led some over-eager therapists to try to unearth a story of abuse in every case of a teenager who was cutting herself, including many cases where abuse never occurred. Psychiatrist Armando Favazza, one of the leading researchers in this field, wrote in 1998 about having to "rescue patients from therapists who were frustrated at not being able to find *the* cause of an individual's self-mutilation and therefore assumed that he or she must have been abused."[52]

In most cases, as Dr. Favazza writes, cutting and other forms of self-wounding can begin as "morbid forms of self-help because they provide rapid but temporary relief from distressing symptoms such as mounting anxiety, depersonalization, racing thoughts, and rapidly fluctuating emotions."[53] But when a girl repeats that behavior over and over again, it can—as Favazza observes—become an "overwhelming preoccupation." That transcendent feeling, the feeling of being above it all, can be supremely satisfying. Researchers have actually found that for these girls, the act of cutting her own flesh may trigger the release of endogenous opioids in her brain, giving her a kind of opiate high.[54] And so the obsession becomes stronger.

All the obsessions we have discussed in this chapter are linked to one another, in various ways and with varying degrees of affinity. As Dr. Favazza observes, a girl who is cutting herself for a period of months or years may stop doing that and instead begin abusing alcohol or develop an eating disorder.[55] There is now strong evidence that girls who cut themselves are likely to develop an eating disorder, although the process can also work in the other direction: girls who have eating disorders are more likely to become girls who cut themselves.[56]

Girls who exercise excessively are more likely to be anorexic. Anorexic girls are more likely to be cutters. Girls who are obsessively perfectionist are more likely to abuse alcohol. At some level of analysis, these are different manifestations of the same problem, which earlier in this chapter we heard one mother call "anorexia of the soul." If you don't know who you are, then you become vulnerable to obsessions.

Many parents become frustrated when they seek help for a daughter struggling with any one of these problems. The generalist pediatricians and family physicians often don't know much about these topics, and the specialists are over-specialized. One mother told me that she found a psychiatrist who specializes in eating disorders, but the psychiatrist insisted on referring her daughter to somebody else when he found out that she was also a cutter. Another psychiatrist, widely respected as an expert in helping teens struggling with alcohol abuse, refused to accept a teenage girl I referred to him after I told him that she was a straight-A student. "If she's a straight-A student, then her drinking is not an impairment. She is not impaired. Without impairment, there's no ground for a psychiatric diagnosis." He talked like a robot. *Of course* she's impaired, I argued, she's abusing alcohol and she talks about suicide. But he wasn't interested. It was frustrating for me as the referring physician, but it was agonizing for the parents, who couldn't find a specialist who would take their daughter's problem seriously just because her grades were good.

I am not suggesting that these obsessions are interchangeable with one another. Many girls who suffer from one of these obsessions may never have the misfortune of suffering from any of the others. Each of these obsessions has its own causes, its own risks, and different outcomes. But, like so many other parents I have known, I am frustrated by the compartmentalization of our current system of healthcare. This compartmentalization rewards each professional for focusing on his little piece of the elephant without seeing the whole picture. As Mark Taylor, a professor at Columbia University, recently observed, "There can be no adequate understanding of the most important issues we face when disciplines are cloistered from one another."[57]

The big picture is a growing proportion of girls who don't know who they are. So they fill the black hole with an obsession. Because something is better than nothing.

life out of synch

Lily Allen, a British pop star who has been an overachiever since middle adolescence, recently shared her plans with an interviewer: "What I'm going to do is work really hard, trying to make as much money as I can, then retire when I'm 30 and have my childhood. I'll just sit in the country-side, ride quad bikes all day, and have my own paintball course."[58]

That sort of comment is an extreme example of the role reversal that has become typical in the lives of many girls and young women today. More and more girls are trying to be adults too early, while hoping, as Lily Allen hopes, that some day, as adults, they might have a chance to enjoy the childhood they never had. I have listened to an 8-year-old girl of normal weight as she explained to me why she needs to go on a diet. I have listened to a 14-year-old girl tell me why she doesn't have time for even six hours of sleep a night. I have handed a box of Kleenex to a 17-year-old girl who was barely able to breathe because she just found out that she didn't do well on the SAT, which she believed dooms her chances of getting into the right university.

What all these stories have in common are girls whose lives are out of synch. It's similar to the problems of premature sexualization that we discussed in Chapter 1. Girls who are 8 or 9 years old trying to dress like teenagers. Teenage girls who want to drink like adults. Girls of every age who are obsessed.

One key to a healthy, happy, and fulfilled life is to live each stage of your life to its fullest. When you are a child, do the things that children are meant to do. Be silly and carefree. When you become an adult, then it's time to put those childish things away, for the most part, and to assume the responsibilities of an adult. By pushing girls to act like adults before their time, our 21st-century culture is robbing them of their girlhood and often condemning them to an unhappy adulthood.

How did we get here? Why are girls getting older younger? Part of the answer may have to do with toxins in the food they eat, the beverages they drink, and the creams and lotions they put on their skin.

environmental toxins

The childhoods of U.S. girls have been significantly shortened. . . . About half of all U.S. girls show signs of breast development by their tenth birthday.

DR. SANDRA STEINGRABER[1]

bra at 8

Olivia's parents were concerned when Olivia began developing breasts shortly after her eighth birthday. Olivia's Mom, Vanessa, was sure that Olivia would be the only girl at school wearing a bra. She worried that the other girls might tease her daughter. So Vanessa was surprised to discover there were two other girls in the class who were already wearing bras. That made a total of three girls, out of twelve girls in the classroom, who had begun the process of puberty.

The parents of the other two girls were not concerned, but Vanessa took Olivia to the pediatrician, who said that Olivia's early development was "within the range of normal." Vanessa insisted on a referral to a pediatric endocrinologist. The specialist ordered some blood tests. At the follow-up visit to discuss the test results, the specialist confirmed that Olivia had begun puberty, but he said that there was no need to do anything about it. "There's nothing wrong with your daughter," he said. He explained that the definition of "normal puberty" had been revised in

1999 and that breast development beginning at age 8, or even age 7, is now considered normal for American girls.

The specialist was correct. According to the current guidelines, a girl who has begun to develop breasts at age 7 is now considered "normal."[2] Indeed, roughly half of the girls in the United States today will begin breast development before their tenth birthday.[3] But as Dr. Sandra Steingraber observers, "what has become the new norm is not necessarily normal or good. Whether or not a 7-year-old with breasts is labeled with a disorder and treated, the falling age of puberty raises serious public health questions. . . . The fact that 'normality' may have changed does not negate the possibility that the physiological processes leading to these changes are neither normal nor benign."[4]

By the time she was 11, Olivia could easily pass for a girl of 15 or even 17 years of age. She was attracting whistles and comments and other unwanted attention from boys at the mall. Her body might have looked like the body of a 15-year-old, but she had the emotional maturity of an 11-year-old, because she *was* an 11-year-old. Most 11-year-old girls who look 15 are not ready to handle the attention they may attract when they go to the mall or the beach. It's often confusing and embarrassing to them. It may even be frightening.

The harm of early puberty goes beyond an increased risk of sexual harassment by older boys. We're talking about the loss of middle childhood, that special period from roughly age 8 to age 12 when girls in previous generations were able to figure out who they were and who they wanted to be. That's the age of Pippi Longstocking and Peppermint Patty and Harriet the Spy. That's the age when previous generations of girls were able to develop a sense of self without regard to their sexuality, without being overly concerned about how they looked in the eyes of boys or whether this skirt or that top was too "hot" or not hot enough.

A long childhood is one of the features that define us as a species. In most mammals, the juvenile period is short. Once an infant is no longer dependent on its mother's milk, the objective in most species is to start reproducing as soon as possible. The period between the time when a mouse is weaned and when it is ready to start reproducing is only a few weeks; likewise for a rabbit. Horses—which are larger in size and weight than humans—can begin reproducing at 2 years of age, although most veterinarians recommend that owners of female horses wait until the filly is 3 or 4 years old. A 2-year-old female horse is still growing. Pregnancy can interfere with healthy development. A 4-year-old mare is ready.

A 4-year-old human still has a long way to go.

"Childhood" can be defined from a biological perspective as the period between weaning from the breast and the onset of puberty. Humans have the longest childhood of any mammal on the planet.[5] How come? What is the benefit of a long childhood? The answer seems to be that children need that time in order to expand their potential before the onset of puberty.

Because puberty changes everything.

the price of puberty

Prior to the onset of puberty, the human brain is incredibly plastic. A normal 5-year-old can learn any language and become fluent in it, acquire a new physical skill such as riding a bicycle with relative ease, and achieve age-appropriate proficiency in a new sport within a few weeks. After puberty is complete, the potential to learn completely new things is reduced. You can still learn a foreign language in your teens or as an adult, but you will probably speak it with at least some trace of an accent.[6] If you want to speak another language effortlessly and without an accent, your best bet is to learn it before the onset of puberty. There has been much talk in recent years about "neuroplasticity," the ability of the adult human brain to rewire itself.[7] But the mental agility of even the most intellectually nimble adult can't compare with a child's.

It's a trade-off. "Pubertal re-sculpting of the brain's circuitry is believed to make possible the emergence of abstract thinking, values, autonomy, adult social behaviors and the capacity to consider alternative viewpoints," writes Dr. Steingraber. But, she adds, "The development of higher-order thought does not come without a price: during the course of sexual maturation, the brain loses plasticity and cognitive flexibility. The ability to assimilate complex new skills—such as playing a musical instrument, riding a bicycle, or achieving athletic prowess—declines dramatically after puberty."[8]

The Philip Pullman trilogy illustrates this point in a poignant way. In the first book of the trilogy, *The Golden Compass* (originally published under the title *Northern Lights*), Lyra Belacqua is 12 years old—and for her, unlike most modern girls, the process of puberty has not yet begun. She discovers that she has an extraordinary talent that enables her to use an ancient instrument, the golden compass, to discover hidden truths about the present and the past, and even to glimpse the future. Her unique ability shapes the plot of the first two books. In Pullman's third book, *The Amber Spyglass,* Lyra goes through puberty. She experiences a sexual awakening and falls in love with a teenage boy, Will Parry. As their relationship progresses and Lyra matures, her special ability slips away. She can no longer read the compass. Pullman is careful to make clear that the loss of her gift is not a punishment but is rather an inevitable consequence of her maturity. She gains a great deal as she undergoes the transition from girl to woman, but something precious is irretrievably lost along the way.

This is not a new insight.

It is not now as it hath been of yore;—
Turn wheresoe'er I may,
By night or day,
The things which I have seen I now can see no more . . .

What though the radiance which was once so bright
Be now for ever taken from my sight,
Though nothing can bring back the hour
Of splendour in the grass, of glory in the flower;

We will grieve not, rather find
Strength in what remains behind . . . [9]

Puberty has different significance and different consequences for girls compared with boys. As boys progress through puberty, they become more satisfied with their bodies; as girls progress through puberty, they become less satisfied with theirs.[10] Girls in puberty are much more likely to have problems sleeping compared to boys in puberty or to pre-pubescent girls.[11] Prior to puberty, there is no difference between girls and boys in the incidence of depression; once puberty is underway, girls are much more likely than boys to become depressed.[12]

Girls who begin puberty earlier are at risk for many adverse consequences that don't apply to boys who begin puberty earlier.[13] Girls who go through puberty earlier are at greater risk of being sexually victimized as teenagers.[14] For many years it was thought that a girl who began puberty early was more likely to be sexually abused in her home; however, it now appears that the arrow of causality points the other way, with childhood sexual abuse *causing* an earlier onset of puberty.[15] (We will come back to the explanation for this later in the chapter.)

Girls who begin puberty earlier are more likely to develop eating disorders.[16] They are more likely to smoke cigarettes and to abuse drugs and alcohol as teenagers.[17] They are more likely to engage in delinquent and criminal activity.[18] They do less well in school compared to girls from the same neighborhood who go through puberty later.[19] They are more likely than other girls to suffer from clinically significant anxiety or depression, not only as teens but as adults.[20] They are more likely than other girls to develop cardiovascular risk factors such as high blood pressure, even if they're not overweight.[21] They are also more likely to develop breast cancer as adults;[22] and if they do get breast cancer, recent evidence suggests that their cancer may be more aggressive and more lethal than the cancers that develop in women who experience later onset of puberty.[23]

And then there's fat.

a matter of fat

There are close links between overweight and early puberty. Girls who become overweight early in childhood are more likely to go through puberty earlier. Girls are heavier today, on average, than they were 30 years ago.[24] Could that be the whole story? Maybe girls are going through puberty earlier than girls did 30 years ago simply because girls today are heavier than girls were back then? It seems plausible, but the truth may be more complicated.

Certainly there is a strong association between overweight early in childhood and the subsequent early onset of puberty. Researchers in Louisiana found that fatter girls typically experience their first menstrual period earlier than thinner girls.[25] In a study of 181 girls in Pennsylvania, girls who were fat at age 5 were more likely to begin puberty at age 9, compared to other girls in the group.[26] In another study, researchers at the University of Michigan periodically examined more than 300 girls for nine years, beginning at age 3. They found that the girls who had more body fat at 3 years of age were more likely to begin puberty earlier. In this study, the girls who gained weight the fastest between ages 3 and 6 were at highest risk to have begun puberty by age 9. In this study, nearly half of the girls had begun puberty by age 9.[27]

But an association between overweight and early puberty doesn't prove that overweight *causes* early puberty. In fact, recent evidence suggests that the association between overweight and early puberty may not be causal at all.

In one study published in 2009, Danish researchers described a group of 1,100 girls who had been examined in the early 1990s; the same researchers then looked at a different group of about 1,000 girls, from the same neighborhood and with the same demographics, who were examined between 2006 and 2008. The average age of breast development for the girls in the early 1990s was 10.88 years. In the group of girls examined between 2006 and 2008, the average age for breast development was 9.86 years of age. That's an acceleration of one full year in less than two decades. But the girls in the later group, in this particular study, were not heavier than the girls in the early 1990s. As the Danish researchers wrote, "we do not believe that the increasing incidence of obesity among children can explain our findings."[28]

Other researchers agree that the hypothesis that early puberty is caused by overweight is "far from compelling."[29] Instead, they believe that some other factor or factors are causing both the obesity epidemic and the acceleration in the onset of puberty; and/or that overweight *mediates* some other factors that are actually causing earlier puberty. What could those other factors be?

In the study I just cited, the Danish researchers suggested that "increased exposure to endocrine-disrupting chemicals . . . may be involved in the observed trends" of earlier breast development in girls.[30] Those "endocrine-disrupting chemicals" are man-made substances that can mimic the action of hormones in the human body. For reasons still not fully understood, most of these endocrine-disrupting chemicals mimic the action of *female* hormones.[31] Almost all of the endocrine disruptors are fat-soluble, which means that the more fat you have in your body, the more you will accumulate these chemicals.[32] In addition to concentrating within fatty tissues, these chemicals may actually change the metabolism of fat cells, making fat cells more resistant to shrinkage or breakdown.[33] In other words, these man-made substances not only make it easier for you to get fat, they also make it harder for you to lose the fat once you've gained it.

So, if you are overweight, you are likely to have more endocrine-disrupting chemicals in your body compared to someone the same age and height who has less fat on board. That means that heavier girls might go through puberty earlier, not because they are heavier per se, but because their extra fat translates into an extra dose of endocrine-disrupting chemicals.

What your daughter eats also seems to make a difference, independent of her body weight. Girls who eat high-fat and high-calorie diets are at higher risk of early puberty, even if they aren't fat themselves. Pediatric endocrinologists Dr. Melvin Grumbach and Dr. Dennis Styne conjecture that this "effect of fat in the diet may be compounded by the effect of estrogen added to commercial beef production cows, which is concentrated in fatty tissue."[34] In the United States, beef cattle are given hormone supplements. In Europe, such supplementation is prohibited. That may be one reason why girls in the United States begin puberty earlier than girls in Europe, even after adjusting for any differences in weight between European and American girls.[35] Conversely, a high-fiber diet appears to postpone the onset of puberty in girls.[36]

Breastfeeding also seems to be a factor in the timing of the onset of puberty. There are at least two possible reasons why. First, formula-fed infants grow up to be heavier than breastfed infants.[37] The second reason is that babies who are fed with formula are fed entirely with bottles. Thirty years ago, those bottles would have been made of glass. Today, they are often made of hard plastic, or they have soft plastic liners, both of which can be sources of endocrine disruptors, as we will see.

Even parents who breastfeed their infants often use bottles with pumped breast milk. If you are such a parent, then you may need to be vigilant about what kind of bottle you are using. Glass bottles are better than plastic, particularly if the milk is warm rather than cold. When you put warm milk or any hot beverage into a plastic liner or a plastic bottle, it's easier for the chemicals to leach out of the plastic and into the liquid (more about that in a moment).

The low rate of breastfeeding in the United States may be one of the reasons why American girls begin the process of puberty earlier than girls in other developed countries. The United States has the lowest rate of breastfeeding in the developed world.[38]

So how can you reasonably avoid these endocrine disruptors without fleeing with your family to the wilderness and living in a tent?

what's in your tuna?

Medical experts are famous for disagreeing. The old joke is that if you get five medical experts in a room, they'll give you six opinions. So expectations may not have been high when the National Institutes of Health (NIH) convened a panel of 38 leading medical experts, mostly from around the

United States but also from Germany, Italy, Japan, Spain, and the United Kingdom, to see if they could reach any consensus about the medical risks posed by a particular chemical, a substance known as bisphenol A, or BPA.

BPA is used to make just about every kind of hard plastic, such as a typical baby's bottle. It's also the main ingredient in the resin that lines the inside of the can in most canned foods such as soup, ravioli, tuna, and vegetables. It's produced in staggering quantities: more than six billion pounds are manufactured every year.[39] Many studies suggest that humans are exposed to BPA in doses that can mimic the action of female hormones.

Remarkably, the expert panel convened by the NIH agreed that BPA acts like a female hormone in the human body at the kind of exposures that normal people encounter in everyday life, such as eating half a small can of tuna fish, or eating half a small can of pasta. They agreed that BPA acts like a female hormone in the human body in concentrations of one part per *trillion*. They concluded that at least 90 percent of people in de-veloped countries have BPA in their tissues at concentrations at or above the threshold at which BPA acts like a female hormone.[40] (A recent Centers for Disease Control study of children and adults in the United States found significant levels of BPA in 92.6 percent of the sample: children had higher levels of BPA than adults, and females had higher levels than males.[41]) The expert panel concluded that there is "great cause for concern" that exposure to BPA is contributing to the "early onset of puberty in girls."[42]

Can we say with 100 percent certainty that BPA is contributing to the early onset of puberty in girls? Maybe not, but the likelihood is very high.[43] Lobbyists for the plastics industry (which includes the manufac-turers of BPA) are still arguing that BPA is not harmful.[44] Outside of the plastics industry, there isn't much doubt. In 2008, Canada banned all baby products, such as plastic bottles and sippy cups, made with BPA; in 2009, Minnesota became the first state in the United States to implement a sim-ilar ban. These are only the first steps needed to eliminate BPA from your daughter's foods and beverages, because most girls older than 3 years of age don't drink from sippy cups. Also in 2009, the state of Connecticut passed a broader ban on almost all consumer products containing BPA; and comparable bills are under consideration in other states.[45]

If you insist on waiting until everybody agrees 100 percent about the risks and until every state and every nation has comprehensively banned BPA from food containers, your daughter may be grown up. In my opinion, if there is reasonable doubt about the safety of BPA, then we shouldn't use it.

Fortunately, it's easy to prevent your daughter (and yourself) from being exposed to BPA. Here's what I recommend:

- Avoid canned foods, particularly canned pasta, canned soup, canned beans, and canned tuna. In one recent study, 50 percent or more of these canned foods contained dangerous levels of BPA.[46] Eat fresh or frozen foods instead.
- Never heat food in any kind of plastic container, either in the microwave or in a conventional oven. If you buy a frozen entrée in a "microwave-ready" plastic container, don't use the container. Put the food in a bowl made of ceramic or glass and use that instead. For a conventional oven, use a metal tray or pan.
- Don't put plastic containers in the dishwasher. Wash them by hand instead. The detergents used in dishwashers—even the most environmentally friendly detergents—will increase the leaching of bisphenol A from plastic when you subsequently use that item.[47]
- Don't drink hot beverages like coffee or tea out of any kind of plastic cup. Instead, use a cup made out of ceramic, glass, porcelain, or steel.
- Avoid any container with the number "7" in the recycle triangle (see Figure 4). "7" can stand for "other" or for polycarbonate (PC). Polycarbonate is made from BPA. However, certain other containers made out of hard plastic may also leach BPA, even if they don't have the number 7 on them.

Figure 4

gimme some skin

The phthalates, pronounced THA-lates, are synthetic chemicals used to make lotions and creams softer and creamier (among other uses). Phthalates may be as hazardous as BPA, but they haven't received nearly as much press, perhaps because they are harder to spell. Just remember that these substances used to be called "naphthalates," but then somebody decided to drop the "na," maybe as a prank to confuse kids in spelling bees. Phthalates have a complex action on the human endocrine system, disrupting sexual development and increasing the risk of obesity, possibly via a direct action on fat cells.[48]

In order to avoid the various phthalates, you must be careful about what your daughter puts on her skin. Many lotions and creams on the market today contain phthalates. When you rub those lotions and creams onto your skin, the phthalates get into your system. A recent study of babies from several sites across the United States found that more than 80 percent had *seven or more* phthalate metabolites in their system. As the authors observed, "in the United States, there is no requirement that products be labeled as to their phthalate content. Parents may not be able to make informed choices until manufacturers are required to list phthalate contents of products." These investigators—from the Centers for Disease Control, the University of Washington, and the University of Rochester Medical Center—came to this conclusion: "Until additional information is available on infant care product phthalate content . . . we recommend limiting [the] amount of infant care products used and not to apply lotions or powders unless indicated for a medical reason."[49]

Creams and lotions aren't the only sources of phthalates. Until quite recently, baby pacifiers and other soft plastic toys for infants were also commonly made with phthalates. That's changing. California governor Arnold Schwarzenegger signed a law that took effect in 2009 banning phthalates in baby products in California. Canada has had a voluntary industry agreement in place since 1998 likewise banning phthalates in anything marketed for use by babies and toddlers, and phthalates have been banned in baby and childcare items in the European Union since

Figure 5

2005.[50] It's usually not too difficult nowadays to find a baby's toy or pacifier with a label stating that the product is BPA-free and phthalate-free, even if you don't live in California or Canada or Copenhagen.

When you're buying any skin lotion or cream for yourself or for your daughter—or a sippy cup or pacifier for your baby or toddler—I recommend that you look for a label like the one shown in Figure 5. Make sure that the product is *both* BPA-free and phthalate-free. Fortunately, it's getting easier to find these products. Many websites now sell lotions, baby bottles, and other products for babies and children that are both BPA-free and phthalate-free: I have used www.thinkbabybottles.com, www.thinksportbottles.com,www.bpafreekids.com, www.greentogrow .com, www.naturemoms.com, www.safemama.com, and others. If you don't see any documentation that the product is both BPA-free *and* phthalate-free, try to get more information before buying the product.

who is PETE?

Just as BPA is used to make *hard* plastic as well as resins, many kinds of clear *soft* plastic today are made from a substance called PETE: polyethylene terephthalate ethylene. This includes the clear plastic bottles that bottled water is usually sold in, plus just about every kind of soda and sports drink that's sold in a clear plastic bottle, as well as soft clear plastic squeeze bottles of peanut butter and salad dressing.

Chemists have found that containers made from PETE can leach phthalates into whatever's inside them, whether it's bottled water, soda, or salad dressing.[51] In one recent study, the water inside clear plastic bottles made from PETE contained phthalates at levels nearly 20 times higher than water in glass bottles.[52] That leaching is most likely to happen if the container is exposed to sunlight under warm conditions. So don't leave your clear plastic water bottle in your car.

Conversely, the container is less likely to leach if it is kept cool and in the dark. The problem is, you don't know where that container of bottled water has been on its long journey to your neighborhood store. It may have sat out on a loading dock, exposed to the sun on a hot afternoon. The warmer the temperature, the more leaching will occur.[53] "If you heat up [these] plastics, you could increase the leaching of phthalates from the containers into water and food," says Kellogg Schwab, PhD, director of the Center for Water and Health at the Johns Hopkins School of Public Health.[54]

German researchers recently looked to see whether the water in a clear plastic bottle made of PETE did in fact have estrogenic effects. They bought bottled water in PETE containers, emptied out the water, and poured in ultra-pure water instead. They then put 100 little snails into the plastic bottles filled with ultra-pure water. As a control, they put another 100 little snails in *glass* bottles filled with the same ultra-pure water. The female snails who were in the PETE bottles produced more than double the numbers of embryos per female, compared with the female snails in the glass bottles. "It is obvious that the observed effects can only be attributed to xenoestrogen leaching from these plastic bottles," these authors concluded. (A "xenoestrogen" is a substance in the environment that acts like estrogen, a female hormone.) They suggested that their findings were just "the tip of the iceberg" regarding the endocrine-disrupting effects of bottled water sold in PETE bottles.[55]

It's easy to tell if a particular container is made out of PETE. Just look at the underside of the container for the "1" in the recycle triangle. Unlike the case with BPA, you can be fairly confident that if there is a number other than "1" in the triangle, then the container does not contain PETE.

What do you need to do in order to avoid exposure to phthalates and to PETE?

- Pour water directly from the faucet into a glass. If you are concerned about impurities in tap water, install a filter. If you insist on purchasing bottled water, buy it in a glass bottle, not in plastic. Bottled water is available in glass bottles at most health-conscious grocery stores such as Whole Foods and Wegman's. If you must carry bottled water with you, make sure that your bottle is BPA-free and phthalate-free. There are many light-weight stainless-steel bottles available on the market now for just this purpose.
- If you want to drink soda, buy it in glass bottles. Yes, Coke and Diet Coke and many other soft drinks are still available in glass bottles, though you may have to go to a beverage distributor to get them. (In Chapter 6 I will try to persuade you and your daughter to avoid cola beverages altogether; if you want fizz, drink seltzer water instead.)
- When you microwave food, don't allow the food to come into contact with the plastic wrap you put over the top. Instead of putting the food on a plate, put the food in a deep bowl, so the plastic wrap across the top won't come in contact with the food. Or, instead of using plastic wrap, you can cover the food with a plate (that's what I do).
- Even better, avoid using plastic wrap altogether: use waxed paper or parchment paper instead. You can find natural waxed paper at www.letsgogreen.biz and other websites promoting organic and natural products. (Don't put any kind of waxed paper in a conventional oven or it will smoke; parchment paper is fine in a conventional oven. Both waxed paper and parchment paper are safe to use in the microwave.)

All these warnings about hidden toxins in our food and beverages can be a little overwhelming. But there's actually a simple fix to this problem, which Michael Pollan outlines in his book *In Defense of Food.* Pollan summarizes his recommendations in just seven words: "Eat food. Not too much. Mostly plants."[56] When Pollan recommends that you eat food, he means whole foods your grandmother would have recognized, like artichokes and asparagus and broccoli and cabbage and cucumbers and oatmeal. None of those foods are shipped in PETE bottles or BPA containers. None of them pose any risk of endocrine disruption if you buy them whole at the store and prepare them yourself.

So you're going to drink water out of glass bottles, or poured straight from the faucet into a glass. Good. That's what I do, and that's what my family does.

What about milk? First, we need to clear up some common misconceptions. Livestock raised for beef in the United States are often injected with hormones, especially bovine growth hormone (BGH), to make them grow faster. However, it's illegal to administer any kind of sex hormones such as estrogens or testosterone to dairy cattle, even in the United States. We do know that cows' milk contains natural cow estrogens, but the concentration is so low that it almost certainly cannot affect a girl's endocrine system. In the most recent study, the highest concentration measured from any cow was 10 nanograms per liter.[57] A nanogram (ng) is one-thousandth of one-millionth of a gram. That's how much estrogen you would ingest if you drank a liter of milk at one sitting. It's not much. (And most of the cows tested had less than that amount — 10 ng per liter was the highest reading.) You would have to drink 1,000 liters of milk in order to ingest one-millionth of a gram of estrogen. Second, the natural estrogen in cows' milk is highly protein-bound. It's not easily absorbed by the body, and it's likely to be broken down in the digestive process. Third, there's no evidence that girls who drink lots of milk are at any risk of earlier onset of puberty. Between the 1970s and the 1990s, consumption of milk by American girls fell by 36 percent.[58] If milk were a significant cause of early puberty, one would expect that fewer girls would be experiencing early puberty today than was the case 30 years ago — but of course the opposite is true.

How about juice? It's fine to buy *fresh* juice in plastic bottles in the refrigerator section of the grocery store, because fresh juices are shipped in refrigerated containers. Those juices are not allowed to come to room temperature. That means the plastic can't leach into what you're going to drink.

Other juices, such as white grape juice and apple juice, are often sold in clear plastic bottles or even plasticized cardboard boxes and are shipped and stored at room temperature. Don't buy them. Don't buy any beverage in a plastic bottle or plasticized box that has been shipped at room temperature. Maybe that bottle sat in a hot truck for a week. Maybe it didn't. You have no way of knowing.

But we're not finished. There's more to the story of early puberty than just environmental toxins. Another factor may be something that used to be a part of almost every girl's life but has become less common today: a Dad in the house.

life with father

Here are two facts:

1. Girls who grow up without their biological father go through puberty earlier. The absence of the mother, by contrast, does not appear to affect the timing of puberty.[59]
2. Girls today are more likely to grow up without their biological father. As recently as 1960, only 17 percent of children grew up without their biological fathers; by 1990, that proportion had more than doubled, to 36 percent.[60] A girl today may grow up with a man in the home, but more often than ever before, he's not her *biological* father.

First, some disclaimers. I am not suggesting that mothers aren't important, nor am I suggesting that fathers are more important than mothers.

I am just noting that on this one parameter—the timing of puberty in girls—the presence of the biological father appears to matter more than the presence of the mother.

Second: I am not suggesting that stepfathers can't do a great job of parenting girls. Indeed, some recent research suggests that stepfathers, on average, do as good a job, on most objective measures of parenting, as biological fathers do.[61] Nevertheless, the presence of the biological father appears to have a protective effect, delaying the onset of puberty in the father's daughter. What's going on?

Scientists have been debating the roots of this phenomenon for more than 30 years.[62] Back in the 1980s and 1990s, many people thought that a father's absence might merely be a marker for poverty. Poverty, these researchers thought, might be the actual reason why girls raised without their fathers go through puberty earlier. Girls who grow up without their biological fathers are more likely to be in low-income households,[63] and some research suggests that girls who grow up in low-income households may indeed go through puberty earlier.[64] Therefore, girls who grow up without their father go through puberty earlier because there's less money around, right?

Probably not. In more recent studies, investigators have carefully controlled for household income, and they have found that the father-absence effect is still highly significant.[65]

Others have conjectured that maybe the absence of the father somehow leads girls to be overweight, and that it's the overweight—not the absence of the father—that is to blame.[66] Again, recent research has disproved that theory: girls who grow up without their father are not more likely to be overweight than girls who grow up with their father.[67]

The quality of the father's involvement matters as well. If a girl has a Dad who is loving and physically affectionate with her, giving her hugs, then she will, on average, go through puberty at a later age.[68] If a girl has a Dad who is emotionally distant, then she will, on average, go through puberty earlier. If a girl has a father who abuses her sexually or physically, then she is at greatest risk and will go through puberty even earlier.[69]

Dad's presence will protect his daughter against early puberty only if Dad is more or less a normal guy. If Dad abuses his wife or daughter; if he's addicted to drugs; or if he is a violent criminal offender, then there is no protective effect with regard to early onset of puberty associated with Dad being in the home.[70]

Stepfathers don't seem to be able to substitute for the biological father on this one parameter, the timing of puberty. In fact, there is some evidence that the presence of a stepfather may actually *accelerate* the onset of puberty in girls, compared to girls raised without any man in the home.[71]

But we still haven't answered the question, What's going on? How come the presence of the biological father, but not the biological mother, plays a role in the timing of puberty in girls?

Some people think that the answer has to do with pheromones.

something in the air

A pheromone is basically an airborne hormone: a form of hormonal communication wafting in the air between individuals. Many people confuse pheromones with odors. Although some pheromones have odors, and some odors may act as pheromones, pheromones do not necessarily have any smell. There's good evidence that many vertebrates, including humans, have a special cranial nerve that is devoted solely to detecting pheromones, even if we can't detect those pheromones as odors.[72]

Pheromones can influence the pace of sexual development. [73] In many species, females raised in the presence of an *unrelated* male will reach sexual maturity *earlier* than females who are not exposed to males.[74] Researchers have also found some cases where female laboratory animals raised in the presence of their *biological* father will reach sexual maturity *later*;[75] that is of course similar to the effect biological fathers have in human families.

Why do adult humans have hair in their armpits? Part of the answer appears to be because the armpit is the number-one place where adult humans manufacture pheromones. The armpit is where you find the apocrine glands, the glands that produce most of the substances believed to act as pheromones in humans. Children don't have hair in the armpits until the process of puberty begins, because prepubescent children don't manufacture pheromones. Armpit hair, as one researcher eloquently puts it, helps "provides a warm environment where the action of commensal bacteria can volatilize the precursor molecules released from apocrine glands."[76] Bacteria in the armpit turn your pheromones into an aerosol, which the armpit hair then wafts into the air.

Makes you want to take a shower, doesn't it?

Robert Matchock and Elizabeth Susman at Penn State University are convinced that pheromones are the mechanism whereby the presence of the biological father slows down the tempo of his daughter's sexual development. They believe that this phenomenon is hardwired in our species, as it is in many other mammals, in order to decrease the likelihood of a father having sex with his daughter.[77] "Biological fathers send out inhibitory chemical signals to their daughters," says Matchock. "In the absence of these signals, girls tend to sexually mature earlier."[78]

It's a plausible hypothesis. We do know that we humans can distinguish degree of kinship, from close family members to total strangers, by using chemical clues: and we know that males and females process these chemical clues differently. Women can distinguish a male relative from an unrelated man, just by sniffing some hair snipped from each man's armpit.[79] (I wonder how much they paid those women to participate in that experiment?)

But there's still a great deal we don't know about why girls are going through puberty earlier. For example, in their study of about 2,000 college girls, Matchock and Susman found that girls who grew up in the city went through puberty earlier than girls who grew up in the countryside, even after adjusting for any difference in the father living at home. They aren't sure why. Urban girls aren't any fatter than country girls. My guess would be that girls in big cities are exposed to BPA and phthalates more than girls in the countryside, but for now that's just a guess.

Another group of investigators found that girls who drink lots of soft drinks are more likely to begin puberty earlier.[80] Maybe that's because girls who drink lots of soft drinks are fatter than girls who don't. Maybe it's because endocrine disruptors are leaching out of the plastic bottle and into the beverage. Maybe it's because biological fathers don't let their daughters drink lots of soft drinks. Maybe it's something else altogether. We just don't know.

what can parents do?

Let's get practical. What can you do to prevent your daughter from going through puberty too early? The following measures may reasonably decrease the likelihood that your daughter will go through puberty before she should:

- **Avoid exposing her to the environmental toxins** which we discussed earlier in this chapter. That means avoiding plastic bottles, avoiding heating any food in a plastic container, and being mindful of what lotions and creams go on her skin.
- **Engage her in appropriate exercise programs**. "Exercise is protective against early puberty," Dr. Steingraber observes.[81] Your daughter doesn't have to exercise herself skinny to enjoy this benefit. Girls who are involved in swimming, for example, decrease their risk of early puberty, even though girls who swim do not weigh less, on average, compared with other girls.[82] In Chapter 6 we will return to the question of what's "appropriate" exercise.
- If you're a Mom, and you live with your daughter's father, then **encourage her Dad to be a warm and loving father.** If you're a Mom and your daughter's father doesn't live with you and your daughter, then try to create opportunities for your daughter and her father to have fun together—as long as he's not abusive, alcoholic, or a criminal.
- **If you're a Dad, be there for your daughter.**

But what if your daughter has already begun puberty—if she is 7 or 8 and she's definitely developing breasts? As Dr. Grumbach and Dr. Styne observe, "Puberty is not an immutable process; it can be arrested or even reversed."[83] Even if your daughter has begun the process of puberty, the process is not complete until she has begun menstruating regularly. It is possible to slow the process down or stop it.

There are now special medications that can slow the tempo of puberty. These medications are known as gonadotropin releasing-hormone (GnRH) analogs. Various GnRH analogs are available today, including nafarelin, buserelin, leuprolide, deslorelin, histrelin, and triptorelin. Their popularity is growing rapidly. They are available not only in once-daily formulations but also as once-monthly injections and even as once-a-year implants. Of course, the decision to start your daughter on such a medication should be made only after careful consultation with a physician who understands your daughter's situation and who is experienced with these medications.

Many parents are understandably reluctant to consider putting their daughter on such medications, but we are living in a new world. Until 50 years ago, most girls never came in contact with the environmental toxins I've been talking about. In most human societies, most girls have grown up in the vicinity of their biological fathers, unless their fathers were dead. That's no longer the case. Girls growing up today are exposed to uniquely 21st-century toxins, so I think it's appropriate at least to consider 21st-century solutions. I want you to be aware of your options.

If your daughter begins the process of puberty between 6 and 8 years of age, and your doctor prescribes GnRH analog medications for her, then you may be giving her at least one or two, and maybe even three, extra years of childhood. You may also be increasing her adult height. Girls who begin receiving these medications between 6 and 8 years of age for the purpose of slowing the process of puberty will grow up, as adults, to be about two to three inches taller than girls who began puberty at the same age but who do not receive these medications.[84]

In 2009, 30 experts gathered to consider the growing popularity of these agents. They agreed that GnRH analog medications generally have "a favorable record of safety and efficacy" but that more experience is needed before these medications can be recommended for routine use in girls with early onset of puberty, particularly in girls over 8 years of age.[85] There's not much controversy about using these medications if a girl is 7 years old and developing breasts. Most experts agree that's OK. But there is much less agreement about whether these medications should be used for a girl who has begun breast development at age 10. If you are interested in learning more about GnRH analog medications, you might start by reading the consensus paper, which you can download for free at the *Girls on the Edge* link at www.leonardsax.com. As updates become available, I will post them on the site as well.

Up to this point, we've considered the challenges facing 21st-century girls from the perspective of the four factors that are driving this new crisis for girls. Now we're going to change direction. Instead of focusing on the problems, we're going to focus on *solutions*. We're going to consider how other parents have helped their daughters develop a healthy mind in a healthy body, and more.

mind

And then a Plank in Reason, broke,
And I dropped down, and down—
And hit a World, at every plunge,
And Finished knowing—then—

EMILY DICKINSON

mozart *in utero*

I admit it: I used to believe in the benefits of playing music to babies while they are still in their mothers' wombs. When my wife, Katie, was pregnant with our daughter, I made a playlist of classical music on Katie's iPod. We purchased little curved speakers for Katie to put on her tummy. Katie and I both thought it would be a good idea to play the music with the speakers face-down on Katie's belly so that our daughter-to-be could listen to classical music while waiting to be born. The playlist included only soft, slow music such as Brahms' "Lullaby," the first movement of Beethoven's *Moonlight* Sonata, or the second movement from Mozart's 21st Piano Concerto. We played the music a lot.

"Do you think she likes it?" I asked my wife once, late in the third trimester.

"Well, I can feel her kicking," she said.

What was the result? Our daughter, Sarah, loves music. She especially loves to dance. She also has strong preferences in music—and has since she was an infant. She loves fast, up-tempo songs. She doesn't care for most classical music. And she absolutely hates soft, slow music like Brahms' "Lullaby," the first movement of the *Moonlight* Sonata, or the second movement from Mozart's 21st Piano Concerto. Even as a little baby, she would become almost hysterical with tears and anger whenever we would try to play any of that music for her. We'd have to turn it off before she choked.

In fact, there is no good evidence that playing music to your baby in the womb has any benefit whatsoever.[1] But our behavior was characteristic of more than a few American parents. Many of us tend to equate "earlier" with "better." I recently went to a store that sells educational toys, where I saw a display promoting a series of DVDs and flash cards promising to "Teach your baby to read!" This particular program assures parents that their 2-year-old can learn to read if they just purchase the DVDs ($199.95), ideally with the help of the upgrade kit ($89.95).[2] As I noted in the previous chapter, the brain of a pre-pubescent child is astonishingly nimble. You might be able to train a 2- or 3-year-old to do all sorts of things. But is this a good idea? *Should* we be pushing 2-year-olds to read? If kids acquire academic skills earlier, do they do better in the long run? Many parents I have spoken with across North America often assume that the answer to that question is "yes." Parents in Europe, Australia, and New Zealand typically are more cautious on this point.

In fact, the answer to that question depends on the context. Certainly kids who are not fluent readers by, say, age 10 are at increased risk for long-term academic difficulties. But kids who can't read well by age 10 (fifth grade) often have a learning disability or other problem that makes it difficult for them to excel. You can't use that finding to argue that drilling your 3-year-old with flash cards will have any long-term benefit.

Over the past 40 years there has been a general acceleration in elementary education in the United States (and to a lesser extent, internationally). Forty years ago, kindergarten was about playing duck-duck-goose or finger-painting or singing in rounds. Today, the kindergarten curriculum looks very much like the first-grade curriculum of 1970 or 1980. The primary emphasis is on learning to read and write.[3]

Proponents of the idea that "earlier is better" point to research showing that kids who know their alphabet by the time they're in kindergarten are more likely to be fluent readers by fourth grade.[4] These advocates proudly note that the average fourth-grader in the United States earns higher scores on reading tests today than was the case in 1980. That's true. But the average twelfth-grade reader is not reading better than the average twelfth-grader was reading in 1980.[5] In fact, the average twelfth-grader nowadays doesn't read books for fun at all. There has been a substantial decline over the past three decades in the proportion of American teenagers who read for fun.[6] The average American teenager today spends only nine minutes a day reading a book or magazine outside of school.[7] I think part of the reason may be that pushing kids to read earlier, before it is developmentally appropriate, disengages some of them from reading altogether.

a short history of kindergarten

The French philosopher Jean-Jacques Rousseau, writing in 1762, insisted that "reading is the plague of childhood." Rousseau believed that young children need to experience the world firsthand before reading about it. "Books are good only for learning to babble about what one does not know. I am convinced that in matters of observation, one must not read, one must see," he wrote.[8] Rousseau recommended that books should be avoided completely until children were 12 years old, so that children might interact with the world as explorers and adventurers, discovering the world for themselves.

Rousseau never tried to establish a school built on his ideas. Swiss educator Johann Heinrich Pestalozzi did. His school, which he launched in Frankfurt, Germany, in 1804, featured several innovations for his time: no lectures, almost no books, and no whipping of students. He believed that the best way to educate young children was to take them on long walks through the countryside, using the outings as opportunities to teach about plants, animals, and rocks.

One of Pestalozzi's students, Friedrich Wilhelm Froebel, took the idea one step further. In the 1800s, many German states such as Prussia prohibited children under 7 years of age from attending any school. Pestalozzi's school enrolled children as young as 7, but no younger. In 1837, Froebel opened the first school specifically for children 3 to 6 years of age.* He invented the word *kindergarten* to describe his new school. *Kindergarten* in German can mean either "children's garden" or "garden of children." "Children's garden" was particularly appropriate for Froebel's school, because every child was assigned a small plot of ground to cultivate under the teacher's supervision. There was also a larger plot that all the children worked together. This communal plot was organized with legumes in one corner, cereal grains in another, and oil plants in another. Froebel's idea was that kids would learn these categories firsthand, in the dirt, rather than from a book.[9]

By the 1860s these ideas had spread throughout Europe and into North America. Some educators tried to appropriate the word *kindergarten* without abiding by Froebel's principles. They were teaching young children how to read. Elizabeth Palmer Peabody, the leader of the kindergarten movement in the United States from the 1860s until her death in 1894, denounced these "false kindergartens [that] cater to adults who want to see young children learn to read and write and study school subjects at an early age."[10] For Peabody, as for Froebel, the objective of educating young children should be to awaken their love of learning. Don't start formal classroom education until age seven, Peabody and her followers insisted. The precious years from 3 to 6 should be spent chasing tadpoles, digging in the mud, and watching clouds scud across the sky.

Froebel and Peabody had the right idea. The girl who has spent hours chasing tadpoles in a pond at age 5 will be fascinated, at age 8, to learn how tadpoles turn into frogs. The girl who has never chased tadpoles or frogs in a pond but has only watched animated frogs on educational television is much less likely to have that interest.[11] Forty years ago, even 30 years ago, the kindergarten experience itself would have offered many

---

* In 1837, Froebel was living in Blankenburg, in the German state of Thuringia, which had no law prohibiting the education of children under 7.

opportunities for this kind of outdoor experience. Not anymore—at least, not in most North American schools.

Some schools are exceptions to this rule. Schools that follow the Waldorf model, or the Reggio Emilia philosophy, as well as many Montessori schools, generally endorse the Froebelian ideal in education, emphasizing hands-on learning for kids at ages 4, 5, and 6, deferring most book-learning until age 7.

does "earlier" equal "better"?

What's so bad about teaching kids to read and write at age 5? For some kids I'm sure it's fine. Some 5-year-old girls are perfectly happy to sit still for a 30-minute session and learn how to read. But I have met other 5-year-old girls who couldn't possibly stay attentive for that long. If you insist that they do so, they may sit still, but they're not paying attention. They may come to regard school, and books, as boring.

Those negative attitudes, once formed, are hard to change. The early years of school strongly influence the subsequent educational trajectory of the child. Kids who are enthusiastic about school because they love to learn are more likely to do well in school than kids who hate school. Ellen Skinner and her colleagues interviewed more than 1,600 elementary-school kids. They asked them how they felt about their teachers and their school. Then Skinner and her associates followed these kids for three years to see how well they did in school. Not surprisingly, kids who liked school and liked their teachers in third grade were much more likely to be doing well three years later, compared with kids in the same classroom who didn't like school or the teacher.[12] Pushing kids to do schoolwork that's not developmentally appropriate for them may cause some of those kids to develop negative attitudes toward school, as well as negative ideas about their own ability, what researchers call "academic self-concept."

Those negative ideas about their ability can become a self-fulfilling prophecy. Kids who do well in school early are more likely to be high achievers years down the road. Kids who struggle in school early are less likely to become high achievers later, and that effect remains strong even after researchers control for differences in family backgrounds.[13]

I am not saying that books are bad for kids. I think it's great for a parent to read to a child, maybe for older kids as well as younger kids.[14] I remember when I was a boy at sleep-away summer camp, the summer before ninth grade. Our counselor would read Sherlock Holmes stories to us each night. Imagine sixteen boys in a cabin in northern Michigan, after dark, the only light coming from the counselor's flashlight pointing at his book as he read. We were all fascinated by the story. An adult reading to a child, or to a group of children, is sending the message that reading is fun, that adults like to read, and that reading opens up a door to a different world. The problem is not with books, but with pushing kids to read on their own before they are ready.

Success in early elementary education is all about doing the right thing *at the right time.* The academic focus that may be right for first grade may be wrong for kindergarten.[15] There's a big difference between what's best for a 6-year-old and what's best for a 5-year-old. Individual differences also are huge in early childhood: a phonics-intensive reading curriculum that may be fine for one 6-year-old girl may be a bad choice for another.[16]

There's a well-known program in the United States called Head Start. It provides all kinds of educational experiences to kids from low-income households who otherwise might spend most of their day stuck in front of a TV set. What I don't like about the program is its name, which implies that education is a race, and so there's an advantage to having a "head start." Developing a love of learning is not a race. Getting a "head start" on the curriculum is less important than inspiring a child to be inquisitive about the natural world.

Results from other countries provide good evidence that earlier does not equal better. The Program for International Student Assessment (PISA) is one of the largest programs designed to allow comparisons in academic achievement across countries. Here are some of the results from the latest round of international testing in science literacy[17] (a score of 500 is considered "average"):

Finland: 563

Sweden: 503

Denmark: 496

United States: 489

Norway: 487

When I look at those numbers, the first question that pops into my head is, What's so special about Finland? Finland consistently finishes highest in the PISA comparisons, way ahead of the rest of the pack, including its Scandinavian neighbors Norway, Sweden, and Denmark.

There are several factors that may contribute to Finland's consistent supremacy on these international comparisons.[18] One is the fact that children in Finland are not allowed to attend formal school until 7 years of age. Little kids in Finland are either at home or attend what we might recognize as preschool. They're playing games. They're playing outdoors. They're looking at clouds. They are not learning to read and write.

The PISA test is administered to students when they are 15 years old. Children in the United States start formal education at age 5 whereas Finnish children start at age 7. We have a two-year head start—so why do the kids in Finland blow American kids away? Perhaps it's because kids in Finland were not required to sit still and be quiet in a classroom at 5 years of age. A 5-year-old who is asked to sit still may do as you ask her to do, as I just said, but she may come to regard school as a sort of prison. In her free time at home, the last thing she will want to do is read a book.

If you give that girl two more years of childhood, she is less likely to regard school as a prison. She may be more eager to learn, and more likely to read in her spare time. An avalanche of research demonstrates that kids who read in their spare time do better in school.[19]

The acceleration of the early elementary curriculum has been harmful to both girls and boys, but in different ways. We're seeing a growing proportion of boys who have decided, by second grade in many cases, that they hate school and that school is a total waste of time. Some of them don't even *want* to do well in school. By the time they're in middle school, they will make fun of any boy who cares about getting good grades (see *Boys Adrift* for more about the growing proportion of boys who regard academic achievement as unmasculine).

I see that result with girls occasionally. But girls are more likely to do the homework and study for tests, in some cases because they don't want to disappoint their parents, in other cases because they care more about getting good grades than boys do. They are more likely to be working in school not for the intrinsic rewards of learning, but for the extrinsic rewards of good grades and parental approval.

I have seen too many fourth- and fifth-grade classrooms where the teacher is ready to throw her hands up in despair. "The boys ignore me, and the only question the girls ask is, 'Will this be on the test?'" one teacher said to me. "I've been teaching for 19 years. When I started, I never had a 10-year-old girl or boy ask me whether something was going to be on the test. Now it happens every day."

So how can you help your daughter? For any girl, or any boy for that matter, under eight years of age, my first recommendation is: turn off the TV set. While you're at it, turn off the computer. Educational television and video games are not the best way to inspire a lifelong love of learning in your child. Instead, get your child outside, playing in the dirt, exploring his or her world. Postpone the grind of 21st-century elementary education as long as possible.

When you buy a toy for your preschool-age daughter, choose a toy that doesn't have an on-off switch. Choose a toy that requires her to be in complete control. A dump truck is a great toy as long as it's a dump truck that she has to push with her own hands. I'm seeing too many kids with remote-controlled gizmos, where all the kid does is push buttons and the toy entertains her. When the batteries die, she says "It's broke." I've watched girls playing with complicated toys based on characters from educational television such as *Dora the Explorer*. The girls press some buttons and Dora starts talking to them on a little screen. Because Dora is doing something instructive, like counting in Spanish, parents think this stuff is great, but all I see is more TV. Girls who spend hours playing these games, pushing the buttons to make Dora jump and run, are atrophying their own imaginations. These girls need to be jumping and running themselves, not watching an animated doll jump and run on a little screen. Simpler toys with no video screens and no remote controls encourage girls to be more imaginative in their play. Girls can create whole worlds in their minds. And the richer their firsthand experience of the world, the more likely they are to do well when they finally begin school.

Which brings us to the next question: When is your daughter *ready* to start school?

For decades it was axiomatic that children should start kindergarten at age 5. That was fine 40 years ago, when kindergarten actually resembled what Froebel and Peabody had in mind. Now that kindergarten has become first grade, I have seen girls who have been labeled (incorrectly) as having ADHD or as having below-average intelligence simply because they don't like to sit for an hour or more.

For some girls, then, the best age to start kindergarten may be 6 rather than 5. Which girls should start at age 6? The girl who has trouble sitting still for more than 20 minutes at a time. The girl who seems to listen better when she is standing than when she is sitting. The girl who makes buzzing noises while she is listening to you. If you enroll this girl at age 5 in a typical American kindergarten, you run a high risk of getting a phone call from the teacher: "Have you thought about having your daughter tested for ADHD?" It's not the teacher's fault. She's just doing her job. If you're the teacher, and your job is to teach 20 5-year-olds to learn to read and write, then the kid who won't sit still, the kid who won't even sit down, the kid who insists on making buzzing noises—that kid becomes the problem kid.

The scariest thing about all these kids being diagnosed with ADHD is that the medications most often prescribed for ADHD—Adderall, Ritalin, Concerta, Metadate, and Focalin—will work even if these kids don't have ADHD. The response to treatment can be misleading. I've spoken with many parents who say, in essence, "That medication for ADHD really helped my kid; *therefore* my kid must have ADHD, because the ADHD medication helped, right?" Wrong. These medications improve the attention and behavior of normal kids as much as they do for kids with ADHD. But these medications may damage an area of the developing brain responsible for drive and motivation. Prolonged use of these medications may result in a child who is apathetic and disengaged. (See *Boys Adrift* for more evidence on these points.)

You don't want to put your daughter in a situation where the teacher is going to need to make that referral. When in doubt, give your daughter another year of childhood. Postpone kindergarten to age 6.

Unless you are among the few parents who are willing and able to home-school your child, the next question is, Which school is best?

The best school for Emily might be a disaster for Melissa, and vice versa. In choosing the right school for your child, you have to know your child, and you have to know the school. Ideally your school should inspire your daughter to care about learning, not just about getting a good grade. Education and learning should be seen—by students, teachers, and school administrators—as worthwhile ends in themselves, not primarily as means to other ends such as getting into a good college or university.

The question of how to choose a school should be an issue for *every* parent, not just for parents who send their kids to private schools. Fifty years ago, public schools had pretty much the same approach to parents that the telephone company had to its customers: the telephone belonged to the telephone company, so you took whatever the company gave you, and everybody had pretty much the same telephone. That may have been acceptable in that era, but not anymore. One truism of the 21st century is that big entities—whether they be telephone companies or public school districts—have to be responsive to their consumers.

I have worked with hundreds of public school administrators over the past nine years, and almost every one of them has been eager to hear from parents. Don't hesitate to ask tough questions. In choosing a school for a girl in kindergarten through fifth grade, or when speaking to administrators at a local elementary school, I would suggest that you ask these questions:

- Does every student spend some time outdoors every day, even in inclement weather?[20] As the Germans say in this context, "There's no such thing as bad weather, just unsuitable clothes." Most young kids love to play outside in the rain and the snow. It's we grown-ups who grumble when the weather is "bad."
- Does the school offer recess, or other unstructured free time, at least once a day?
- Does the school offer daily physical education? (I'll address the importance of this in the next chapter.)
- Does the school try to accomplish at least some curriculum items outdoors—such as learning about farming by actually planting seeds in the soil, rather than by looking at pictures on a computer screen?
- Does the school have a thoughtful and intentional program to encourage each child's creativity and curiosity? "Draw a picture of whatever you want; then tell me a story about it" is a better assignment for this purpose than "Please draw a picture of a tree, a flower, or a dog."

I would not be impressed by an elementary school that boasts about having a computer for every child, especially if we're talking about 5- or 6-year-olds. On the contrary, I would be concerned that the leadership of that school doesn't understand what's developmentally appropriate for young children. Most kids will pick that computer stuff up quickly enough when it's time. Just because 50-year-olds need to take courses in how to use the Internet doesn't mean 7-year-olds do. The greater danger for girls today is that they will put too much emphasis on the virtual world, and not enough on the real world. Kids in second grade need to understand dirt—what it's made out of, what it feels like, and how it helps plants to grow—much more than they need to understand the Internet. A school that boasts "a computer for every kindergartner" may not be the best school for your 5-year-old daughter.

You have to shift gears as your daughter grows up and moves into middle childhood and early adolescence, in the years just before and just after the onset of puberty. One of the great challenges of parenting a daughter is helping her to achieve her potential and become the woman she is meant to be—when you have no idea what she is meant to be. Maybe she would be happiest as an astrophysicist, or as a plumber, or as a computer scientist. How are you and she going to discover that? You have to ensure that her horizons are broad; and you have to empower her to explore.

"all our girls love physics"

I had the privilege of visiting Korowa, a girls' school in Melbourne, Australia. While there, I spoke at length with Jenn Alabaster, the physics instructor. Physics is an elective course at Korowa, but more than half the girls sign up for it. "And they love it, they all love it, even the girly girls who are into Paris Hilton and *Gossip Girl,*" Ms. Alabaster told me. I know the schools in Melbourne pretty well, having visited many of them. Schools in Melbourne, as in most major cities throughout the English-speaking world, typically don't have a majority of girls signing up to take physics. How does Jenn Alabaster do it?

Walk into just about any school anywhere in the world where physics is being taught. Visit during the first weeks of class. Chances are high that the instructor will be explaining that part of physics known as *kinematics*: concepts like velocity, acceleration, and change in momentum. That means you're talking about drag cars accelerating on a racetrack, or football players colliding, or bombs exploding. Boy stuff.

That's not how Jenn Alabaster starts the school year. The first question she asks her students is, "What is light? It's all around us. It's how we see. But what is light *made* out of?" Then her students get out the ripple tanks and study how ripples in water interfere with each other. They discover how to use the ripple tanks to demonstrate reflection, refraction, and diffraction of water waves. Then they study the same phenomena—reflection, refraction, and diffraction—with light.

"So light is a wave?" the girls ask.

"Yes," Jenn Alabaster answers. Then she gets out the laser. In 30 minutes, the girls discover that light is a particle.

"But how can that be? How can light be both a wave and a particle?" the girls ask.

"Good question," Ms. Alabaster says.

The girls go on to learn that light is not only both a wave and a particle—a particle with no mass—but also that light itself is invisible. When they shine the laser into the vacuum inside a sealed glass container, they see nothing. It's only when the laser beam emerges from the vacuum into the (dusty) room air that they can see the beam. The girls are fascinated.

Alabaster teaches kinematics—it's part of the required curriculum, as it is everywhere—but she teaches it toward the end of the school year. In most other schools I have visited, the physics course begins with kinematics, while the wave-particle duality of light is pushed back into the final weeks of the school year.

So one aspect of girl-friendly physics may be as simple as the sequence in which the various curriculum items are taught. Beginning the school year with the wave-particle duality of light is a more girl-friendly approach than starting with kinematics and momentum transfer. It's not better. It's not worse. It's just different. Most schools teach physics using the boy-friendly sequence of topics, starting with football players colliding and bombs exploding. Then they wonder why more girls don't want to take the class. Girls may not sign up because they may not know how fascinating physics can be once you get past the collisions and the explosions. "If you're not aware of something that at some point might interest you, how can you choose it?" asks Karen Peterson, the principal investigator for a National Science Foundation–funded project that is investigating why girls and women are still underrepresented in subjects like physics.[21]

Figure 6

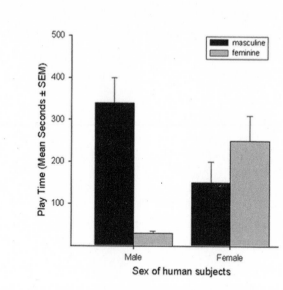

Sex of human subjects

would you rather play with a truck or a doll?

Why does Jenn Alabaster's approach work so well? I believe it works because it touches on a much deeper principle.

If you took a course in developmental psychology at almost any university in the past 30 years, odds are good that you learned about a number of classic experiments done in the 1960s through the 1990s. All these experiments were some variation on the following: the experimenter offers a young child, perhaps 3 or 4 years old, a choice of playing between a doll (or some other "girly" toy) and a truck (or some other "boy" toy). Girls typically show a slight preference for the doll over the truck. Boys typically show an overwhelming preference for trucks rather than dolls.[22]

When I learned about those studies as a graduate student earning my PhD in psychology at the University of Pennsylvania, we were taught that "the social construction of gender" is the appropriate framework in which to understand these results. Figure 6 shows a typical result from one of these studies. The black bar indicates the amount of time the child spent playing with a "masculine" toy such as a truck. The gray bar indicates the amount of time the child spent playing with a "feminine" toy

Figure 7

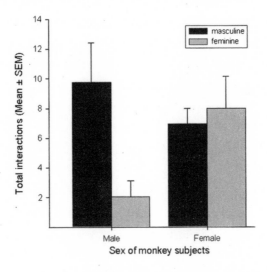

such as a doll. Girls spend slightly more time playing with the doll than with the truck. Very few boys spend even a minute playing with the doll. The boys greatly prefer the truck; the girls slightly prefer the doll.[23]

My professor at Penn, Justin Aronfreed, explained it to me this way: "We give girls a fairly consistent message that girls are supposed to play with dolls, and not with trucks. So when offered a choice, girls will be more likely to play with dolls rather than trucks. But if a girl picks up a truck, it's not a catastrophe." With boys, Professor Aronfreed explained, the stakes are higher. "We send boys a much stronger message about what a boy is and is not supposed to do. Boys are NOT supposed to play with dolls. Boys get that message loud and clear. So boys are much more likely to play with trucks rather than dolls." When Professor Aronfreed gave me that explanation 30 years ago, it seemed like common sense.

Kim Wallen and his colleagues at the Yerkes National Primate Research Center in Atlanta recently decided to do this familiar study again, with a little twist: instead of offering human children a choice of playing with dolls or trucks, they gave that choice to monkeys. Their results are shown in Figure 7.

As you can see, the basic pattern of results was similar to the pattern seen with human children.[24] The females slightly prefer to play with dolls rather than trucks, and the males substantially prefer to play with trucks rather than dolls.

It is difficult to invoke the social construction of gender to accommodate this finding. You would have to assert that a monkey in authority, maybe a parent, is saying to a young male monkey, "Don't let me catch you playing with a doll!" But in fact nothing of the sort happens. Monkeys don't appear to care whether other monkeys, female or male, are playing with trucks or with dolls. And yet the main effect is clearly present in monkeys as it is in human children. The social construction of gender may be playing some role, because the magnitude of the sex difference is clearly greater in human children than it is among monkeys. But the social construction of gender cannot reasonably be invoked to explain this effect in humans, in view of the fact that a similar effect is present in monkeys.[25]

So what's going on?

monkeys, girls, boys, and toys[26]

Developmental psychologist Gerianne Alexander thinks she might know. Professor Alexander was the first to offer monkeys a choice of playing with "boy toys" or "girl toys." Like Dr. Wallen's group, Alexander found sex differences among monkeys that are similar to the sex differences we see among human children.[27] In 2003, one year after she published her monkey study, Alexander published her theory explaining *why* female and male monkeys—as well as female and male humans—might prefer to play with different toys.[28]

Scientists have known for roughly three decades that our visual system actually comprises two separate systems operating in parallel, beginning at the level of the ganglion cells in the retina and extending back to visual cortex and visual association cortex.[29] One system is devoted to answering the question "*What* is it?—what's its color, what's its texture?" The other system is devoted to answering the question "*Where* is it going?—and how fast is it moving?" These two systems in the brain are often referred to as the "what" system and the "where" system.[30]

Professor Alexander was the first to suggest that hardwired sex differences in the visual system may explain the observed sex differences in the toy preferences of children as well as monkeys. She conjectured that maybe girls have more resources in the "what" system and boys have more resources in the "where" system. Her hypothesis accommodates a number of findings that otherwise are hard to explain: for example, that baby girls ages 3 to 8 months, but not baby boys, prefer to look at dolls rather than toy trucks.[31] Researchers in Germany recently reported dramatic sex differences in the anatomy of human visual cortex in adults, with more resources devoted to the "where" system in men compared with women.[32] That finding also fits Alexander's suggestion.

Professor Alexander's hypothesis helps me understand the gender differences I have seen firsthand, in schools from Edinburgh to Calgary to Dallas to Auckland, in gender-specific best practice for teaching not only physics, but also creative writing, visual arts, and even modern foreign languages. The best way to teach physics to boys is pretty much the way we usually do teach physics in coed classrooms: with a focus on *action*—cars accelerating, football players colliding, and so on, which engages the "*where* is it going?" system. The best way to teach physics to girls appears to be to focus on answers to questions like: *What* is it? *What* is light made out of? *What* is matter made out of? *What* laws govern the universe? *Why* those laws and not others?

How we see influences how we perceive the world and what we like to read and how we like to write, particularly when we are young. In my book *Boys Adrift* I explored how a lack of awareness of this point disengages boys in subjects such as creative writing and visual arts. Some boys want to write stories with an emphasis on action, but they lose their enthusiasm when the teacher says, "Tell me more about your characters, Justin: What do they look like? What kind of clothes are they wearing?" The teacher wants Justin to emphasize the features that engage the "what" visual system, but Justin wants to tell a story that engages the "where" visual system.

Most teachers don't know anything about sex differences in the visual system. Very few schools of education provide any instruction on this topic, or on anything related to sex differences in best practice for teaching various subjects.[33] The general lack of awareness of gender differences disadvantages both girls and boys. The result too often is a school where the boys think creative writing is for girls, while the girls believe that physics is for guys. When teachers do understand these gender differences, you can break down gender stereotypes. As Jenn Alabaster and others have found, girls love physics if you know how to teach it to them.

the unity of everything

Benjamin Hutto, the director of music for the National Cathedral School, a girls' school in Washington, D.C., has a unique perspective on how to teach girls and boys—in part because he is also director of music for St. Alban's, the boys' school that is the brother school to the National Cathedral School. When I met with Mr. Hutto, he told me how he prepares both the boys and the girls to perform selections from Mozart's *Requiem*. He rehearses the boys and girls separately on their respective campuses, then brings them together for the final rehearsals. He told me that the girls were fascinated by his stories about Mozart's personal life: how Mozart had written letters to his friend Michael Puchberg begging for money; how Mozart was dying even as he was trying to compose the *Requiem*, which was unfinished upon his death; how his widow Constanze managed to have another composer, probably Franz Xaver Süßmayr, complete the *Requiem* under cloak of secrecy so that Constanze could collect the full commission that had been promised to her husband. "The girls can't get enough of those stories," Hutto told me. "And it really increases their interest in the music."

Not so the boys. "The moment I start telling these stories to the boys, they get fidgety," Hutto said. "They start looking at their watches. Make no mistake, these boys love music, they love to sing, but they're not interested in how sick Mozart was when he wrote the music or how his widow had to struggle to have the work completed." Hutto finds that putting music in historical context, linking the music to stories or to literature, engages the girls. "But the boys are there to sing. They don't want a history lecture."

I have heard similar stories from other teachers. Breaking down boundaries between the subject areas, linking the disciplines whenever possible, works well for many girls but not so well for many boys. However, you generally won't find such differences between adult women and men. There are big differences between the best ways to teach girls and boys, but only small differences between adult women and men. We all get to the same point, eventually, by about 30 years of age.[34] After all, Mr. Hutto himself found these stories interesting, and he's a man.

I discussed these questions with teachers at the Academy of the Sacred Heart, an all-girls school in New Orleans. They told me how, for example, when they're teaching the history of the Inca, they merge the history of the Inca with the teaching of Incan stories and literature, alongside Incan art. The girls try to create their own art in the style of the Inca. "Whoever came up with the idea of teaching history in one room, literature in a different room, and art in a third room didn't know anything about how to teach girls," one teacher said.

I think that's right. For most of recorded history, "education" has meant "the education of boys." The tradition of teaching history, literature, and art as separate subjects arose in part because that's probably the best way to teach those subjects to most teenage boys. But teenage girls will often be more interested, and will learn the subject better, if a team of teachers approaches the same topic—in this case, Incan history—from the different perspectives of the historian, the teacher of literature, and the artist, all at the same time, ideally all in the same classroom.

If girls and boys are seeing subtly different worlds—and if the best way to teach most girls is different from the best way to teach most boys—then maybe we should be educating girls and boys in separate classrooms, or at least making that option more widely available.

Certainly there is plenty of evidence that girls do better academically in an all-girls classroom. In one recent study from UCLA, investigators examined data from more than 20,000 young women across the United States. They found that girls who graduate from single-sex private schools do better academically when compared to girls with comparable demographics who graduate from comparable coed private schools on a wide variety of parameters, including time spent doing homework, discussing course material with teachers outside of class (a measure of motivation), higher SAT scores, and higher academic self-confidence, particularly in math, computer science, and engineering.[35]

An even larger study from the United Kingdom included data from about three-quarters of a million girls: 71,286 girls who attended non-selective public girls' schools, and 647,691 girls who attended nonselective public coed schools. (Girls' schools are widely available in the public sector in the United Kingdom.) These researchers used a sophisticated method called "contextual value added" to determine how much a girl would typically gain from attending one type of school compared with how much the same girl might gain from attending another type of school. They found that girls in girls' public schools "race ahead of those [girls] who learn alongside boys" in comparable coed public schools. Specifically looking at the gains made by girls between 11 and 16 years of age, they found that 11-year-old girls who subsequently attend a girls' public school achieve gains about *six times greater* than girls of the same academic ability who attend a comparable coed public school.[36]

"it's not the real world"

When I share findings like these with parents, one common response is, "Fine, maybe girls do better *academically* at a girls' school, but real life is about more than academics. The real world is coed. Women and men need to know how to work together. School should prepare kids for the real world, so school should be coed, right?"

That question is based on the assumption that the coed school resembles the real world. That assumption is false. The coed school is a peculiar world where what really counts—if you're a girl—is who's cute, who's wearing the cool clothes, and who likes whom. Johns Hopkins sociologist James Coleman was one of the first to study the question of what girls really care about at school. He interviewed girls at coed high schools and at comparable girls' high schools. He found that girls at many coed high schools were concerned first and foremost with how they looked, and with which boys liked which girls and which girls liked which boys. Girls from the same neighborhood who attended girls' high schools were more likely to be concerned about their academic achievement and less likely to be obsessed with their appearance. He wrote, "It is commonly assumed, both by educators and by laymen, that it is 'better' for boys and girls to be in school together during adolescence, if not better for their academic performance, then at least better for their social development and adjustment. But this may not be so. . . . Coeducation in some high schools may be inimical to *both* academic achievement *and* social adjustment."[37]

Coleman found that girls at coed schools were often more concerned with being pretty and wearing fashionable clothes, as well as having what he called "an enticing manner." At the coed schools, Coleman reported, "These superficial, external attributes of clothes and good looks do pervade the atmosphere to the extent that girls come to feel that this is the only basis or the *most important* basis on which to excel." But in no area "of adult life are physical beauty, an enticing manner, and nice clothes as important for performing successfully as they are [for girls at a coed] high school. . . . The adult women in which such attributes *are* most important are . . . models, movie and television actresses, and call girls. In all these activities, women serve as *objects of attention* for men and even more, objects to *attract* men's attention. . . . If the adult society wants high schools to inculcate attributes that make girls objects to attract men's attention, then these values of good looks and nice clothes are just right. If not, then the values are quite inappropriate."[38]

In fact, the greatest benefits of single-sex education for girls may have nothing to do with grades or test scores. These nonacademic benefits may include a lower risk of alcohol abuse,[39] a lower risk of teenage pregnancy,[40] and, most important of all, a focus on who you *are* rather than how you *look*.

American psychologists Jacqueline Granleese and Stephen Joseph went to Belfast, Northern Ireland, because Northern Ireland, unlike the United States, offers single-sex public schools in most cities. Parents can choose to enroll their daughters either in single-sex or in coed public schools. Granleese and Joseph interviewed girls from the same neighborhood, some of whom attended the girls' public school, others who attended the coed school. They found that the most important determinant of self-esteem for girls at the coed school was appearance. If a girl is pretty and she attends a coed school, then her self-esteem is high; if she's not pretty, her self-esteem is low. At the girls' school, by contrast, these researchers found that self-esteem was related to *behavior* more than to appearance: what you do and how you behave counts for more than how you look.[41]

By now you may have guessed that I'm a big believer in girls' schools. In fact, I helped to found the National Association for Single Sex Public Education (NASSPE, www.nasspe.org) back in 2002, when only a handful of public schools in the United States offered single-sex classrooms. At this writing, more than 500 public schools in the USA offer single-sex classrooms. Nevertheless, I don't assert that every girl should be educated in a girls-only classroom. But I do believe that every parent should have a *choice* between single-sex and coed. That's why I think it's important for more schools in the public sector to offer this option. If there's only one school in the neighborhood, then I think that school should, if possible, offer parents a choice between single-sex classes and coed classes.

I also don't believe that you should blindly choose a girls' school over a coed school. A good coed school is always a better choice than a bad girls' school. And don't assume that all girls' schools are alike. The difference between two girls' schools can be as great as the difference between a girls' school and coed school. For example, I visited two girls' schools, Laurel and Hathaway Brown, both in the same suburb of Cleveland,

Ohio. Hathaway Brown (HB) and Laurel are both selective private girls' schools, less than 3 miles apart. But the two schools are quite different. For example, girls at Laurel are required to wear uniforms whereas girls at HB are not. I asked the girls at Laurel how they felt about the requirement to wear uniforms. "I love it," one girl said. "I can wake up 20 minutes before the carpool comes, throw on my uniform, and I'm ready to go. I don't have to think about what I'm going to wear." Every girl I spoke to at Laurel expressed similar support for uniforms, even when no adult staff were within earshot.

When I asked girls at HB about uniforms, the girls were equally unanimous—and dismissive. "I could never go to a school that required uniforms," one HB girl told me. "What I wear is totally a part of who I am. I would feel like a *robot* if I had to wear a uniform." I reminded this girl that Laurel requires all girls to wear uniforms. She shrugged. "That's fine if you're a Laurel girl. Laurel girls should go to Laurel. HB girls should go to HB."

Laurel girls come from the same demographics as do HB girls. Girls at Laurel have no interest in making the case that their school is better than HB; likewise for girls at HB and for administrators at both schools (in fact, my visit was sponsored jointly by both schools). In order to choose the right school for your daughter, you need to know the school and you need to know your daughter. If your daughter is an HB girl, don't send her to Laurel.

Here are three questions that parents have found useful when visiting a prospective middle school or high school:

Do the teachers sit with the students at lunch? Schools where teachers sit with the students tend to be schools where the teachers are more involved in the lives of the students, where there is a genuine sense of community. We will explore the importance of community at greater length in Chapter 7.

Dress code and enforcement: what are the girls wearing? Is there a fashion show going on, or worse, a contest?

Interactions between girls and boys: If the school is coed, what policies and strategies are in place to ensure that girls and boys interact respectfully? If it's a girls' school, what programs are in place to ensure that girls have plenty of opportunities to interact and collaborate with boys in quiet, low-stress settings?

the best of both worlds?

Let's expand on that last point, "interactions between girls and boys." It's important for girls and boys to be comfortable interacting with each other. It's also important that the focus in the French classroom should be on learning French, not on whether or not Emily likes Justin. How to balance those two objectives?

I was impressed by one example I saw in Auckland, New Zealand. St. Cuthbert's is a girls' school that partners with a nearby boys' school. The girls study French in an all-girls classroom. The boys study French in an all-boys classroom. However, the instructors at these schools bring the girls and boys together on a regular basis. Speed-dating is one such exercise. The girls sit down on one side of a long table, with the boys on the other side. Each girl is facing a boy. The instructor says *"Alors, commencez!"* (Begin!) Each girl and each boy now has five minutes in which they can talk about whatever they want, as long as they're speaking in French. After five minutes, the instructor rings a bell. The girl moves one seat to her left, the boy moves one seat to his left. Now you've got another five minutes in which to talk with a different boy. And so on, for 30 minutes.

Afterward, the class moves outdoors, where instructors from both schools teach the girls and boys how to play *petanque*, a Provençal game similar to bocce ball. The students can play if they want to, but they don't have to. If they prefer, they can just sit on the grass and talk. I think this gets it exactly right. The kids aren't being graded on their French during the speed-dating exercise or while they play petanque. The focus of the exercise is not on French at all, but rather on creating a situation where girls and boys can interact without pressure.

Though it's important for girls and boys to learn to work together, we have to remember that we live in a sexist society. When you put girls and boys together in a classroom to learn how to add resistors in parallel or capacitors in series, sexist stereotypes often infiltrate the classroom, even with the best teachers at the best schools. I have seen an intelligent teenage girl at an elite private high school say, "I just don't understand how to add resistors in parallel . . . but Jason, you're so smart, you can explain it to me, OK?"

The real world is very different from the world of the coed middle school or the coed high school. In the real world, you are often working with people who vary widely in age. You may be working with someone 15 years older or 15 years younger. The majority of your coworkers are not available to you as potential romantic partners, either because they are already in committed long-term relationships or married, or because they're much older or younger than you are.

The coed school is an artificial hothouse in which nobody is married, everybody is in your age group, and everybody is a potential romantic partner. This situation basically hasn't existed anywhere in the world for most of human history. The idea that you can put 14-year-old girls and boys in the same classroom and expect them to focus on Spanish grammar, rather than on one another, would have seemed ridiculous to educators before the late 1800s.[42]

I'm not saying that coed schools are bad. I've visited some wonderful coed schools, both public and private. I myself attended only coed public schools growing up in Ohio, and I turned out OK, I hope. But it's important to keep in mind that coeducation for kids over 12 years of age is still a fairly new idea, historically speaking. The all-girls option may be a better choice for some girls, including your daughter.

parents unite!

What to do if an all-girls classroom is not an option where you live? Maybe there isn't a girls' private school anywhere nearby, or maybe you couldn't afford one even if there were, and the public schools don't offer single-sex classrooms?

First, here's what you should NOT do. Do NOT start by making an appointment to talk to the principal about offering single-sex classrooms at her school. One parent with a crazy idea is just an annoyance. Single-sex classrooms sound like just another crazy idea to most principals.

Here's what you should do instead:

Step One: organize a meeting of your fellow parents. The easiest way to do this is to contact the president of your school's parent-teacher organization and ask for permission to speak for a few minutes at the next meeting. Explain to parents how the all-girls format can broaden educational horizons, engaging more girls in subjects like physics and computer science.[43] Show how the girls-only classroom makes it possible to create an environment in which the focus is on who you *are* rather than on how you *look*. Conclude the meeting by asking for a show of hands, or better yet, signatures on a petition to give to the principal and the school board. You need the support of the parents of at least five other children at your school in order to move on to Step Two.

Step Two: NOW it's time to make an appointment to meet with the principal. Show her your petition, or at least make sure she understands that there are at least half-a-dozen students at her school whose parents would like a single-gender option to be available. Explain to her that offering single-gender classrooms doesn't cost anything, at least not if the school already has at least 75 kids in each grade. You can have one class of 25 girls, another class of 25 boys, and a coed class of 25 students for parents who prefer the coed option. Same number of classrooms, same number of teachers. Zero cost.

Step Three: Work with your school or your parent-teacher organization to offer an evening event for parents on this topic. Explain the benefits of single-sex education for girls, in particular how the single-sex format can shift the focus from how you *look* to who you *are*. You can also describe the benefits for boys, such as creating an alternative counterculture in which it's cool to be smart (see *Boys Adrift* for more on this point).

Step Four: Make sure your teachers get some training. Most schools in developed countries require teachers to have ongoing professional development. Try to persuade the principal to include this gender-specific training during some of the days set aside throughout the year for the required professional development. NASSPE serves as a clearinghouse for appropriate training for single-sex classrooms; ask the principal to check it out at www.nasspe.org. If you offer an all-girls classroom but your physics instructor is still beginning the year by talking about bombs exploding, football players colliding, and trucks crashing into each other, then you're not likely to accomplish much. Also, if you put the girls together in one room, and teachers don't know how to lead an all-girls classroom, you may increase the risk of Mean Girls.

mean girls

I had the privilege not long ago of sharing a podium with Rosalind Wiseman, author of the book *Queen Bees and Wannabees*. Wiseman's book was the basis for the 2004 movie *Mean Girls*. In the movie, Lindsay Lohan plays the part of Cady Heron, a girl who was literally raised in the jungle. Her character's parents are anthropologists who have been doing fieldwork in the African jungle for many years, so Cady has spent most of her life being homeschooled by her parents. She doesn't know the rules of Girl World, as Wiseman puts it. At the beginning of the movie, her parents have returned to the university campus back home, so Cady enrolls in a large public school.

The first day, one of the girls says to her, "You're really pretty."

Cady answers, "Thank you."

Wrong answer. The first rule of Girl World is, "I'm no better than you, I have the same concerns you have." The correct answer would have been, "Oh my God, my butt is getting so huge, I'm so embarrassed I think I might just start wearing sweatpants, and I'm getting this awful muffin top so I can't even wear a midriff anymore, and I think I'm getting another pimple."

When Cady says, "Thank you," the girls pounce. "Oh, so you think you're prettier than anyone else?" they say. But Cady learns quickly. Part of the fun of the movie is seeing how rapidly Cady progresses from novice to expert in the Machiavellian art of pretended friendships and the stab-in-the-back betrayals that are the worst aspect of Girl World.

Why do some girls become bullies? It's useful to turn once again to research with other primates to understand the answer. For decades, primate researchers believed that only male gorillas and male chimpanzees had social hierarchies. When you study the male of these species, it's easy to see who the alpha male is after just a few minutes' observation. The alpha may not be the largest; the alpha male is the one who's not smiling.[44] The subordinates are all smiling and chattering at the alpha male, but the alpha isn't smiling back.

When you watch a group of female gorillas and female chimpanzees, they are all smiling and chattering at each other, so it might seem the females don't have hierarchies. But they do; they're just more subtle than the male hierarchies.[45]

If you understand the subtlety with which girls establish and maintain the hierarchy, then it's not difficult to see why a girl might become a bully. Let's imagine that you're a popular girl at your school. Now a new girl comes to town—let's call her Alyssa. All the girls in your group are gushing about Alyssa and what a sweetheart she is. Alyssa is jeopardizing your status. She's the new favorite.

If you were a boy, you could pick a fight with the newcomer and slug it out in the schoolyard. If you beat him up and he cries uncle, then you've reestablished your supremacy.

But you're not a boy. If you punch Alyssa in the mouth, the other girls will think you have gone completely psycho. Instead, you call up Alyssa one Saturday morning and say, "Hi Alyssa, a bunch of us girls are going shopping at the mall this afternoon; would you like to join us?"

Alyssa says, "I'd *love* to join you, but I already told some other girls that I'd go see a movie with them this afternoon."

You say, "OK thanks, bye," and hang up. Now you call up your other friends and you say, "You know Alyssa, the girl who thinks she's Miss

Popular? I called her up and asked her to come to the mall with us this afternoon, and she said, 'Oh dear, you'll have to join the line, there's just so many of *you* and just one of *me*, I couldn't possibly go out with all the *zillions* of people who want me to do things with them, sorry but I'm just *too* busy.' So you know what? I think we should show Miss Popular that she's not so popular. How about if we give her the silent treatment? How about if none of us sit with her at lunch? How about if none of us invites her out?"

That's how it can start. If you're a girl and you feel that Alyssa is jeopardizing your position, then organizing a boycott may be a rational response to the threat you feel Alyssa poses. This is an important distinction between girl-on-girl bullying compared with boy-on-boy bullying. Some boys become bullies because they enjoy beating up smaller boys. They enjoy inflicting pain.[46] That's much less common with girls.

If any girl can become a bully when the situation is right, how do you prevent it?

I'm going to share with you a strategy I first learned from Marsha Marko, a counselor at Woodlands Academy of the Sacred Heart, a Catholic girls' school north of Chicago. I have since seen this strategy deployed in a diverse variety of schools, both public and private, in schools serving affluent suburbs as well as low-income inner-city neighborhoods. It begins on the first day of school when the teacher says, "Before we start working on our subject area, let's talk about how we're going to get along with each other during the year. Let's agree about some rules we're going to follow." The teacher doesn't lay down the rules for the class (although she has a good idea of what she wants the final rules to look like). Instead, she leads a discussion, starting with a question like, "Should we allow texting in the classroom?"

Of course some of the students will shout "Yes!"

The teacher then points out that if everybody is allowed to text in the classroom, it's going to be really distracting. If you see your friend texting somebody, but she's not texting you, you're going to wonder what she's texting about, and to whom. That makes it harder to focus on geometry, which is what the class is supposed to be about. So the teacher says, "Can we all agree that we're not going to do any texting during class?" Reluctantly the class agrees. Slowly the teacher guides the class toward a consensus. Here's what a typical list looks like, with the preamble followed by the promises:

We the undersigned hereby agree:

- That everyone has the right to attend school with a feeling of security.
- That school should be a place both for learning and for fun.
- That no one should be denied the opportunity to experience everything the school has to offer.
- That that no one should be excluded regardless of race, religion, sexual orientation, weight, style of clothes, favorite music,* etc.

We the undersigned solemnly promise that we will:

1. Treat each other with respect.
2. Treat each other as we would want others to treat us.
3. If we have a problem with another girl, we will approach that girl directly; we will NOT organize boycotts, "silent treatments," etc.
4. If we can't approach the girl, we will approach a teacher or counselor.
5. If a bullying situation arises, we will intervene and/or get help from a teacher or school administrator or counselor.
6. We will facilitate communication between students, teachers, and parents.
7. We will not pass notes in class; we will not send texts during class; we will not use cell phones, etc., during class.

---

* Many girls today are generally very tolerant with regard to issues like race and religion. But music—that's something they fight about. A girl who loves the Jonas Brothers and hates Shakira may insist on excluding another girl who loves Shakira and hates the Jonas Brothers.

By signing this contract, we, the students, understand the importance of implementing these goals in our classroom and our school, and we pledge to fulfill this contract.

The teacher prints out the contract on a poster-size piece of paper. All the students sign it and the teacher posts it on the wall of the classroom.

That's the first part of this program. In the second part, the teacher has to emphasize—not only on the first day of the class, but frequently throughout the school year—that she is available to every student to talk about *anything*, even about issues that have nothing to do with geometry or whatever the class subject is. If a girl wants to talk with the teacher about her concerns about her parents' impending divorce, that's OK. If she wants to talk with the teacher about how other girls are giving her the silent treatment, that's OK.

Not all teachers can do this. I gave a presentation on this topic to some teachers a while back. After my talk, one teacher came up to me—after waiting until everyone else had left the room—and said, "Dr. Sax, I'm not this girl's Mommy, and I don't want to be. I am not her social worker, and I have no desire to be. My job is to teach this girl algebra."

I later spoke with the school principal, who told me that this teacher is a hardworking and dedicated professional. But she won't be effective implementing this strategy. She would do better in an all-boys classroom.

The second part of this program begins when Alyssa comes to the teacher to tell her how the other girls are ignoring her, giving her the silent treatment, and the like. Alyssa will only do this if the teacher has clearly and repeatedly said that she wants to hear about personal issues. Girl-on-girl bullying can be subtle. You may not know it's happening unless you are told about it.

Cindy Rudman teaches girls in all-girls classrooms at Carman Trails Elementary School, a public school in St. Louis. She shared with me her little trick for encouraging her girls to share their secrets with her. She calls it "the tattle box." Other teachers have told me about this approach as well. You can use a little lockbox with a slit on top, like the wooden suggestion boxes you can pick up at an office supply store. Ms. Rudman explains to the girls that if there's anything they want her to know, but they don't feel comfortable coming directly to her to talk about it, they can write it on a slip of paper and put it in the tattle box. "I've never actually seen any girl put anything in the tattle box," Cindy told me. "But somehow they manage to do it when nobody's looking. At the end of the week, there's always a few notes in there." She reads every note. Sometimes a girl will use the tattle box to tell the teacher about how one girl is bullying another. Teachers who have a heart for girls will use either this method or some other method to make sure that their girls can share with them what's really happening in their lives. (Cindy recently let me know that she has also added a second box, for girls who want to give other girls secret compliments. At the end of the week the compliment box is always full, while there are only a few notes in the tattle box.)

So now Alyssa has shared with the teacher what's happening. Sometime within the next few days, the teacher has a talk with the bully, let's call her Samantha. The teacher shows Samantha the contract, which is still hanging on the wall. The teacher reminds Samantha that she signed the contract. "You promised that if you had a problem with another girl in this class, you would come to me or to another teacher rather than organizing a boycott or giving her the silent treatment. But you didn't do that. So here's what's going to happen."

The teacher then gives Samantha an assignment to do with Alyssa. At Woodlands Academy, the assignment was for the bully and the victim to do a community service project together each Saturday for the next three weeks in the city of Chicago. They then had to give a report jointly to the class about what they had learned. If you're the teacher, you have to use your judgment in choosing the assignment. If these girls are talking about slashing each other with razors, then you can't assign them to do a project outside the classroom. Instead you have to assign a classroom project, possibly under your close supervision.

The bullying evaporates.

The reason Marsha Marko's strategy works so well is that it builds on the fact that most girls don't want to be bullies. They welcome a way out that doesn't cost them status within the group. In this case, after Samantha and Alyssa do their assignment together, it's easy for Samantha to say to the other girls, "Hey, remember how we thought Alyssa is so conceited and stuck up? Well, that evil witch of a teacher made me do that after-school assignment with Alyssa, and it turns out that she's really not so conceited. She's actually been feeling pretty left out since we stopped talking to her. So . . . how about if we invite her to sit with us for lunch?"

I have seen this program work both to prevent bullying, and to eliminate it after it has started. But it works reliably only in girls' schools or girls' classrooms. If you ask a coed group of middle-school or high-school student kids to discuss what rules should govern behavior in the classroom for the coming year, it takes only one boy to disrupt the process. In a coed class of 20 or more students, there's almost always at least one boy who will argue each point, or another boy who will insist on the right to use his cell phone during class. It's rare to find a girl who will stubbornly defy the majority and the teacher with regard to a perfectly reasonable rule, but it's common for there to be at least one boy who seems to take satisfaction in gumming up the works. Another reason this strategy is less likely to work in the coed classroom is that if you put the boy bully and boy victim together, you may just be creating another opportunity for the bully to torture his victim.

do women make better teachers for girls?

Over the past nine years I have led professional development workshops for more than three hundred schools and school districts. I firmly believe that any teacher who is dedicated to the profession can be a great teacher for boys, because being an effective teacher for boys is mostly about what you *do*—how you present the material, constantly moving around the classroom, frequently interrupting yourself to call on students, and so on. Teachers can learn that stuff in a workshop.

Not so with girls. If the teacher cares about each girl as a person and truly wants to listen to what's going on in each girl's life, the girls will know it. Girls will work harder for such a teacher, even if they don't much like algebra or geometry, because they don't want to disappoint the teacher.[47] If a boy finds a subject boring and doesn't care about getting a good grade, then he's not likely to worry much about disappointing the teacher, even if the teacher is kind and caring. But for a girl, knowing that a teacher really cares about her is a powerful motivator.

You can't fake this kind of genuine caring and concern about the personal lives of girls. Even the youngest girls can tell if you're faking it.

The most successful girls' schools are well-endowed—not with money necessarily, but with teachers who care about girls. I have listened to teachers who get tears in their eyes as they tell me stories about their girls. And I have found that some of the best teachers for girls are, occasionally, men. There are some men who have a true ability to empathize and to care about a girl's problems; there are some women who don't have that ability.

There has been growing interest in gender and education in recent years. Sometimes that interest is expressed in simple-minded ways, with principals assigning women to teach girls and men to teach boys. I've seen many such programs fail. In order for girls to do their best, you need to make sure that you have a teacher who has a heart for teaching girls, regardless of whether the teacher is a woman or a man. Try to make sure the principal at your school understands that. Try to make sure the right kind of teacher is in your daughter's classroom.

body

Sport is like religion. Many follow, but few understand.

LARRY GERLACH[1]

Which is better, hopscotch or baseball? Jump rope or soccer?

Better for whom? Better for what?

Physical education for elementary-school kids in North America usually includes instruction in baseball: learning how to swing a bat to hit the ball, run the bases, and so forth. It's much less common for kids to receive formal instruction in hopscotch. We encourage kids to play competitive soccer far more often than we encourage them to play competitive jump rope. How come?

Eight-year-old boys are, on average, better than girls at tasks that require targeting a moving object in space[2]—which means that boys are likely to have an edge in games that involve swinging a bat to hit a pitched ball, or kicking a moving soccer ball into a goal. Eight-year-old girls are, on average, better than boys at tasks that require balance[3]—which means girls will have the edge in games such as hopscotch or jump rope. Our physical education programs for children usually promote sports where boys have the advantage while deemphasizing or simply ignoring sports where girls have the advantage.

When surveyed, girls typically think boys are better athletes than girls.[4] One reason is surely because our physical education programs emphasize sports such as baseball, football, and soccer, in which boys enjoy advantages, while devaluing or ignoring activities where girls enjoy the advantage, such as the balance beam, hopscotch, or jump rope.

I don't think this bias in favor of boys' sports is deliberate. In the gym, as in the classroom, we teach girls pretty much the same way we teach boys simply because there hasn't been much serious consideration that maybe what works best for boys might not always be the best way for girls. I still encounter suspicion when I suggest that girls should be taught differently, either in the classroom or on the playing field. Any such suggestion may elicit the response, "Are you suggesting that girls can't do what the boys can do?" But ignoring differences between girls and boys doesn't provide a level playing field—as we will see, it often puts girls at a disadvantage and at risk.

A second reason that so many girls believe that boys are better athletes is probably because the boys tell them so, beginning in elementary school. Many boys boast about their athletic prowess. As one team of investigators recently reported, "Girls are more realistic about their competencies while boys overestimate their physical competence, especially in the early years."[5] Most adult women, and many teenage girls, have figured out that boys often exaggerate their athletic skills. But most 8-year-old girls haven't yet discovered that boys are less trustworthy than girls regarding self-assessment of athletic ability.*

What's the point of physical education? Why should we bother? Surely a top priority should be to improve physical fitness and coordination, to teach children the joy of movement. But the movements that bring joy to a child may be different for girls compared with boys. And the best

---

* I am not suggesting that boys are less trustworthy than girls in general. But specifically with regard to self-assessment of athletic ability, the average young boy has a tendency to overestimate his ability, a tendency much less common among same-age girls.

way to engage most girls in physical activity and sport is often quite different from the best way to engage most boys. The majority of coaches for most team sports are men; in fact, the proportion of coaches who are women has actually declined significantly over the past 30 years. In 1972, 90 percent of coaches of women's teams at American colleges and universities were women. As of 2006, the proportion of coaches who are women had dropped to 42 percent.[6]

We have more girls and young women playing sports today but proportionately fewer women coaching them. That's true at every level, from beginner leagues for 7-year-olds right up through college. As Michael Sokolove writes in his book about girls in sport, "The unspoken feeling in many settings is that men know sports—they've been at it longer—so if you want your daughter's travel team to succeed and the girls to get scholarships, you'd better have a male coach."[7] Among parents who have kids playing competitive sports, more than 27 percent of fathers coach their child's sport team; less than 4 percent of the mothers are coaches.[8] That imbalance leads to a third reason why so many girls assume that sports are, fundamentally, male territory: the experts—the coaches—are overwhelmingly male. The fact that so many girls think that males are better at sports may also explain why girls attach more weight to their father's opinion about their own athletic ability than they do to their mother's opinion.[9]

Gym teachers matter. Coaches matter. The style of the coach or the P.E. teacher may have a big influence on how your daughter views sports and her own ability to play. Some coaches have a relentless focus on playing to win. That's not helpful for most kids, but it's particularly harmful for many girls. The research consistently shows that girls are more likely to be engaged in sports when coaches focus on helping kids master skills, praising good performance and offering encouragement and supportive criticism when girls make mistakes.[10] Coaches or gym teachers who make fun of the klutzy kids, or coaches who ignore kids who aren't athletically talented, will not make good coaches for most girls. We also know that coaches who play favorites can turn girls off a sport very quickly.[11] If the girls believe that the coach has favorites, then the non-favored girls may quit.

Girls should be active and as athletic as they can be, within healthy limits. As a parent, you can help your daughter choose the sports and physical activities she most enjoys and where she can fulfill her athletic potential with the greatest benefits and lowest risks.

All sports carry some degree of risk, of course. You must understand the risks and balance them against the benefit. In helping your daughter choose a sport, the first question you need to answer is:

which are the most dangerous sports?

On August 9, 2005, Ashley Marie Burns was just a few weeks away from starting ninth grade. She was one of 12 incoming freshmen girls chosen for the cheerleading team at Medford High School in Massachusetts.[12] She and three other girls were rehearsing a stunt called an arabesque double down. The three other girls were to throw Ashley in the air and then catch her. Ashley had previously executed the stunt without a problem; indeed, she was renowned as one of the best "fliers" on the squad.[13]

At 4:51 P.M. that afternoon, the girls tried the stunt. Ashley came down awkwardly, landing in the other girls' arms chest-down instead of on her back.[14] She didn't appear to be injured—nothing was broken or dislocated— but she complained of feeling short of breath. The coach told her "to stretch her hands over her head, and then sent her to the bathroom to splash cold water on her face."[15] Ashley still didn't feel right, but nobody called 911 until she passed out half an hour later. She never regained consciousness. She was pronounced dead at the hospital at 6 P.M. An autopsy revealed that she had lacerated her spleen when she fell. She died of internal bleeding.

Unfortunately Ashley's story is not unique, nor was her injury an incredibly rare accident. Girls' cheerleading is by some measures the most dangerous sport kids do today—more dangerous even than football or ice hockey if the measure of danger is the number of serious injuries per

Which sport is the most likely to cause catastrophic injury? Football? Ice hockey? No, it's cheerleading. Like most cheerleading squads at basketball games, this squad is executing a gymnastics stunt over a bare wooden floor.

Photo courtesy of Andres Valenzuela, www.andresvalenzuela.com

thousand athletes. The National Center for Catastrophic Sports Injury Research (NCCSI) publishes an annual report chronicling deaths and serious injuries sustained by high school and college athletes. Between 1983 and 2008, the NCCSI documented a total of 156 serious injuries* or deaths among high-school girls and college women. Of those, 97 occurred in cheerleading—that's more than in *all* other girls' sports *combined*.[16]

Dr. Robert Cantu, a professor of neurosurgery at Boston University School of Medicine and a coauthor of the NCCSI report, says, "What's staggering, really, is that the single most dangerous activity in sports in schools is to be a flier in cheerleading," he says. "The chance for catastrophic injury is exponentially higher than for any other sports activity."[17]

---

* A "serious injury" in this report is an injury with the potential of causing permanent disability of life-changing significance, such as a fractured cervical vertebra leading to paralysis. A sprained ankle or ruptured ACL does not count as a "serious injury" in the NCCSI report.

In my judgment, cheerleading epitomizes some of the worst aspects of sports for girls. To begin with, the focus is on how you *look* rather than on who you *are*. If you are playing volleyball, the coach isn't going to care (and shouldn't care) whether your socks match or whether your gym shorts have a smudge of dirt on them. But in cheerleading and related sports like drill team and dance team, you not only have to execute the stunt; you have to look pretty and smile while you do it.

In most jurisdictions, cheerleading is organized as an "activity" rather than a bona fide sport. That means that the safety requirements for the cheerleading squad are no different from the requirements for the chess team or the debate team. The chess team isn't required to have a certified athletic trainer in attendance; neither are the cheerleaders. The coach of the debate team isn't required to be certified in injury assessment; neither is the coach of the cheer squad. Ashley's life might have been saved if the adults in attendance had understood the risks of splenic injury after a fall and had called 911 immediately rather than waiting until Ashley lost consciousness.

Cheerleading has changed dramatically over the past three decades. Thirty years ago, cheerleaders were usually girls who jumped up and down on the sidelines, leading cheers. Nowadays the emphasis, beginning around age 10, is on high-flying stunts. Today, "cheerleading most closely resembles the sport of gymnastics, only without the mat and safety regulations," says Massachusetts state representative Peter Koutoujian, who is trying to make cheerleading safer. Kimberly Archie, executive director of the National Cheer Safety Foundation, says that the emphasis is on "death-defying, gravity-defying stunts. That's a long way from shaking pom-poms on the sidelines like I did in the '80s."[18]

If your daughter is 5 or 6 years old, you may think that this advice doesn't apply. Nobody is going to ask your daughter to do an airborne somersault anytime soon. But there are long-term consequences to the choices that young girls make about which activities and sports they will participate in. Ask any girl over 8 years of age which sports she likes the most, and the answer will almost invariably be whatever sports her friends do. If she joins the Midget Poms at age 6, she will probably want to carry on with her friends to Junior Cheer. At age 10, when she's been with the same girls for four years and the coach is beginning to teach them some airborne stunts, it may be difficult for you to suggest that she switch to a safer sport. She will say, "But all my friends are on the cheer squad!" — and she may be right. It's much easier to steer your 6-year-old daughter in a healthy direction than it is to ask your 10-year-old daughter to change her sport, and her friends.

Encourage your daughter to choose sports in which the emphasis is on what she *does* on the field of play, not on how she *looks* while she's doing it. Volleyball, field hockey, swimming, and archery are good choices by that criterion. Cheerleading, gymnastics, and figure skating are not good choices. The risks in these sports outweigh the benefits of exercise; the focus on appearance, on looking cute, is often relentless.

Don't allow your daughter to specialize too early. Specializing in a sport before the onset of puberty appears to increase the risk of physical injury and mental burnout. According to an official policy paper from the American Academy of Pediatrics (AAP), "Those who participate in a variety of sports and specialize *only after reaching the age of puberty* tend to be more consistent performers, have fewer injuries, and adhere to sports play longer than those who specialize early."[19] A second committee from the AAP, examining the same question, came to the same conclusion: "Young athletes who participate in a variety of sports have fewer injuries and play sports longer than those who specialize before puberty."[20] In his book about girls who get hurt playing sports, Michael Sokolove writes that "nearly every injured athlete I met in the course of researching this book played one sport exclusively, beginning at age ten or younger."[21]

Don't allow your daughter to compete in the same sport year-round. In the 1980s it wasn't possible to play the same sport year-round. There was soccer or field hockey in the fall, basketball in winter, and lacrosse or track or tennis in the spring. But beginning in the early 1990s, club teams and travel teams began to grow in popularity. Now it's common to find girls playing on a club team all year around. But the evidence strongly suggests that specializing in one sport, and competing in that sport year-round, greatly increases the risk of injury. Each sport uses a particular group of muscles. Overdeveloping one set of muscles, while neglecting the others, throws the body out of alignment.

There's a second reason, aside from the risk of injury, why your daughter should not compete in the same sport year-round: if she's playing the same sport winter, spring, summer, and fall, she's likely going to be with the same group of girls for a great deal of time. Being respected and liked by those particular girls may become the highest priority in her life. If she sustains a minor injury, she will be less likely to mention her injury to anyone for fear that the doctor might restrict her participation. Her enthusiasm for the sport itself may wane, but she won't consider quitting the team, because that's where her friends are. The time commitment may cause her grades to suffer, but she doesn't want to let her friends down.

It's all about balance. Sports are great, but when a particular sport becomes an obsession, it's time for you to step in. You and your daughter have to find a sensible balance between risk and benefits. As Sokolove observes, "We can't prevent every injury, but what we are currently doing is manufacturing them. If you *intended* for a girl to suffer a major injury, you would take away all her other sports before puberty, make her play her one sport all year round . . . and then you would just wait."[22]

The earlier you make your intervention, the easier it will be. Too many parents today go with the flow until it's too late. We all want to be supportive of our daughter's interests. What could be healthier than sports? Sokolove describes parents of highly motivated girls, parents who are supportive of their daughters but bewildered by the culture. "The children, as often as not, are the ones leading the way," Sokolove found. "They do not so much put pressure on themselves as they absorb it from the youth sports culture. The parents get subsumed in ways they never anticipated. 'We had no idea what we were getting into,' says one parent. 'You just feel your way as you go.'"[23]

Don't be that parent. Know what your daughter is getting into before it's too late. Don't be intimidated by the coach or by the culture. You know better than the coach what is best for your daughter. Your coach has a different agenda. He* is concerned about winning. If your daughter is injured, emotionally or physically, it's not his problem. It's not going to keep him awake at night. There are other girls who can take her place.

In the name of safety, **don't allow your daughter to focus only on sports that involve the same muscle groups**. A girl who plays soccer in the fall and runs track in the winter and spring is running all the time. Swimming would be a better winter sport for her, because swimming exercises different muscle groups, complementary to those used in running.

Many parents, especially in the United States, assume that early specialization in a particular sport will give their daughter a competitive advantage. This assumption is related to the notion we explored in Chapter 5 that "earlier is better." In sports as in academics, however, the evidence doesn't support that notion. Colleen Hacker, team psychologist for U.S. Women's Soccer, told Sokolove, "The big misconception is thinking that there is a linear connection between the development of a young athlete and the time spent being coached, attending organized practices, and playing organized games. There's no support for that. There may be belief and a hope, but not evidence." The most successful athletes, the ones who make it to the Olympics, usually have a history of playing many sports, specializing only once they reach their early teens. Diversity of experience—cross-training—makes the body stronger, better-coordinated, and less prone to injury. Hacker expresses frustration that so many parents don't understand this basic reality about the developing human body. "This message [about the importance of athletic diversity] is not getting across," she says. "We need to encourage parents, coaches, sports leagues, [and] the culture itself to go back to multiple sports participation. And there needs to be real off-seasons with unstructured play. No adults. No rules. No leagues. No registration cards. One of the best sentences a parent can utter is 'Go outside and play.' One of the worst is, 'It's 9 A.M. Get in the car, we're going to practice.'"[24]

---

* I have noted earlier in this chapter that most coaches of girls' teams are, unfortunately, men.

Not all girls care about team sports. Some girls do care passionately about team competition, about victory and defeat. For those girls, the traditional sports of soccer, basketball, and baseball/softball may be a good match. But many girls are not particularly motivated by the opportunity to bash the other team. If you have the sense that your daughter might be such a girl, **try to expose her to a wide range of activities,** including those that don't necessarily involve team competition: aerobics, yoga, martial arts, fencing, and archery, to name a few.[25] (Some of these sports, such as fencing and archery, *can* be done in a team-competitive way, but they don't have to be, and often are not.)

a girl's knee is not a boy's knee

The most popular team sports, such as soccer, baseball, and basketball, were developed mainly by men to be played by men and boys. In the past 40 years, girls have begun playing these sports in record numbers. For the most part they are playing boys' sports according to boys' rules, and they are usually coached by men. Few people have asked whether these sports should be modified to make them safe for girls. Many people bristle when this question is raised. "Are you suggesting that girls are not as tough as boys?" one parent asked me.

On the contrary, girls seem to be tougher, if the criterion of toughness is how severe an injury is needed to knock the athlete out of the game. Girls and young women appear to be more willing to play while injured compared to same-age boys.[26]

But girls are different. When researchers tested girls and boys at 8 years of age, they found that girls' quadriceps were very strong relative to their hamstrings, while boys had more of a balance between their hamstrings and quadriceps.[27] (In case you're a bit weak on the terminology: the quadriceps is the four-headed muscle that straightens your leg; the hamstrings are the muscles in the back of your thigh that bend your leg.)

Puberty exacerbates these differences. As a girl's hips widen, her "Q angle" increases. The Q angle is the angle formed by the femur (the thigh bone) in relation to the vertical. The widening of the pelvis that is a normal part of puberty in girls leads to a larger Q angle for young women. As a result, activities that involve the quadriceps—activities such as running, jumping, or kicking a ball—create a more severe torque on the anterior cruciate ligament (ACL) in girls than in boys.

Fatigue stresses the female knee differently, and more severely, compared with the male knee.[28] A girl's leg responds differently to a "run and cut" maneuver compared with a boy's executing the same maneuver.[29] As a result, girl gymnasts are more than *five* times as likely to injure their knees than boy gymnasts; girls playing basketball are more than twice as likely to rupture their ACL than boys playing basketball.[30] College women are four to six times more likely to injure their ACLs than men playing the same sport at the same level of competition.[31]

The consequences of knee injuries can be significant and long-lasting. If your daughter experiences an ACL injury, there is more than a 50–50 chance that she will develop significant arthritis in that knee within 7 to 20 years after the injury.[32] She may need a knee replacement by the time she's in her 30s.

Girls who are injured are more likely to be reinjured, compared with boys who suffer the same injury playing the same sport.[33] This is not because girls are more fragile than boys, but because the entire culture of sport has developed around what works for boys, not what works for girls. For example, consider how coaches usually warm up their players before a game. Generations of men have prepared boys before a game by having the boys run a few laps around the track, or doing some jumping jacks or simple stretching exercises. That may be fine for boys, but it's not particularly helpful for girls. For example, sports medicine specialists have discovered that a completely different warm-up routine is more effective in preventing knee injuries among girls. The girls' warm-up routine should involve, among other things, running backward while slapping your heels.[34] It doesn't cost any more money or time than the boys' routine. It doesn't require special equipment. But it's different. When girls do these girl-specific routines before practice and competition, the risk of ACL injury is reduced by 88 percent compared with girls on comparable teams doing the traditional warm-up.[35]

Ask the coaches of your daughter's team whether they are aware of this research. If they aren't, make sure they learn.

a girl's head is not a boy's head

Samantha Firstenberg is, or was, a top-ranked lacrosse player. In a high-school game in September 2007, she was sprinting with the ball toward the opposing goal. Three girls defending the goal tried to stop her. At least one girl whacked her in the head with a lacrosse stick. Samantha never lost consciousness, but she didn't feel right. She sat out of the game for a few minutes. Then she went back in.

Samantha had suffered a concussion. By the usual criteria—based on decades of research on concussions in boys and men—Samantha's concussion would be classified as mild, because she never lost consciousness. For several days, though, she was nauseated, dizzy, and had difficulty thinking clearly. Her parents took her to see a specialist at Children's Hospital in Washington, D.C.; when her symptoms persisted, Samantha and her parents traveled to consult with another specialist at the University of Pittsburgh. Even three weeks later, her symptoms were nearly as bad as they had been the day after the game. She couldn't focus for more than 10 or 15 minutes at a time. It took months for Samantha to recover fully.[36]

In April 2009 Samantha sustained a second concussion during a lacrosse match. That was the end of her high school career as a lacrosse player, but she wouldn't give up the sport. She was recruited by Colgate to play NCAA Division I lacrosse. However, in August 2009, just a few days before she was to leave for Colgate, she bumped her head against her brother's head while they were tubing on a lake. The dizziness and the foggy sensation returned. After consulting with specialists and talking things over with her coaches and her parents, Samantha decided to sit out the 2009–2010 season. "I have decided to take a step back from the lacrosse world for a least a year or two in order to allow myself to heal not only physically, but emotionally and mentally as well," she wrote in an e-mail to me. "My doctors have said that in a year or two, if I am not only ready, but dying to play lacrosse again, they would allow me to do so. Despite having had three concussions that each lasted for a while, the door still hasn't been completely shut."

Most team sports are played by the same rules for girls and for boys at the high school and college level. Lacrosse is a notable exception. Boys are required to wear helmets while playing lacrosse; girls aren't. The reason given is that boys' lacrosse is a contact sport: boys are allowed to make physical contact with other boys. Girls' lacrosse is supposedly a non-contact sport, because girls are not supposed to make intentional physical contact with other girls.

Many coaches are still opposed to girls wearing helmets for lacrosse. Joe Caruso coaches girls' lacrosse at Barlow High School in Connecticut. He doesn't think girls are strong enough to hurt other girls with their sticks. "No female is big or strong enough to cause a concussion," according to Coach Caruso. "I can see it [a concussion] from a ball. I can't imagine it happening from a stick."[37]

I asked Samantha Firstenberg whether she would like to have an opportunity to whack Coach Caruso in the head and see whether she might be able to change his mind. She politely declined, although she did suggest that Coach Caruso "needs to take a look at the way girls are training and preparing to play sports these days." Samantha herself said that she "can't even count" how many hours she has spent in the weight room, building her upper body strength. Samantha has no doubt that a high-school girl swinging a lacrosse stick with all her might could certainly give another girl a concussion.

I should add that Samantha doesn't believe that the solution is for girls to wear helmets. She's concerned that if all the girls are wearing helmets, some girls might interpret that as permission to play the game more violently than before. Instead, Samantha thinks that referees should be better-trained, and perhaps there should be more referees on the field, to ensure that the game is played according to the rules. When Samantha was struck in the head back in September 2007, no player on the other team was penalized, even though the rules of the game require issuing at least a yellow card if the blow to the head was ruled unintentional, or a red card if it was intentional.

Until just a few years ago, research on sports-related head injuries meant research on sports-related head injuries *for boys and men.* Even though girls and women have been playing competitive sports for decades, the first attempt at a thorough investigation of the risk for girls, compared to boys, wasn't published until 2007. That study, undertaken by the NCAA in association with Ohio State University and based on data from 100 high schools and 180 universities across the United States, demonstrated that girls playing high school soccer have a risk of concussion 60 percent higher than boys; girls playing high school basketball have a risk of concussion 300 percent higher than boys.[38]

Which NCAA sport has the highest concussion rate? If you said "football," you'd be wrong. The college sport that carries the highest risk of concussion is women's ice hockey. Women playing ice hockey have more than double the risk of concussion than men playing college football.[39] In every sport played by both girls and boys—basketball, soccer, ice hockey, lacrosse—girls' risk of concussion is significantly higher than the risk for boys.

One can imagine several possible explanations. However, the most plausible explanation is that *girls' heads are built differently from boys' heads.* Consider the lateral ventricles, which are basically big holes in the brain that contain nothing but cerebrospinal fluid, the watery liquid that encases and insulates the brain. These fluid-filled holes in the brain are significantly bigger in boys than in girls, even after adjusting for any differences in overall body size.[40] These empty spaces act as shock absorbers. If a boy's head collides with a soccer ball, the odds of damage are lower than if a girl's head collides with the same soccer ball.[41] That makes sense if the boy's lateral ventricles are bigger than the girl's: he has more empty space in his head to absorb the blow.

Some have suggested that maybe the reason that girls have a greater risk of concussion is merely because girls are, on average, smaller than boys. That hypothesis doesn't fit the facts. Girls are more likely to have a concussion compared with boys of the same size, and girls are more likely to suffer lasting cognitive deficits after concussion than boys are; these sex differences are not attributable to differences in overall size or body mass, according to researchers who have carefully controlled for these variables.[42]

Dr. Joseph Bleiberg is a clinical neuropsychologist with a particular interest in head injuries. He says that comparing the male and female skull and brain is "like comparing an SUV and a VW bug. The same level of impact is probably not going to cause the same level of damage."[43]

What should we, as parents, do to minimize the risk of our daughters suffering a significant head injury?

First: I think it's wise to try to steer your daughter away from the highest-risk sports such as ice hockey, figure skating, and gymnastics.

Second: If your daughter is going to play an intermediate-risk sport such as soccer or lacrosse or basketball, I think you should insist that she wear one of the new headband-style helmets. These devices look like overgrown headbands, but they act like helmets. One example is the Full 90, www.full90.com, which comes complete with an opening for your daughter's ponytail in the back. Just make sure that she doesn't regard the helmet as a license to kill.

Third: Insist that the coach and staff have appropriate training in recognizing the signs of concussion, including sex differences in the presentation of concussion. Male coaches whose experience has been mostly with boys may not be aware that girls are at higher risk for concussion. They may not be as thorough in assessing a girl for concussion after she has been knocked in the head but hasn't lost consciousness.

I discussed this issue recently with Suzanne Firstenberg, Samantha's Mom. Suzanne pointed out that she can go online and easily obtain all sorts of data about the quality of a baby's car seat. "But where can I go to get information about the man who's coaching my daughter's lacrosse team?" she asked. While many parents know which coaches have won the most games, or which high school coaches have placed the most players at NCAA Division I colleges and universities, "Nobody keeps track of which coaches are most likely to have players who get injured, or whose players are most likely to injure kids on the *opposing* team," she said. Suzanne and Samantha both told me about lacrosse matches in which high-school girls became so violent, whacking each other with sticks, that the referees had to end the game early. A lacrosse game going out of control, becoming violent, suggests both bad coaching and bad officiating. Better coaching and better officiating might prevent some of the injuries in girls' lacrosse. If the refs are well-trained and in control of the game, girls are less likely to be whacking each other in the head.

So maybe we need programs to certify coaches, and referees, in gender-specific safety issues and in gender-specific concussion awareness. Or maybe, as Suzanne Firstenberg suggests, we should have an online rating system for coaches—a system that would prominently indicate which coaches are more likely to have players injured, or whose players cause injuries. Such a system might give coaches an incentive to take injury prevention more seriously.

a girl's bones are not a boy's bones

When I was a medical student at the University of Pennsylvania back in the early 1980s, we were taught that osteoporosis—brittle bones—is something that happens mostly to older women. Today doctors recognize that although osteoporosis usually *manifests* in women over 60 years of age, it is best understood as a disease that begins in *childhood*, caused by the failure to build sufficient bone in childhood and adolescence. A girl makes most of her bone between 6 and 17 years of age. By the time she's 17, a young woman has acquired more than 90 percent of all the bone mineral she will ever have. After about age 24, it's mostly downhill.[44]

I'm not saying that women in their 40s can't do anything about their bone density, but if your bones are strong at age 20, you're in good shape. If your bone density is significantly below-average at age 20, it's going to be a real struggle to make up the difference when you're in your 40s or 50s. It's much easier for women over age 30 to *maintain* their bone density than to try to *build* bone they should have built when they were younger. So your daughter needs to exercise right, and she needs to eat right.

Researchers at Oregon State University randomly assigned children 6 to 8 years old either to jumping or stretching exercise. The jumpers were asked to jump off a two-foot box 100 times, three days a week, for seven months. The stretchers did stretching exercises for an equivalent length of time. There were no differences in bone density between the two groups of kids when they enrolled in the study, but at the end of the seven months the kids who had been assigned to the jumping exercise had significantly stronger bones than the kids who were assigned to the stretching exercise. Even more important, significant improvements in bone density, relative to the control group, were still in evidence seven *years* after the intervention ended—for girls as well as for boys.[45]

In a separate study by Canadian researchers, 10-year-old girls were randomly assigned either to high-impact exercise (lots of jumping) for ten minutes at a time, three times a week, or to participate in regular physical education for the same amount of time. After two years, the girls who had been assigned to be jumpers had stronger bones than the girls who had been assigned to regular P.E., even though there was no difference in bone density at the beginning of the study.[46]

Every able-bodied girl can do jumping exercises. It doesn't require any special athletic talent, or any special training for staff, or any expensive equipment.

So your daughter needs to exercise—and so do you. You have to practice what you preach. It's great if your school's P.E. instructor is familiar with this research, but you can do these exercises with her yourself. Don't rely on your daughter's school, or the coach of her team, to make sure she gets enough exercise. It's *your* responsibility to get her out of the house, jumping up and down in the field or the pool or at the park or wherever. The earlier you start, the better. By 8 years of age, girls who are more active have significantly stronger bones than girls who are less active.[47]

As with every other aspect of development we've considered here, balance is important. Girls who over-exercise and get too skinny put themselves at risk for stress fractures: that's especially true for girls in track, gymnastics, and cheerleading.[48] Too much of one kind of exercise, without cross-training, is not a good thing.

As for eating right, forget everything you've learned from studies of boys or men. Diet doesn't seem to matter as much in building boys' bones, compared to girls.[49] Girls, for starters, must drink plenty of milk and avoid cola beverages. Consumption of cola beverages is linked to lower bone density and fractures in girls.[50] (This appears to be true of older women as well.[51]) Drinking soft drinks is associated with brittle bones in teenage girls, but not in teenage boys.[52] Girls who drink plenty of milk have stronger bones compared with girls who are equally well-nourished but who don't drink much milk; other sources of calcium in the diet do NOT appear to be able to compensate for not drinking milk.[53] There may be more to the story than just calcium; recent research suggests that there are some as-yet-unknown factors in milk that help to build strong bones, especially in girls.[54]

Your daughter needs to drink milk. Milk from a cow. Or a goat. Soy milk doesn't count.[55] If necessary, you can let her drink flavored milk. Girls who drink flavored milk do not become fatter than girls who drink unflavored milk.[56] Girls who are lactose-intolerant need to take special measures.[57]

So give your 5-year-old daughter her very own little bottle of strawberry-flavored milk. Don't wait until puberty. In one study, investigators measured bone density in 8-year-olds, then followed the children until they were 16 years old. Girls who have brittle bones at age 8 are significantly more likely to break their bones by the age of 16, compared with girls who have strong bones at age 8.[58]

the promise and perils of exercise

The evidence suggests that girls who are involved in sports are more likely to remain active through adolescence, when other girls generally become less active.[59] Girls who are involved in vigorous physical activities, including but not limited to organized sports, also appear to be at lower risk for becoming depressed—and that protective effect holds true regardless of body mass index or even fitness. In other words, an overweight girl who exercises regularly is less likely to become depressed than an equally heavy girl who doesn't exercise.[60] And girls who exercise regularly are less likely to feel tired.[61] Exercise has all sorts of benefits that have nothing to do with how much you weigh or how you look.

But some girls exercise too vigorously or for the wrong reasons. One study of girls age 9 to 16 years found that 46 percent of girls want to look like a female celebrity, and that's part of the reason why they exercise.[62] That's not a healthy motivation. It's *other*-referenced rather than *self*-referenced. The goal should be "to help girls have realistic and healthy body images and recognize the importance of physical activity for overall health and well-being—not just for appearance-focused reasons."[63]

Many girls are on the edge of an unhealthy obsession when it comes to exercise. Some girls fall over that edge. Obsessive exercise can be hazardous to your health. Researchers at San Diego State University interviewed girls at six different California high schools and found that 18 percent of girls playing interscholastic sports reported disordered eating attitudes or behaviors.[64] Almost one in four (23.5 percent) had irregular menstrual periods; more than one in five (21.8 percent) had low bone density. In another study, young women who participate in sports where leanness is desirable—sports such as gymnastics—were almost twice as likely to have irregular menstrual periods compared to young women participating at the same level of competition in sports such as softball, where leanness is not essential (24.8 percent of girls in "lean" sports compared with 13.1 percent of girls in other sports).[65] We discussed the "athletic triad"—the association of excessive exercise with brittle bones, disordered eating, and loss of the menstrual period—back in Chapter 3.

On the one hand, you don't want your daughter to obsess about her weight. On the other hand, girls who are out of shape are at greater risk not only for overweight and obesity but also for depression and fatigue. How can you encourage the right kind of healthy exercise without pushing your daughter over the edge? In order to answer those questions, we need to understand the role that culture plays, and the role played by something psychologists call *social contrast effects.*

what do girls in chicago have in common with hopi girls in new mexico?

Carol Cronin Weisfeld and her colleagues wanted to understand how much of the difference in girls' and boys' interest in sports is due to culture, and how much might be due to other factors—perhaps psychological rather than cultural. They decided to watch girls in Chicago playing dodgeball, first girls against girls, then girls and boys together. Then they did the same thing with Native American children on a Hopi reservation in New Mexico.

When Chicago girls played against other Chicago girls, there was lots of variation in the style and quality of play. Some of the girls were really serious about the game: as soon as play began, those girls would adopt what coaches call the "athletic stance," knees bent, arms flexed, eyes focused, ready to jump for the ball. When play got under way, these girls were real competitors: they would jump for the ball, grab it, sometimes even wrestling the ball away from another girl. The girls who were most engaged were, not surprisingly, the highest-skilled girls at playing the game. Other girls were not particularly excited about the game and certainly were not jumping and grabbing for the ball; again, not surprisingly, these girls were less skilled. Weisfeld and colleagues found the same variation in engagement and skill among the Native American girls in New Mexico.

When boys were brought into the gym so that there were an equal number of girls and boys playing, the picture changed dramatically. The

New Mexico Hopi girls still participated in the game, but the high-skill girls no longer demonstrated their skill. They didn't want to fight the boys for the ball. When the boys were playing, the high-skill Hopi girls looked very much like the low-skill girls. Most of the high-skill Chicago girls didn't even hang around for the game when boys were playing. Instead, they left the playing area altogether and went off in little groups to dance with one another or to snack on potato chips. Most of these kids, girls and boys, were 12 years old. In this study, the average girl in Chicago and in New Mexico was bigger and taller than the average boy in Chicago and in New Mexico, respectively. Nevertheless, the high-skill girls seemed to lose much of their enthusiasm for the game when boys were playing.

In a peculiar twist, the investigators—who had previously rated the skill of each girl and each boy in single-sex competition—arranged a game in which high-skill girls played against low-skill boys. The girls didn't do well. They didn't try hard. Only one Chicago girl, and only one Hopi girl, seemed to be comfortable fighting the boys for the ball.

This study illustrates what psychologists call *group contrast effects*.[66] When members of two different groups are present, members of each group tend to exaggerate the differences between the two groups. Boys and girls will categorize themselves as "boys" and "girls" and will be more likely to behave according to the prevailing cultural stereotype. When girls are around, boys are less willing to exhibit any behavior that might be considered feminine; when boys are around, girls are reluctant to exhibit behaviors that might be considered boyish. I've seen this phenomenon myself while visiting coed schools and single-sex schools, for example with regard to displays of affection for the teacher. At coed elementary and middle schools, it's common to find girls giving the teacher hugs, but you won't find many boys hugging the teacher. At coed schools, hugging the teacher is something girls do. But if that school adopts the single-sex format, with boys in all-boys classrooms, all of a sudden you will find boys hugging the teacher as though it's the most natural thing in the world for a boy to do—which of course it is, as long as there aren't any girls around.[67]

Likewise in the study of Hopi girls and Chicago girls. If grabbing the ball out of somebody else's hands is something the boys do, then girls will be less likely to do that if boys are present. When the girls are by themselves, you see a wider range of individual differences, from the competitive athlete to the disengaged girl. When boys are added back into the mix, group contrast effects kick in, and most of the girls act more "girly"—less competitive, more talkative. **The coed format has the effect of homogenizing the girls**: variations among the girls fade away, and differences between the sexes are exaggerated.

And here's what I found strangest of all about the Chicago/New Mexico study: when the investigators asked the girls which format they preferred, all-girls or coed, the girls in both locations overwhelmingly said that they preferred the coed format, even though the video showed clearly that the girls were less engaged and did much less well when the boys were playing.[68]

That's important. *Asking* girls which format they prefer isn't a reliable indicator of which format is actually best for them, in terms of athletic engagement. What girls say they prefer may not always be what is best for them. Nowadays it wouldn't be cool for most girls to say, "No, I would prefer to do my physical exercise just with other girls, no boys." Such a comment might make a girl vulnerable to the charge of being a baby or, worse, a prude.

But there's good reason to believe that for most girls, particularly after the onset of puberty, the all-girls format is usually preferable for physical activity. Part of this has to do with the "swimsuit becomes you" phenomenon we considered in Chapter 1. When the boys are around, "you can feel them looking at you," one girl said.[69] Some girls might worry about how they look in the eyes of the boys; other girls are simply annoyed by the way boys rate girls' bodies, as some boys are wont to do. There is good evidence that girls from kindergarten through high school are more likely to exercise when offered a single-sex gym class rather than a coed class.[70]

Before 1980 it was common for girls and boys to take their physical education classes separately, even if all other classes were mixed. Today, most coed schools have coed P.E. classes. There are many other reasons why this may not be such a good idea beyond the changes just discussed. The best way to provide instruction in physical education may be different for girls than it is for boys. For example, one strategy that is often effective for girls is to have one girl, more experienced in the sport, teach the sport to a novice girl. The more-experienced girl is more likely to be sensitive to the needs of the less-experienced girl, and more interested in really helping her to learn the sport. Girls seem more interested in sharing their knowledge for the sake of sharing whereas the boys are generally more interested in showing off, so this strategy works less well for boys.[71]

The reasons kids play sports are often different for girls than boys. For many boys, the thrill of victory and the agony of defeat is what sports are all about. But "many girls may be more interested in developing their personal capacities through sport than they are in establishing personal superiority over others," according to a recent report from researchers at the University of Minnesota.[72] Many boys engage in sports because they want to win. The best way to get them engaged in a P.E. class is to have a real game with clearly defined winners and losers. Though some girls have that same competitive drive, for other girls a win-at-all-costs mentality may be less appealing—and may even push them away from sports. Girls are more likely to enjoy sports when the emphasis is on having fun and getting in shape rather than on beating the other team.[73]

You can begin to appreciate how a physical education program with girls and boys in the same gym class might result in zero-sum choices for the instructor. If you, the instructor, organize a winner-takes-all competition, then you may engage many of the boys but you risk disengaging many of the girls. If you structure the class along the lines of "everybody gets a trophy, everybody's a winner," then you may disengage at least some of the boys.

In Chapter 5 we saw that a lack of understanding of gender differences can exacerbate gender stereotypes. This holds true in sport as well. If you ignore gender differences in best practice, the end result is boys who think ballet is for girls, and girls who think playing to win is for guys.

Conversely, the single-sex format can broaden horizons for boys as well as for girls. Again, group contrast effects may be part of the explanation. Several years ago I was interviewing a boy at an all-boys school in Perth, in Western Australia. I asked him whether he saw any advantages to attending a boys' school. Was he doing anything at the boys' school that he wouldn't be doing at a comparable coed school?

"Ballet," he responded without hesitation. This young man was the top football player at the school.* He was tall and muscular and handsome—imagine a younger, friendlier, more Australian version of Mel Gibson and you've got the picture. "But there's no way I'd do it if the class were mixed." He explained that when it's just guys in the ballet studio, and some of those guys are his teammates on the football team, then it's OK to work on balance and poise and fourth position.

"If girls were around, you wouldn't feel as comfortable doing a deep plié?" I asked.

He shook his head. "I just wouldn't be there," he said. According to him, at coed schools, the only students who study ballet are "either girls or fags. That's it."

I have found that parents are often receptive to the idea of single-sex physical education for teenagers, provided that the same facilities and resources are available to the girls and boys. That willingness seems to arise in part because so many parents are concerned about the sexual overtones that might kick in when teenage girls and boys engage in strenuous physical activity in close proximity. Too much heavy breathing.

But many parents balk at the idea of single-sex physical education for younger kids. "I don't see the point of separating girls and boys for gym class in second grade," one parent told me. "Seven-year-olds don't have a sexual agenda at that age, do they?" she asked. Seven-year-olds hopefully do not have a sexual agenda, but they certainly do have gendered notions

---

* We're talking Australian rules football of course—a much faster-paced game than American football.

about physical activity. As I said earlier, 7-year-old boys are more likely to boast about their (imaginary) physical prowess, and 7-year-old girls may believe them, so girls may get the notion very early that the gym and the playing field are the boys' domain. An all-girls physical education program, beginning in kindergarten, might enable more girls to take ownership of the whole domain of physical activity.

We need to help our daughters take that ownership, to feel comfortable on the playing field. By the time kids reach adolescence, "boys are much more comfortable than girls in basketball courts, playing fields, streets, local parks, and other public spaces conducive to physical activity," according to researcher Dr. Kandy James. "Girls often see these places as belonging to boys, and they fear being teased, excluded, or hurt if they try to join in. Instead they sit on the periphery as passive spectators or avoid these active spaces altogether." Many of the girls surveyed by Dr. James said they would use their school basketball courts if the courts were located where boys could not watch them.[74]

Work with your school to ensure that all-girls athletic options and all-girls physical education are available. But the all-girls format won't be so great if you have a male instructor screaming at the girls. We parents need to insist that the instructors who are teaching our daughters understand and respect gender differences, in order to help each girl to fulfill her physical potential.

In her book *Perfect Girls, Starving Daughters,* Courtney Martin describes her own years-long struggle to accept her body, to move beyond her obsession with what she ate and how she looked. Her body was her enemy. She began to glimpse a resolution to her struggle one day while taking a yoga class. The instructor told her to "meet your body where it is." This was a new concept for her. *Meet your body where it is.* Be comfortable in your body. Work on your fitness, but be at home in your own body.[75]

Psychotherapist Madeline Levine writes that many communities "overvalue a very narrow range of academic and extracurricular accomplishments."[76] Many parents sign their daughters up for soccer or basketball without investigating whether those sports are really the best choice for their daughter. For some girls, yoga or aerobics might be a better way of connecting with their own bodies. Or maybe canoeing.

I recall Shannon, a teenage girl from my own practice, who discovered on her own at the age of 13 that she had a passion for canoeing and kayaking. Her father asked if she wanted to join a kayaking club so that she could compete against other teenagers. She had no interest in competing. She didn't want to beat anybody. She just enjoyed the feeling of being on the river, gliding along the water on her own power.

During the summer between tenth grade and eleventh grade, Shannon spent two weeks canoeing the Snake River in the Northwest Territories (Canada) with a group of other girls. She told me later how much she valued that experience. "We spent all day every day either canoeing or portaging our canoe. By the time it was evening and time to make camp, I was *so* hungry. You can't believe how good fresh river trout tastes after you've spent six hours canoeing and two hours portaging your canoe and your gear."

Then after a pause, she said, "It's the most spiritual thing I've ever done. Out there in the wilderness, on the river, where there's no trace of anything human—it's so easy to believe in something more. Paddling on the river became a kind of prayer for me, you know?"

I nodded, because that's what doctors do, but I wasn't sure I understood.

"The physical . . . becomes spiritual," Shannon said, and then shook her head as though she had said something wrong, or as though she were on the brink of tears.

spirit

Except for the point, the still point,
There would be no dance, and there is only the dance.

T. S. ELIOT[1]

Up to this point, we have addressed areas where I think and hope we can all be in agreement. Every girl should develop her intelligence to the best of her ability, fulfilling her academic potential. Every girl should strive to be physically fit and as athletic as she can be, within healthy limits. While we may not always agree about the best strategies to achieve these objectives, we all agree on the objectives: for every girl to fulfill her physical and intellectual potential.

But when we turn to matters of the spirit, some parents are uncomfortable. When I'm speaking to parents and I say something like, "For some girls, life is about more than just mind and body; the core of their identity is all about the *spiritual* journey," I see some parents grow visibly restless. It's easy to understand why. Ten or 20 or 30 years ago, some of these parents were themselves teenagers who rebelled against their own parents' attempts to indoctrinate them into a particular religion. Often they don't see the point of religious involvement in the 21st century.

Your daughter is not your clone. Nowhere is this more true than in matters of the spirit. I spoke with one father who takes pride in having broken free of the religious conventions to which his parents adhered.

He believes that most organized religions are sexist, patriarchal, and out-of-date. So this father was baffled when his 14-year-old daughter, Zoe, told him that she had become an evangelical Christian. He thought at first that her religious devotion must be her form of rebellion against his parental authority, just as he had rebelled against his own parents. That might be true for some girls, but in Zoe's case teen rebellion just wasn't part of the story.

Other parents say, "My daughter simply has no interest in spiritual or religious matters." Maybe she doesn't. But if your daughter is younger than 14 years of age, you don't really know yet who she is going to become on this dimension. I don't think anybody can reliably tell what the spiritual or religious proclivities of a girl will be, prior to the completion of puberty.

Age matters. Girls on average are more concerned with pleasing their parents than boys are,[2] so a young girl will often follow in her parents' footsteps, particularly in areas where Mom and Dad are in agreement. If Mom and Dad are both devoutly religious, then their 8-year-old daughter is likely to appear devout. If Mom and Dad both think religion is an antiquated relic of a bygone era, then their 8-year-old daughter is not likely to be interested in religion, except perhaps as it affects her peer relationships: "Sarah and Jessica are going to Vacation Bible School; how come I don't get to go?"

A girl's willingness to follow in her parents' footsteps may change during puberty, when girls often question the spiritual foundations of their lives. For some girls, those are the years of "spiritual awakening."[3] That's when they may struggle to figure out what they really care about.

Puberty is often disorienting for girls and for their parents. So much is changing at once. The girl who used to enjoy going to church services and Sunday school now stubbornly refuses. Or, as in Zoe's case, the girl who never wanted to go to church during the first 13 years of her life now insists on going every Sunday—and on Wednesday evenings for Bible study, and most Saturday evenings too for the youth prayer meeting.

Mix sexuality into the brew, and everybody's confused. Once Dad accepted that Zoe's religiosity was not a form of rebellion against him personally, he seized on the idea that she must have a crush on a boy—probably Luke, a 15-year-old boy in the church youth group. Luke's parents were driving Zoe to church for the Saturday evening prayer service—with Luke in the car, of course. And maybe Zoe did have a bit of a crush on Luke. She certainly blushed when I asked her about it. Maybe Zoe herself wasn't sure how much of her zeal for the Saturday evening prayer service was due to religious fervor and how much was due to Luke. It's easy for 14-year-old girls (and boys too) to confuse the sexual realm with the religious or spiritual domain.

I think it's important to support and nurture our daughters' spirituality, even if it's not easy. It's especially difficult if your daughter wants to go in a spiritual direction different from your own. It can feel like a personal rejection if, like Zoe's Dad, you have no interest in the spiritual life, and your daughter does. Don't take it personally.

Because parents do matter. Researchers have consistently found that the greatest single influence on children's spiritual development is their parents. "Contrary to popular misguided cultural stereotypes and frequent parental misperceptions," wrote the authors of a recent large survey, "the evidence clearly shows that the single most important social influence on the religious and spiritual lives of adolescents is their parents." To be sure, teens often deny outright any possibility that their uncool parents could possibly influence them in any way, and particularly in regard to religion. But the teens are mistaken. Parents are the most important determinants of their children's spiritual life—or lack thereof.[4]

If you fail to nurture your daughter's budding spirituality, it may be extinguished. And if that happens, then your daughter will be at risk for the all-too-common substitution of sexuality in place of spirituality. The spiritual and the sexual are often tightly linked, especially for teenagers and young adults. Some girls will try to find the deepest meaning of their lives in a romantic or sexual relationship. They will be disappointed, because no young man (or woman) can fill the niche in the heart that belongs only to the spirit. But those girls don't know that. In the first thrill of sexual awakening, they may plunge into sex and romance with the zeal of a new convert.

Those girls are in jeopardy of falling into the wrong kind of relationship, one in which a girl gives her boyfriend a kind of spiritual authority over her soul, surrendering her own voice to his. And some boys are all too willing to take that authority. Deborah Norris was 17 years old when she started dating Joshua Bean. It wasn't long before her Mom became concerned. "When he would call or text her, she had to answer right away or there was trouble," Ms. Norris said. "She became quiet and withdrawn around him, and that wasn't like her." After three years, Deborah tried to break off the relationship and escape from Joshua. He stabbed her to death, dismembered her body, and stuffed the pieces into garbage bags.

Deborah's horrific death was a rare tragedy. But the underlying dynamic is all too common. Stephanie Berry, who manages a community health center in Indiana and leads a program to stop abuse in teenage relationships, reports seeing similar cases frequently. They rarely end in violent death, but the destruction done to a girl's spirit is nonetheless devastating. As Berry explains, teenage girls often "see the jealousy and protectiveness as 'Oh, he loves me so much.' Girls make excuses for it and don't realize it's not about love, but it's about controlling you as a possession." Dr. William Pollack, a psychologist who directs the Center for Men and Young Men at McLean Hospital in Belmont, Massachusetts, sees it too. "Usually when adolescent boys get involved with girls, they fall into the societal model which we call 'macho,' where they need to show they are the ones in control. Actions like nonstop texting or phoning often are efforts to gain control back," said Dr. Pollack.[5]

Bereft of good guidance from parents and other adults, many girls struggle to find their spiritual voice. Disentangling spirituality and sexuality is often a major challenge for these girls. "The degree and kind of a person's sexuality reaches up to the pinnacle of the spirit," wrote the philosopher Friedrich Nietzsche.[6] For many girls, finding their spiritual voice is also about figuring out how to express and to balance their inner masculinity and femininity.

Robert Bly is a poet and philosopher. Dr. Marion Woodman is a psychoanalyst. Together they have been trying to figure out the relationship between femininity, masculinity, and spirituality. They believe that our modern culture leads young people to what they call "the ready-made masculine and the ready-made feminine,"[7] by which they mean the caricatures of masculinity and femininity presented in so many movies and magazines. Bly and Woodman believe that each girl must work out for herself what "feminine" will mean for her, what kind of woman she will be; and likewise, each boy must discover and create what "masculine" will mean for him.

Most enduring cultures of which we have any record have taken this process—the transition from childhood through adolescence to a *gendered* adulthood—very seriously. We ignore it. American parents seldom speak to their children at all about the meaning of *womanhood* or *manhood*, as opposed to generic, ungendered adulthood. Many parents today don't know what to say.

But girls still want to know, What does it mean to be a woman? Boys still want to know, What does it mean to be a man? Because parents don't tell them, the marketplace fills the vacuum, providing ready-to-wear images of "the ready-made masculine and the ready-made feminine" that are unrealistic and inauthentic—but young people don't recognize them as caricatures, because they have received no guidance.

I think Bly and Woodman have identified a major reason why a growing proportion of girls are anxious, depressed, and tired; why there are so many girls who can tell you a great deal about what they *do* but not so much about who they *are*. Part of a girl's identity as she makes the transition to womanhood is surely *what kind of a woman she will be*, how she will express her feminine side—and her masculine side.

All of us, as human beings, have both feminine and masculine dimensions. Fifty years ago, the conventional wisdom was that masculine and feminine are opposites; and in popular culture, that notion is still prevalent.[8] According to that notion, the more feminine you are, the less masculine you are. It's a one-dimensional either/or:

Feminine ◄──────────► MASCULINE

Today we have a more informed understanding of the importance of gender in the way we construct ourselves. For three decades now, scholars in the field of gender studies have recognized that masculine and feminine are two independent dimensions.[9] Any individual may be very feminine; or very masculine; or both feminine and masculine, *androgynous;* or neither feminine nor masculine, *undifferentiated.* It's a two-dimensional both/and. Masculine and feminine are not exclusive.

Feminine	*Androgynous*
Undifferentiated	**MASCULINE**

At the end of my first book, *Why Gender Matters,* I included two questionnaires: "How Masculine Are You?" and "How Feminine Are You?" Both questionnaires were based on extensive research by scholars in the field. The purpose of those questionnaires was to help readers understand that femininity and masculinity are independent of one another, and different from the biological female and male. A particular girl might be more masculine than she is feminine, while a particular boy might be more feminine than he is masculine. I wanted to make it clear that differences do not imply an order of rank. A feminine girl isn't better or worse than a masculine girl (a "tomboy"). They're just different. We should celebrate those differences; they expand the range of human experience, making all of us more three-dimensional, more real. In my own marriage, my wife fixes the lawn tractor and does most of the outdoor chores, while

I shop for groceries. I like to shop for groceries, and she doesn't. She enjoys taking the time to fix the tractor; I don't. It's all about being who you are.

I must not have done a very good job of explaining this point, because many readers still didn't understand. I received an e-mail from a woman who said that my questionnaires must be wrong because she scored higher on the "How Masculine Are You?" questionnaire than she did on the "How Feminine Are You?" questionnaire. In our ensuing e-mail correspondence, it became clear that the results of the questionnaires were accurate: this woman happens to be quite masculine, and not feminine at all. That's just who she is.

"You should become who you are," is good advice for any teenager.[10] We should help our daughters to understand who they are and who they want to become regardless of the pressures from the society and the popular culture to conform to a particular "ready-made" caricature of the feminine.

Bly and Woodman believe that we have neglected the importance of each individual discovering for herself the right balance of masculine and feminine. The right balance for Emily, who loves reading *Seventeen* and *CosmoGirl*, will not be the right balance for Melissa, whose favorite pastime is wrestling hogs at her uncle's farm—and still different from Sonia, who enjoys both working with farm animals and reading the women's magazines; or from Nancy, who doesn't enjoy either farm work or reading women's magazines but would rather do crossword puzzles.

Figuring out how to express your inner masculine in the right balance with your inner feminine is an essential part of the transition to full adulthood, Bly and Woodman believe. And the way you balance the masculine and feminine within you comes very close to the core of who you are. It's a spiritual journey. "In our essence, the opposites are not in opposition," write Bly and Woodman[11]—because masculine and feminine are not opposites at all, they are simply different, complementary, nonexclusive ways of being human. I can imagine a woman who might enjoy both fixing lawn tractors and shopping for groceries, but that woman is not my wife. My wife hates grocery shopping; she always has and probably always will. Bly and Woodman believe that one aspect of a fully-developed sense of self has to do with how you work out within yourself the balance of your inner masculine and your inner feminine.

Some girls are spiritual by nature. They yearn for spiritual fulfillment, but they find no satisfaction for that yearning in 21st-century popular culture. When they try to find that fulfillment in sex or in romance, say Bly and Woodman, "the result is that the American adolescent tries to receive from sexuality the marvelous ecstasy. . . . But the ecstasy doesn't come. What arrives is disappointment. The adolescent feels horrific despair when the sexual chakra does not deliver the ecstasy that he or she believes will come. Sex is brief and flat. No one can overestimate how huge this Disappointment is."[12] Bly and Woodman observe that some girls then try "to fill the emptiness with alcohol, sexual conquests, clothes, designer drugs, rudeness, flights from home, breakings of the law, self-pity, spiky hair, pregnancy, [or] agreeing to be no one."[13]

Bly and Woodman are, respectively, an older man and an older woman. But their observation is echoed by Courtney Martin, who is herself a young woman chronicling her own struggles and those of her friends. Like Bly and Woodman, Martin has found that much of the obsessive activity of young women today results from an unsatisfied appetite for the spiritual:

Some of us, for lack of a "capital G" God, have searched out little gods. We worship technology, celebrities, basketball players, rock stars, supermodels, video games. . . . These empty substitute rituals, this misguided worship, intellectualization, addiction to moving fast has led my generation to a dark and lonely place. In the inevitable stillness that frightens the hell out of a perfect girl, she must ask herself not *What is the size of my stomach?* but *What is the quality of my soul? What do I believe in? What is my purpose? Is there a black hole where my core should be?*[14]

Two centuries ago, Western culture tried to sublimate the sexual urge into religious practice. The result was a lot of sexually repressed teenagers and young adults. Today, our culture pushes girls to divert their spiritual impulse into a romantic or sexual channel. The result is a growing proportion of young women who are disillusioned with sex. After a few years of hooking up, they wonder: "Is that all there is?"[15]

The sexual is good. The spiritual is good. But they are not the same thing.

the great disappointment

Bly and Woodman describe the spiritual condition of the child before the onset of puberty as characterized by the feeling that "something marvelous is going to happen." Then sometime after the onset of puberty, navigating through adolescence, the teenager "is hit with the awareness that something marvelous is *not* going to happen. That's the moment of The Great Disappointment."[16] In our culture, that moment is often postponed until young adulthood, when the 20-something finally realizes that she isn't ever going to compete in the Olympics or be the next American Idol or a movie star.

Adolescence should be the time when kids learn about their own limits. In a world that contains more than six billion people, 99.999 percent of us are going to have to get used to the idea that we are not anybody special. Becoming a mature adult means reconciling yourself to the fact that you're not going to be a movie star, you're not going to be on the cover of *People* magazine, you're not going to be famous.

Our culture today does a terrible job of preparing kids for this moment and helping them to make the transition to full adulthood. One reason our culture is so lacking in this regard is that we don't understand one key element in the transition to adulthood: kids don't want to be ungendered generic "adults"; rather, girls want to become *women* just as boys want to become *men*.[17] But instead of providing girls with a richer and multidimensional understanding of the feminine and masculine within them, we parents today mostly ignore the topic. We pretend that gender doesn't matter. The consequences of our neglect can be severe.

When boys encounter The Great Disappointment, many of them find solace in the world of video games. If you're a boy or a young man and you invest 20 hours or more each week playing *Call of Duty,* you can indeed become master of that universe. And for many boys, that is satisfaction enough. In *Boys Adrift,* I described how these boys can easily become addicted to video games. The games fill the spiritual void. When *Call of Duty: Modern Warfare 2* launched in November 2009, buyers (overwhelmingly male) purchased more than half-a-*billion* dollars of product in its first five days. The *Call of Duty* series of video games has now sold a total of more than $3 billion worth of video games in the six years it has been on the market. "To put that in perspective," as reporter Tom Slater dryly noted, "James Bond has been a franchise for 47 years and [has] grossed just over $5 billion" in total sales over those five decades.[18] As I wrote in *Boys Adrift,* there are a growing number of boys and young men who are finding their spiritual fulfillment, their ultimate meaning of life, playing video games.

Girls are less likely than their brothers to find satisfaction for their spiritual hunger in the fantasy world of first-person-shooter video games. Girls are more likely to plunge into a real-world obsession—which might be an obsession with athletics, thinness, alcohol, cutting, and/or social networking, devoting dozens of hours a week to their instant messaging or their texting or their social networking page. But none of these obsessions will satisfy. It's like drinking water when you're hungry for food.

buckle your seatbelt, don't smoke cigarettes, and go to church

Girls who are actively engaged in the religious and/or spiritual life are healthier than girls who aren't. That's the conclusion of a years-long survey of more than 3,000 American teenagers, from every region of the country, and representing every religious tradition. The researchers found that teens who are actively engaged and committed to their religious community "are much less likely to smoke cigarettes regularly, drink alcohol weekly or more often, and get drunk. . . . [They] are also more likely to not drink alcohol and not smoke marijuana."[19] The size of the protective effect is startling. For example, only 1 percent of religiously devoted teens smoke marijuana regularly or occasionally, compared with 21 percent of disengaged teens. These differences remain statistically significant even after controlling for teens' age, race, region of residence, parental marital status, parental education, and family income.[20]

The differences in attitude toward sex were particularly dramatic. Only 3 percent of religiously devoted teens think it's OK to have sex "when you're ready for it emotionally," compared with 56 percent of disengaged teens. In other words, disengaged teens were almost 20 times more likely to say that you can have sex whenever you feel ready for it—and in a culture that prizes risk-taking, the pressure is on to say that you're ready even when you may not be.[21]

Religious involvement seems to work as an antidote or as protection against preoccupation with physical appearance and unrealistic standards of thinness. In the survey, 54 percent of religiously engaged teens say they are "very happy" about their own body and physical appearance, compared with 29 percent of disengaged teens; only 1 percent of teens who are involved in religion are very unhappy about their body or physical appearance, compared with 7 percent of disengaged teens.[22] Somewhat surprisingly, nonreligious teens are more likely than religious teens to say that they "feel guilty about things in life fairly often or very often."[23]

Whereas our 21st-century culture often pushes girls to *act* sexual before they *feel* sexual, a religious community can provide an alternative perspective. The survey researchers spoke with Catholic girls at a religious retreat who "seemed exhilarated by the idea that they might actually take charge of their romantic relationships and may not have to barter their bodies simply to get boys' attention."[24] The fact that religious communities almost always bridge the generations, bringing young people together with adults of different ages in many kinds of sharing and social interchange, may be part of the reason why participation in such communities can empower girls to define themselves spiritually rather than sexually. As the researchers point out, "American religion is one of the few major American social institutions that is not rigidly age-stratified and emphasizes personal interactions over time, thus providing youth with personal access to other adult members in their religious communities."[25]

Girls who are fully engaged in the spiritual life are less likely to be depressed than girls with the same demographics who are disengaged from spirituality. The antidepressant effect of being involved in the spiritual or religious life gets bigger, but *only for girls,* after the onset of puberty. In one major study, researchers interviewed 3,356 adolescent girls to understand their degree of religious involvement, and the extent to which they were experiencing depression or depressive symptoms. They found that religious involvement protects girls against depression, but the degree of protection appears to be a function of physical maturity (rather than age per se). Girls who have not yet experienced the onset of puberty, or who have just begun the process of puberty, are about 20 percent less likely to be depressed if they are religiously involved. But for girls who are farther along in the process of puberty, or who have completed puberty, the benefit roughly doubles; among the more physically mature girls, those involved in religion are 40 percent less likely than nonreligious girls to become depressed.[26]

Sociologists have recognized since the 1990s that religious or spiritual involvement has benefits for girls and women that it doesn't have for boys and men—particularly with regard to preventing depression.[27] For example, Shirley Feldman and her colleagues interviewed girls and boys between 13 and 18 years of age about how they cope with stress. Then the researchers came back six years later and interviewed the same people, who were now young women and men. They found that girls who prayed regularly, or who talked to a pastor or other clergy about their problems, were more likely to be doing well and coping better than nonreligious girls. But the reverse was true for boys; boys who "turned to religion" to help deal with stress were actually doing worse than other boys.[28]

In a more recent study, Columbia University researchers Alethea Desrosiers and Lisa Miller suggest that "spirituality experienced in a personal way through a relationship to God may be uniquely protective against depression in girls and women."[29] They interviewed 615 adolescents: girls and boys; Christian and Jewish and Muslim and Buddhist; Asian and black and Hispanic and white. They found that measures of "relational spirituality"—that is, daily prayer to a God who answers back, and/or turning to clergy for help with problems—were associated with a significant protective effect against depression in girls from every demographic group, but this protection was seen only in girls, regardless of race or religion. These researchers believe that the growing "epidemic" (their word) of depression among girls and young women may be due in part to "broad cultural lack of support or validation of relational spirituality during individuation in girls." That's a fancy way of saying that our culture no longer encourages girls to pray every day; and one result, according to these researchers, is that a lot more girls are depressed.

Girls who are especially inclined toward spirituality, but who find no healthy expression for their spirituality, may be particularly at risk. "A psychological propensity may be either cultivated into a source of resilience, or if left uncultivated, pose risk for pathology," these researchers suggest. A girl who is by nature spiritual might harness that spirituality "through prayer to deepen spiritual connection, but if left 'willy-nilly' might account for the previously established increased depressogenic sensitivity to life events."[30] In other words, a spiritually inclined girl who doesn't find a suitable outlet for her spirituality might actually be *more* likely than average to become depressed; whereas if that same girl becomes integrated into a religious community and practices daily devotions, then she will be *less* likely than average to become depressed.

Some people don't want to hear this. I have heard from nonreligious people who say, "So you're telling me I should indoctrinate my daughter into some religion I don't believe in, just because teaching her the religious mumbo-jumbo MIGHT decrease her risk of drug use and depression?"

Religious people are sometimes equally annoyed by any mention of the mental-health benefits of religion. As one pastor said to me, "Religion should not be promoted as a form of public health. Faith is not like a flu shot you can get at the mall. I want people to believe that Jesus Christ is their Lord and Savior because it's the truth, not because it will make them happy or keep them off Prozac."

To the devout pastor I say, "OK, but it's important that you understand the gender differences in what works for tweens and teenagers. Otherwise you may have boys who think that your church is for girls, and girls who are left cold by your services and your youth programs."

To the free-thinking parent I say, "If you want to try to raise your daughter to follow your beliefs, that's your right as a parent. But don't deny *spirituality* just because you can't believe in any *religion*. Commune with Nature if you like. Or meditate in the dark with a candle.* But you have to help your daughter to see that there is more to life than school and sports and her circle of friends. You have to help her to develop all aspects of herself—and that has to include her spirit, not just her mind and her body."

In Chapter 4, while discussing puberty in girls, I mentioned Lyra Belacqua, the heroine of the children's fantasy books *The Golden Compass, The Subtle Knife,* and *The Amber Spyglass.* One of the wacky ideas that give these books their unique flavor is that in Lyra's world, everyone's soul is visible in the form of some animal who always stays near the person to whom the soul belongs. In the first book, depending on Lyra's mood, her soul Pantalaimon is variously a mouse, a hare, a fox, or a badger. In the course of puberty, each child's soul becomes fixed as one particular animal. There is no more shape-changing once puberty is under way.

The dramatic tension in these scary fantasy books is provided by evil grown-ups who seek to excise the soul from children prior to the onset of puberty. The most haunting images are the children whose souls have

---

* A useful "how-to" guide for parents interested in nonreligious meditation is provided by Dr. Herbert Benson's classic, *The Relaxation Response* (New York: Harper Books, 1976).

been excised. Their minds are intact, their bodies are intact, they don't look any different, but they are missing that special thing that animates them. They are dull and listless.

I see such kids every day.

the dark night of the soul

Why is the spiritual journey so important? Because life doesn't go as planned. Because death and loss happen. Because disappointment hurts. Even if a girl has a brilliant mind and has earned top marks in every subject, and she is in great physical shape, those achievements of mind and body will count for nothing when the crisis hits. She will then discover that she has been living on the edge of the abyss. It may not take much to push her over that edge. Achievements in academics and athletics won't get you through the dark night of the soul. If her life is just mind and body, then she may feel her life falling apart. She may experience an awful disorientation as she wonders whether anything is worthwhile, whether life is worth living. Maybe it's not. All her dreams are dust.

But if she has nurtured her spirit, nurtured it because you have taught her to cherish it, then she can endure through that dark night. It still won't be easy, but it won't poison her as it might if her spirit were weak.

Rabbi Sandy Eisenberg Sasso explains why parents—even parents without a strong sense of spirituality themselves—should make this effort. "We want our children to be more than consumers and competitors. We want something much more," she says. "We want them to have courage in difficult times. We want them to have a sense of joy and purpose. That's what it means to nurture their spiritual life."[31]

OK, but how do you do that, exactly?

One place to start, Rabbi Sasso suggests, is with prayer. Maybe you don't believe in a God who answers prayers. Maybe the very idea seems a little juvenile to you; perhaps it conjures an image of an overworked bureaucrat trying to answer too many e-mails. Try it anyhow. As Sasso observes, "Our children are so bombarded with noise and activity, there is very little time for silence and reflection." A quiet time for prayer is a good antidote to all the noise. That quiet moment may allow you and your daughter to discover what T. S. Eliot called "the still point":

> *At the still point of the turning world . . .*
> *At the still point, there the dance is . . .*
> *By a grace of sense, a white light still and moving.*[32]

Remember that the purpose of this exercise is not about you. It's about your daughter. If nothing else, you may find that your daughter is able to say things to God, out loud with you listening, that she would never say directly to you.

Here's what you do. You sit down with your daughter, perhaps in the evening, or perhaps during a rainy indoor afternoon. You take her hands in yours, and you are silent with her for a moment. Then you pray. You first, then her. You pray out loud.

How are you supposed to do that, if you aren't a religious person? Rabbi Sasso makes these suggestions for a do-it-yourself prayer—and remember to say it out loud, so your daughter can hear.

1. Name some of the things you are grateful for.
2. Then name some of the things you hope for.
3. Then ask for protection from some of the things you fear.
4. Then say Amen.
5. Then tell her it's her turn.

You may be surprised at what happens. As Sasso says, "If you can take the hand of your child on that journey, you not only enrich his or her life, your enrich your own. [Children] open part of our lives that maybe has been dormant for a long time." Once that door is opened, there's no telling where it may lead. If nothing else, you are creating new channels for communication with your daughter.*

---

* Rabbi Sasso has written a series of picture books, intended to be read out loud to children, specifically to facilitate this conversation. Two of my favorites are *In God's Name* and *But God Remembered: Stories of Women from Creation to the Promised Land.*

"i believe there is a god and stuff"[33]

You may start with a prayer, but you have to do more. Ideally you want to help your daughter to figure out what she believes about spirituality; that's part of what it means to honor and cherish the spirit. The survey researchers found that most American teens, even religiously involved teens, are remarkably inarticulate on this point. "For many of the teens we interviewed, *our interview was the first time that any adult had ever asked them what they believed and how it mattered in their life.* Very many seemed caught off-balance by our simple questions, uncertain about what we were asking, at a loss to know how to respond."[34]

Here's a verbatim transcript of one of their interviews:

INTERVIEWER: Where do you get your ideas about God?
TEEN: The Bible, my Mom, church. Experience.
I: What kind of experience?
T: He's just done a lot of good in my life, so.
I: Like, what are examples of that?
T: I don't know.
I: Well, I'd love to hear. What good has God done in your life?
T: I, well, I have a house, parents, I have the Internet, I have a phone, I have cable.[35]

This could almost be an interview with one of the zombie-like victims in Pullman's dark fantasy. This is what a child disconnected from her own spirit sounds like.

In Chapter 2 we discussed why your daughter should not have a computer in her bedroom. Now we need to consider whether she should have her own TV. Roughly two-thirds (65 percent) of American kids between 8 and 18 years of age have their own TV in their bedroom.[36] That's a mistake. It's a mistake even if your daughter watches nothing but Nickelodeon and the Disney Channel. Bedtime should be quiet time. No cell phones, no texting, no instant messaging, and no TV. It should be a time for a girl to think about life and death and darkness and time. You can't do that if you're watching reruns of *iCarly*. As T. S. Eliot wrote, the spirit cannot grow and be healthy if "there is not enough silence." [37]

If you want your daughter to develop a strong and healthy spirit, you should do the same as you do to help her develop a strong and healthy body: you should help her to exercise it. Ask her questions. Does she believe in God? How come? If yes, is God male or female? Or both? Or neither? What makes her think so?

Many adults today are uncomfortable discussing such questions with their children. Try to overcome your reluctance. We adults don't hesitate to teach our kids about school or sports.[38] If you know something about the life of the spirit—even if it's just something about deep breathing that you learned in yoga class—share it. If you don't know anything about the spiritual life, then find someone who does to teach your daughter. And go to the classes with her.

You don't learn physics by watching the instructor do physics problems. You have to work out the problems yourself, perhaps with some help from the instructor. You don't learn soccer by watching the coach play. You can't learn religion or spirituality by watching the pastor pray or the monk meditate. In matters of the spirit, as with the mind or the body, we learn by doing.

I have had the privilege of meeting with girls and young women who are walking that journey with love and guidance from their parents, and who have already gone quite a ways. I have found that one of the hallmarks of a truly original spirit is a willingness to do the unexpected not just to be different, but because the different path is the right path for you. Madeline Baay fits the bill.

On October 24, 1998, Tropical Storm Mitch became Hurricane Mitch as it gathered strength over the Caribbean Sea. On October 26, Hurricane Mitch reached its peak strength, with maximum sustained winds of 180 miles per hour. Mitch was moving slowly when it made landfall on the Honduran coast on October 29. Between October 29 and November 3, the hurricane caused torrential rains and flooding throughout Honduras and Nicaragua. The hillsides could not absorb so much rainfall—more than 50 inches in three days. "Mudslide" is an understatement for what happened next. In some cases, the hills themselves slid down and buried villages within minutes; at least four villages vanished that way. More than 10,000 people died.

Chinandega, a Nicaraguan city near the border with Honduras, was severely damaged by the hurricane. Hundreds of thousands of people were displaced, their homes flooded. Many of those people had nowhere to go. "The government relocated the homeless families to a garbage dump and promised that help was coming. It never did," recalls Sue LaFave, an administrator for a nonprofit organization active in Nicaragua.[39]

Madeline Baay was 15 years old when she first traveled to Chinandega with other teenagers for a 10-day mission trip, in the summer between ninth and tenth grade. That trip "really transformed her," her mother, Gigi Baay, told me. "She didn't want to shop for expensive clothes anymore. Instead of going to the malls or the outlet stores, we started going to the thrift shop." (When I asked Madeline about this, she mentioned that she *does* shop at stores like Old Navy and Target, but she does also shop at the Goodwill store.)

Madeline returned to Chinandega after tenth grade and after eleventh grade as well. As a senior in high school, while the other kids were deciding which college they would attend, she was making arrangements to spend a year as a full-time volunteer with Sue LaFave's nonprofit group helping to build homes and provide basic services to the displaced residents of Chinandega. The nonprofit normally doesn't allow people under 21 years of age to serve, but the administrators made an exception for Madeline.

Madeline spent her first year after high school working in Chinandega. She ate beans and rice and plantains with the local villagers. She lived in the mission house, where she shared a room with at least three and sometimes as many as six other women. And she worked: helping to build homes and schools, teaching and playing with the children, directing the efforts of other volunteers who would come down to spend a week or two.

After she finished her year in Chinandega, she chose to attend Warren Wilson College, which specializes in preparing young people for international service work. But Madeline insists that she's not trying to be Mother Teresa. She reads *Rolling Stone*. She likes the *Star Wars* movies.

She enjoyed reading *The Time Traveler's Wife*. When I spoke with her, she sounded to me at first like any other middle-class American girl. Except that she's not anxious. She's not concerned about her clothes or her weight or her grade-point average or her job prospects. She's comfortable in her own skin.

I find it remarkable that a girl raised in a middle-class American family, participating in 21st-century American culture, could still find it within herself to serve others in the way that Madeline has done. Certainly her parents deserve a great deal of credit. Her school and her church also played a role. You've already heard about her school: it's the Academy of the Sacred Heart, the all-girls school in New Orleans I mentioned in Chapter 5. When I visited that school, I found that the school leaders put great emphasis on the idea that school should be about more than grades and test scores and athletics, more than just mind and body; this school explicitly teaches girls how and why they must be mindful of their spiritual development, which the school leaders believe includes a sense of one's place in the world, an understanding of how one can be of service to others.

Another school that does this wonderfully well, but very differently, is Lauriston, a girls' school in a suburb of Melbourne, Australia. For Year 9 (i.e., ninth grade), Lauriston girls don't go to the main Lauriston campus. Every girl in Year 9 spends the academic year at the school's satellite facility, a three-hour drive north then east, deep into the forested hills between Mansfield and Mount Butler. There you will find a collection of cabins set back in the woods.

There's no cell phone service. There's no ready access to any kind of shopping, even for snacks. You eat what the school provides in the cafeteria. If you want candy or chocolate or an espresso, you're out of luck. The girls live in simple wooden cabins with no Internet access. More than a few Lauriston girls dread Year 9, and some of them freak out when they arrive. "My first thought was, How am I going to survive without being able to text my friends on my mobile?" one girl told me when I visited the compound. "And I had no idea what I would do on the weekends. I was so used to going to Chapel Street to shop almost every Saturday. I couldn't imagine what I would do stuck in the middle of nowhere, which is what it seemed like to me."

Slowly, and with some guidance from the staff, the girls start to discover the rhythms of a simpler life. That involves hard work. Manual labor. The cabins are heated by wood stoves; the girls must carry the wood and prepare the fire. Within a few weeks, the hysterics have subsided and the girls are starting to appreciate the experience.

Every girl must do a solitary overnight campout. They are provided with the necessary training over the first few months. The area where the campout takes place is secured and patrolled by adults from the school, so the girl's safety is never in doubt, and she knows this. For many of these girls, however, such an experience is completely unprecedented: alone, outdoors, responsible for making your own campfire, cooking your own meal, pitching your own tent, no electricity, no adults to help (except in case of emergency).

"I was really dreading it," one girl told me. "But when the time finally came, I really enjoyed it. I loved the quiet. It felt *sacred*—more sacred than being in church."

Another girl told me how she started getting up early with her friend to go for a morning run and watch the sun come up over the mountain:

I was one of those girls who really complained about having to do this whole year out in the bush.* And the first few weeks I really hated it. I missed my mobile and shopping and the Internet. I really considered those things to be necessities, and I couldn't imagine not having them. But after about two months, I didn't miss them so much. And then one day, while I was sitting and watching the sunrise, it suddenly occurred to me: the mobile and the shopping and the Internet—those things are not necessary for happiness, they actually get in the way of being happy. It was an epiphany.

---

* "The bush" is Australian for "the forest"—not to be confused with "the outback," which is the term used by Australians for the desert areas of their country.

The girls at Lauriston, like Madeline Baay and the other girls at Madeline's school, come mostly from either middle-class or affluent families. They have all sorts of material advantages.

Not all girls are so lucky.

Not long ago, I visited the PACE Center in Orlando, Florida. The PACE Centers for Girls comprise 17 centers across the state of Florida, serving girls at risk (www.pacecenter.org). Each center includes an all-girls public school, but each center is more than a school. "We're not [just] a school," Jill Gentry, director of the PACE Center in Orlando, told me. "We are a comprehensive center for girls." Roughly half of PACE's services don't fall within the traditional school model. Every girl has a counselor who meets with her frequently, one on one; there's also an extensive network of social workers and other social service providers at each center. Most of the girls are from low-income households; some of the girls are in foster placement.

The motto of the PACE Center in Orlando is: "Honor the female spirit." I asked Jill Gentry what that means.

"The female spirit might mean something different for each girl here," she told me. "But there's one thing we're sure of: 'Honoring the female spirit' means not letting someone else define you: not the media, not a boy, not even the other girls."

She told me about a recent graduate from the school, a girl named Carmen. Carmen has only vague memories of her mother, a drug addict who died when Carmen was young. Carmen was placed in foster care. By age 11 she was using drugs herself. By age 13 she was in state-sponsored drug rehab. From rehab she went to living in a residential group facility for teens. That's when she came to the PACE Center in Orlando.

At the center, for the first time in her life, Carmen was welcomed into a community of women who were looking out for her. "If you're one of our girls, we're going to watch over you," Ms. Gentry told me. "If there's a man waiting for you in the parking lot, we're going to ask you: who's that man? What are you doing with him? What does he expect you to do for him? If a girl comes to school with a bruise on her face, we are going to find out how she got that bruise."

To me it sounded intrusive, but Carmen, and many of the girls, seem to thrive on it. Carmen started arriving at school early, earlier than most of the staff. She would pack her breakfast in a bag and eat it at school. "She felt safe here," Gentry told me.

In her second year at the PACE Center, Carmen told the staff that she wanted to have a funeral service for her mother at the cemetery where her mother is buried. The staff helped her plan the service, and six of them attended. Afterward, Carmen acted as though a weight had been lifted off her chest. She set to work on her academics with renewed energy, she graduated on time, and she is now attending the local community college.

The PACE Centers are strict by contemporary standards. Girls must surrender their purses and cell phones each day when they arrive at school. Some girls try to conceal their cell phones. Gentry told me the story of one girl who hid her phone in a place people used to refer to as *décolletage*. But then her phone rang. The girl looked around as if to say "Anybody hear something? I don't hear anything. Did you hear anything?" The teacher walked over to her, said, "Excuse me, your chest is ringing," and held out her hand for the phone. The girl meekly reached in, pulled out the phone and handed it over.

The teachers eat their lunch with the students. That's unusual in schools that serve kids from low-income neighborhoods, but it's vital. When women of all different ages eat lunch with teenage girls, there's a community being formed.

Gentry told me about another girl, Alejandra, who was "almost invisible" when she came to the school. Alejandra was cutting herself. She seldom made eye contact—not with teachers, not with the other girls. And she never spoke. After a few weeks at the school, she started to make connections, both with the other students and with the teachers and the counseling staff. After a few months, the cutting stopped.

After two years at the school, Alejandra was a shining star: she was doing well academically and had developed a nourishing circle of friends. She spoke to more than 300 adults at a fundraiser for the school—and she spoke from the heart. The fundraiser was a big success. "Once a girl at this school finds her voice, she will not lose it," Gentry told me.

The stories of these girls are very different, just as the girls themselves are different, but they have one important element in common: each girl was part of a close-knit community of girls and women.

a community of girls and women

Community matters. The kind of community in which your daughter engages will shape the person she becomes. In Chapter 2, I described how a girl growing up 40 or 50 years ago was likely to be involved in communities that involved adult women, whether at church, or in her extended family, or just sitting on her neighbor's front porch. Today, a girl's community is more likely to consist primarily of other girls her own age.[40]

That means girls talking mostly with other girls. But Girl Talk can be toxic to girls, even when they don't mean it to be.

When girls talk with one another, the most popular topics tend to include their own personal problems. That's as true of 9-year-old girls as it is of 19-year-old women. All too often, the sharing and self-disclosure can spin into an obsessive rehash of negative emotion. As the old saying goes, rolling in the mud is not the best way of getting clean. "When girls are talking about these problems, it probably feels good to get that level of support and validation," says Amanda Rose, professor of psychology at the University of Missouri. "But they are not putting two and two together, that actually this excessive talking can make them feel worse."[41]

Dr. Rose and her colleagues call this phenomenon *co-rumination*. It seems to be increasingly common among girls today but remains rare among boys. The essence of co-rumination is that talking with same-age peers about personal problems makes girls more anxious. Tessa Lee-Thomas, 13 years old, gave a reporter an example of how it can happen. "Sometimes we get into disagreements. And we have to settle them. My friends think that my other friend did something wrong, but she didn't do something wrong. Sometimes it makes the situation worse than where we were when we began. It spiraled into something bigger than it was."[42]

That's what can happen when girls counsel other girls, because girls providing counsel to same-age girls isn't the right kind of community.

The right kind of community bridges the generations. The right kind of community involves girls learning from women their mother's age and their grandmother's age.

It doesn't have to be anything formal or structured. Sophia was a high-school girl working part-time as a receptionist at a medical clinic when she told me how much she valued the opinions and support provided by her coworkers at the clinic, all women. She had a huge crush on a guy at her high school, and he was taking advantage of her. The other girls at the high school saw nothing wrong with what was going on. In fact, they envied her because he was popular and athletic, and he wasn't being physically intimate with anybody else. But he wasn't making any promises to her either.

When she told the older women in her office about it, they offered a different perspective.

"If you act like a doormat, don't be surprised when he steps all over you," one of them told her.

"If you let him treat you like a piece of meat, don't be surprised if he chews you up and spits you out," said another older woman.

Sophia broke off the relationship—if you could call a series of late-night booty calls a relationship. "He wasn't fazed at all. He was like, 'OK, whatever, I was getting tired of it anyhow.' I think he said that just to be mean, but it proves that the women at work were right. He wasn't serious about us, about having a relationship. He was just using me."

How does a girl become a woman? What does it mean to be a "real" woman?

These are questions that almost every enduring culture has answered by providing a community of women to show girls the way. I'm not talking only about mothers teaching their daughters, but about a community of women teaching the girls. We used to have many such communities in the United States, formal and informal: quilting circles, sewing circles, all-female Bible study groups, all-female book groups, Girl Scout troops, the variety of women's clubs that operated in association with the

Federation of Women's Clubs, and so forth.[43] Remnants of such groups still exist, but girls today are much more likely to hang out with other girls their age than they are to mix socially with women their parents' age.

Girls teaching same-age girls what it means to be a woman is a new phenomenon in human history. It's fundamentally equivalent to the blind leading the blind. Teenage girls don't have the wisdom, experience, and perspective that a 35-year-old woman or a 65-year-old woman can provide.

Many cultures have rituals to mark a girl's passage into womanhood: *quinceañera* in many Spanish-speaking cultures; the relatively recent emergence of *bat mitzvah* in the majority of Jewish communities today; and *kinaaldá* among the Navajo, are three examples. But as the demise of the early-20th-century debutante ball illustrates, these coming-of-age rituals for girls can be empty or even counterproductive if the focus shifts from identity to surface, from a focus on who you *are* to a focus on how you *look*. And even with the best of intentions, a one-day ritual like *bat mitzvah* or *quinceañera* isn't enough. One day or one week isn't enough. Girls need a community that lasts.

One reason I've become a proponent of girls' schools is because a girls' school can so easily provide an authentic community of girls and women—as long as the leadership of the school understands the reality that the school's mission must go beyond academics. Men may be fine for teaching girls English or Spanish or mathematics or social studies. Indeed, some of the most effective and most popular teachers I have met at girls' schools have been men. But only a woman can teach girls what it means to be a woman: how each girl must figure out for herself how she will express her inner feminine and her inner masculine. I have visited a number of girls' schools—such as Madeline Baay's school in New Orleans, Lauriston in Australia, and the PACE Center in Orlando—that consciously, thoughtfully, and intentionally provide that community of women for girls.

But what if your daughter attends a coed school? You can't expect most coed schools to have much interest in creating all-female communities. You may have to take the lead yourself. You need to create an alternative counterculture in which it's cool for girls to spend time in a community of women. If your daughter attends a coed school, then you might look to your church or synagogue or mosque to provide that community. If you don't belong to a local church or synagogue or mosque, consider joining one—not for your sake, but for your daughter's.

If your church or synagogue or mosque doesn't offer an all-female religious retreat, try to organize one. Remind the leaders of your congregation that Christianity, Judaism, and Islam each have long traditions of celebrating all-female religious communions and community. No men allowed.

Most churches and synagogues in the United States offer youth groups for children and teenagers. These groups are usually coed, and stratified by age. But everything we've learned suggests that a better approach might be to offer a single-sex group, not stratified by age. In fact, it might be time to rethink the whole idea of the church youth group or synagogue youth group. These groups should not be about teens hanging out with teens. If teens want to hang out with teens, most of them don't need any help from the church. The church or synagogue should offer opportunities for activities that the kids can't easily arrange by themselves: for example, an all-female hiking trip along a stretch of the Appalachian Trail with girls from age 11 on up to grandmothers.

You don't have to tie into an established organization or religious group to do this. Organize a get-together with half a dozen girls and at least two adult women. Women have been doing something like this with Tupperware for decades. You might create a sewing circle, if you or a friend of yours knows how to knit. Choose a catchy name like "Knit Happens."* If you don't know how to knit and you don't want to learn, choose something else. You could organize a once-a-month cooking or baking club, with the club meeting at a different girl's house each month. In December you make holiday treats, in the summer you make slushies and smoothies—something different each season.

---

* I am aware of at least one recently formed crochet circle whose members call themselves the "Happy Hookers," but I think that name might contradict the message we're trying to send here.

If knitting and baking seem gender-stereotyped to you, then come up with something else, maybe a backcountry hike or a fishing trip. It's not about the activity. The knitting or the baking is only an excuse to get women and girls together under one roof. Use the activity as a jumping-off point to talk about something important, maybe clothes, from the perspective we considered in Chapter 1. Pass around this month's copy of *Seventeen* and *Teen Vogue* and *CosmoGirl.* Ask the girls who's cute and who's just skanky. Ask questions like, "Could a girl look just as hot wearing clothes that don't show her thighs or her cleavage?" If not, why not?

Your group should **bridge the generations.** That means ideally involving not just other parents but also grandparents. Encourage your daughter to develop friendships with women your age and your mother's age.

Sometimes we may just need to rediscover old ways of connecting girls with women. Sewing circles were never primarily about sewing; they were about women and girls helping each other, which included helping girls negotiate the transitions through adolescence and into womanhood. The challenges are different today, of course, but the value of a mature adult perspective hasn't changed.

Your daughter may know more than you do about how to upload photos from a cell phone to a Facebook page, but you know more than she does about how alcohol affects the judgment and behavior of teenage boys. She needs your perspective and the perspective of other adults your age and older.

Don't let your daughter fall into the trap of thinking that her *knowledge* is a substitute for your *wisdom*. As Bly and Woodman observe, the average 12-year-old girl today knows more about the varieties of human sexual experience than the average 60-year-old knew in 1890,[44] for example, regarding oral sex and anal intercourse. But knowledge is not the same thing as wisdom. Most girls today don't fully understand the harm that sex can do to a girl, to her spirit, if it's sex at the wrong time in her life or sex with the wrong person. That understanding is not a matter of knowledge, it's a matter of wisdom. Very few 12-year-old girls (or boys) have that wisdom, and it can't easily be taught in a sex education class. That's why they need you and other adults your age.

"If we choose, we can accept our unique place in history," write Bly and Woodman.[45] For the first time in history, there is an international consensus among educated people that girls and women have a fundamental right to equal opportunity. For the past three decades, most of us have assumed that the best way to ensure equal opportunity is to pretend that girls and women are more or less the same as boys and men; that we should teach them in the same way and in the same classroom; and that we should instruct them in the same sports in the same way.

That assumption hasn't worked very well. In matters of the spirit, as in education, and in athletics, simply lifting the strategies that have been used for boys and applying them to girls, in gender-blind fashion, doesn't work reliably or well for many girls. We have to recognize that girls need girl-specific interventions. Sewing circles might not be the best way to engage boys in a community of men, but I'm hearing about some communities where it seems to be a great idea for girls.

If girls are not healthy spiritually, they may find themselves not so much *living* as *performing*. I discussed in Chapter 2 how easily this can happen in the era of the cyberbubble. The technology of social networking sites, instant messaging, and texting makes it easy for girls to think they are living their own lives when in fact they are really putting on a show for their peers. Even back in the 1990s, well before the modern cyberbubble as we know it today existed, Marion Woodman wrote that most girls "have been performing since they were tiny children. They don't know there's any other way to live except for the voice inside that's saying, 'If this is it, it's not worth living.'"[46] Today that problem is more severe.

In Chapter 3 I shared my encounter with an anorexic girl whom I called Lauren. Lauren seemed to be perfectly at peace. In the context of this chapter, one might say that she had connected with her own spirituality and she was comfortable with it. But it was the wrong kind of spirituality, one based on asceticism and self-deprivation devoid of any larger spiritual context, a spirituality divorced from any purpose or perspective outside of the self.

But I have found other girls who manifest the same peace and contentment Lauren has. Carmen, the girl who graduated from the PACE Center in Orlando, has it. Madeline Baay has it too. Emily, the girl I mentioned in Chapter 3 who dropped out of college to work at the animal shelter, also radiates that same peace and contentment. It wasn't easy for Emily to get to that quiet place, because her parents wanted her to keep on pretending to be somebody she wasn't. They wanted her to keep on performing while she wanted to start living. In Emily's spiritual quest, she explored Roman Catholicism before deciding not to convert; she read the works of Thomas Merton, St. Francis of Assisi, and the Buddhist monk Thich Nhat Hanh. Emily herself believes that her devotional reading, *and* her conversations at the coffeehouse with Rachel and Carol—two women her mother's age—were crucial in enabling her to find her way to that peaceful place in her soul.

In Chapter 4 I mentioned Michael Pollan's book *In Defense of Food.* I noted there that Mr. Pollan summarizes his book in three short sentences:

> Eat food.
> Not too much.
> Mostly plants.

By *food* he means real food, honest-to-goodness food like asparagus and salmon and carrots and oranges, not manufactured food-like stuff such as Twinkies and Cheez Whiz.

I think I can summarize some of the most important advice this book has to offer to girls in three equally short sentences:

Have friends.
Not too many.
Mostly females.

Have friends. Not too many. As I described in Chapter 2, many girls today are concerned with their two hundred friends on Facebook, not the one or two real friends who matter. A Facebook "friend" is not a real friend, any more than Cheez Whiz is real cheese. Girls trapped in the cyberbubble often have trouble making that distinction. As a result they may jeopardize their real friendships, and their connection with their own inner selves, in their frantic quest to entertain the hundreds of acquaintances or near-strangers who might glance at their social networking site.

Mostly females. It's great for your daughter to be friends with boys, and it's wonderful for her to have a close and loving relationship with her father; in Chapter 4 we considered some evidence that a good relationship with her biological Dad may have some unexpected and profound benefits. But the core of a girl's emotional life, for most girls, has to be founded on good friendships with two, three, four, or, at most, five other girls and/or women. That number may include her Mom and/or another relative such as an aunt or a cousin, plus one or two girls her own age, and hopefully at least one woman besides Mom who is not her own age, ideally someone her Mom's age or older. Those friendships can last for decades, long after the boys are forgotten.

As I said earlier: parenting is an art, not a science. Sometimes you have to push your daughter into unfamiliar territory when she would rather be sheltered at home. Sometimes you have to shelter her at home when she would rather spend spring break with the cool kids getting drunk at the beach. And the right decision this year may be not-quite-right next year.

When she is young, you may need to challenge her, gently pushing her out of her comfort zone so that she can explore her world. That may be the only way that she can discover her strengths and her weaknesses. Help her to develop that sense of agency, of being able to create, to imagine, to take the initiative.

The onset of puberty is likely to change her. Don't back away even when she tells you to get lost. Speak to her the words of the poet:

> *Dig into yourself . . .*
> *Go into yourself and find out how deep is the place from which*
> *your life springs;*
> *at its source you will find the answer to your question.*

The goal is to help your daughter to discover and nurture her true self. To accomplish that, you and she may find it useful to draw on other traditions than your own. One of the unique gifts we enjoy as a species is the ability to learn from other people who have lived in other times and other places. The slogan "Think globally, act locally" is usually used in support of environmental programs, but the same basic idea, of drawing on an international perspective in order to create something that can work where you live, might also apply to the idea of creating a community that "honors the female spirit" while transcending location and culture.

The job description of a good parent changes as your daughter grows up. When she's 4 years old, you have to be in charge. As your daughter matures intellectually, physically, and spiritually, your role has to change. You're no longer the captain; you have to help your daughter to take the helm, at first perhaps with your hand on the wheel, but then, as the time becomes ripe, you have to step away and let her chart her own course.

Your daughter's journey, becoming the woman she is meant to be, is a journey to an unknown destination. You don't know the woman she is meant to be. You don't know how she might mix her inner masculine and her inner feminine to find the right balance for her unique spirit. As a parent, it's tempting to think that you know where your daughter's destination should lie. You naturally want to guide your daughter to that destination the way a captain guides a ship. Some parents find it hard to let their daughter take the helm. But that approach is likely, eventually, to lead to shipwreck.

Ultimately only your daughter can be the captain of her own ship. But you can be the lighthouse, warning of unseen dangers. You can be the shipwright, helping patch holes and make the ship stronger and better. And you can be the safe harbor, welcoming the sailor home before she sets out on her next voyage.

acknowledgments

My first debt is to the girls who came to see me as patients during my 18 years as a family physician in Poolesville, Maryland (1990–2008). What I learned from those girls as they progressed through childhood and adolescence and into adulthood became the foundation for everything I have to share in this book. To them, and to their parents, I express my most sincere thanks. I could not have written any sort of book about girls without the firsthand experience I gained as a family doctor serving Barnesville, Beallsville, Darnestown, Dickerson, Poolesville, and Potomac, Maryland.

However, if I had stayed only in my own neighborhood, then this book might be only a memoir of life in northwestern Montgomery County, Maryland. And so I am most grateful to the following schools (listed in alphabetical order) that have opened their doors to me over the past five years for personal, face-to-face interviews and/or conversations with girls and/or their teachers and/or their parents:

- Academy of the Holy Names (Tampa, Florida)
- Academy of the Sacred Heart (New Orleans, Louisiana)
- Agnes Irwin School (Rosemont, Pennsylvania)
- Anne Bailey Elementary School (St. Albans, West Virginia)
- Branksome Hall (Toronto, Ontario)
- Brigidine St. Ives (Sydney, Australia)
- Burlington Central High School (Burlington, Ontario)
- Caddo Heights Elementary School (Shreveport, Louisiana)
- Canberra Girls Grammar School (Canberra, Australia)
- Carman Trails Elementary School (St. Louis, Missouri)

- Chatham Hall (Chatham, Virginia)
- Cheyenne High School (Las Vegas, Nevada)
- City of London School for Girls (London, England)
- Columbus School for Girls (Columbus, Ohio)
- Convent of the Sacred Heart (Greenwich, Connecticut)
- Cunningham Elementary School (Waterloo, Iowa)
- Cypress Heights Academy (Baton Rouge, Louisiana)
- Deerfield Academy (Deerfield, Massachusetts)
- Dent Middle School (Columbia, South Carolina)
- Ellis School (Pittsburgh, Pennsylvania)
- Epsom Girls' Grammar (Auckland, New Zealand)
- Everest Academy (Clarkston, Michigan)
- Foley Intermediate School (Foley, Alabama)
- Gateway Academy (Chesterfield, Missouri)
- Greenwich Academy (Greenwich, Connecticut)
- Hastings Girls' High School (Hastings, New Zealand)
- Hathaway Brown (Shaker Heights, Ohio)
- Hewitt School (New York, New York)
- The Highland School (Warrenton, Virginia)
- The Highlands School (Irving, Texas)
- Independence Middle School (Coal City, West Virginia)
- Irma Lerma Rangel School (Dallas, Texas)
- Jefferson Middle School (Springfield, Illinois)
- Jefferson Montessori School (Gaithersburg, Maryland)
- Kambala (Sydney, Australia)
- Katherine Delmar Burke School (San Francisco, California)
- Korowa Anglican Girls' School (Melbourne, Australia)
- Lake Forest Country Day School (Lake Forest, Illinois)
- Langston Charter Middle School (Greenville, South Carolina)
- Laurel (Shaker Heights, Ohio)
- Lauriston (Melbourne, Australia)
- Mary Institute and Country Day School (St. Louis, Missouri)
- McLain High School (Tulsa, Oklahoma)

- MLC School (Sydney, Australia)
- Mountain View High School (Los Altos, California)
- North Shore Country Day School (Winnetka, Illinois)
- Oak Grove School (Green Oaks, Illinois)
- PACE Center of Orlando (Orlando, Florida)
- Penrhos (Perth, Australia)
- Pinecrest Academy (Cumming, Georgia)
- Porter-Gaud School (Charleston, South Carolina)
- Potomac School (McLean, Virginia)
- Providence High School (San Antonio, Texas)
- Purnell School (Pottersville, New Jersey)
- Randle Highlands Elementary School (Washington, D.C.)
- Riverview High School (Sydney, Nova Scotia)
- Robert Frost Middle School (Hazel Crest, Illinois)
- Rocky Mount Preparatory School (Rocky Mount, North Carolina)
- Royal Palm Academy (Naples, Florida)
- Santa Catalina School (Monterey, California)
- Seymour (Adelaide, Australia)
- St. Aidan's Anglican Girls' School (Brisbane, Australia)
- St. Anthony's School (West Vancouver, British Columbia)
- St. Cuthbert's (Auckland, New Zealand)
- St. Mary's Anglican Girls' School (Karrinyup [Perth], Australia)
- St. Mary's Episcopal School (Memphis, Tennessee)
- St. Michael's Collegiate School (Sandy Bay, Tasmania)
- Thomas Jefferson Preparatory School (Darnestown, Maryland)
- Woodbridge Middle School (Woodbridge, Virginia)
- Woodford House (Havelock North, New Zealand)
- Woodlands Academy of the Sacred Heart (Lake Forest, Illinois)
- Woodward Avenue Elementary School (Deland, Florida)

At various points in this book, I place considerable weight on comments by author Courtney Martin, on the research of Professor Gerianne Alexander, and on the insights of Rabbi Sandy Eisenberg Sasso. I would like to thank each of these women for reading relevant portions of the manuscript and, when necessary, correcting or clarifying the text. Any remaining errors are of course solely my responsibility. I also thank Jill Gentry for reading and correcting my retelling of some of the stories I heard during my visit to her school. I am also indebted to Dr. Bonnie Ellinger for double-checking my translation of Shir HaShirim 8:4. And of course I am grateful to Samantha Firstenberg for sharing her story, and for her thoughtful comments regarding girls' risk of concussion.

I would also like to thank my agent, Felicia Eth, as well as the team at Basic Books: Amanda Moon, who guided this book's development in its early stages; Whitney Casser, who handled all the necessary chores with aplomb; and especially John Sherer, the publisher, for his personal support of the project. Thanks also to Liz Stein, who provided a thoughtful, professional, and constructive line-by-line critique of the entire book. Once again, any errors that remain are my responsibility.

It takes a bit of chutzpah for a middle-aged man, however well-informed, to write a book about girls. My wife, Katie, encouraged me at every step of the way, as well as providing helpful feedback on each chapter. She also helped immensely with all the traveling chores. My hosts were often amazed by my fashionable dress. "... *du seist auch noch so ferne, du bist mir nah ...*"

And finally, thanks to my daughter, Sarah, who gave me the most important motivation to write this book: the hope that what I have learned will make me a better Dad.

notes

Epigraph on page vi: Rainer Maria Rilke, "Letters to a Young Poet" (*Briefe an einen jungen Dichter,* Franz Xaver Kappus), letter 1, written February 17, 1903. The original German reads: "*Graben Sie in sich . . . in sich zu gehen und die Tiefen zu prüfen, in denen Ihr Leben entspringt; an seiner Quelle werden Sie die Antwort auf die Frage finden.*" The translation is my own.

INTRODUCTION

1. Except where indicated, the names of the girls have been changed, and certain details have been changed to protect each girl's anonymity. For example, "Emily" was in fact rejected from both Harvard and Princeton, and she did in fact matriculate at a well-regarded selective university in the eastern United States, but it wasn't the University of Pennsylvania.

2. Andre Sourander, Päivi Santalahti, and associates, "Have there been changes in children's psychiatric symptoms and mental health service use?" *Journal of the American Academy of Child and Adolescent Psychiatry,* volume 43, number 9 (2004), pp. 1134–1145.

3. A Scandinavian study suggests that this increase has continued at least through 2006. The Scandinavian researchers compared use of mental health services in 1997 with 2006. In 1997, 8 percent of boys had visited a psychologist in the previous year, compared with 10 percent of the girls. By 2006, those figures had risen to 12 percent for the boys and 17 percent for the girls. The reference is to Inga D. Sigfusdottir and associates, "Trends in depressive symptoms, anxiety symptoms, and visits to healthcare specialists," *Scandinavian Journal of Public Health,* volume 36 (2008), pp. 361–368.

4. Mark Olfson and Steven Marcus, "National patterns in antidepressant medication treatment," *Archives of General Psychiatry,* volume 66 (2009), pp. 848–856.

5. Sigfusdottir and associates, "Trends in depressive symptoms," p. 366; emphasis added.

6. Sigfusdottir and associates, p. 364, found that "regular visits (six times or more during 1 year) to psychiatrists and psychologists increased significantly over the same period among girls but not among boys." I have made prominent mention here of two European studies—Sourander, Santalahti and associates, 2004; and Sigfusdottir and associates, 2008. Before you dismiss these studies as merely an indicator of how rough life is for European kids, consider that a recent study comparing the European experience with the American experience found that kids in the United States are more than twice as likely to be on psychiatric medications, overall, compared with kids in Europe (specifically in Germany and in the Netherlands). When you break down the results by gender and psychiatric diagnosis, the results are even more stark: American girls age 15 to 19 are about *nine times* more likely than German girls to be taking antidepressants, for example, and American girls age 10 to 14 are more than *30* times as likely as German girls to be taking antidepressants. See Julie M. Zito, Daniel J. Safer, and associates, "A three-country comparison of psychotropic medication prevalence in youth," *Child and Adolescent Psychiatry and Mental Health,* volume 2 (2008); available online at www.capmh.com/content/2/1/26. Table 6 of that study provides the following prevalence rates for depression for girls in the United States compared with girls in Germany:

- American girls age 10 to 14 taking antidepressants: 3.26 percent
- German girls age 10 to 14 taking antidepressants: 0.09 percent
- American girls age 15 to 19 taking antidepressants: 5.21 percent
- German girls age 15 to 19 taking antidepressants: 0.58 percent

I am not suggesting that life is wonderful for German girls. I have met with girls in Germany and have been struck by how similar their experience is in so many ways to the experience of American girls. The biggest difference between the United States and Germany in this regard is not so much in the challenges the girls have to face but with the much greater tendency of Americans to use prescription drugs as a fix.

More generally, the finding that girls and women are more anxious than boys and men is fairly robust across cultures. One of the largest studies ever conducted of personality traits across cultures, led by Robert McCrae at the National Institutes of Health, with a total of 80 investigators from 50 different cultures, was published in 2005. See Robert R. McCrae and associates, "Universal features of personality traits from the observer's perspective: data from 50 cultures," *Journal of Personality and Social Psychology,* volume 88, number 3 (2005), pp. 547–561. Interestingly, they found that the sex difference in anxiety declines with age. In other words, 20-year-old women are much more anxious than 20-year-old men, but 80-year-old women are only slightly, if at all, more anxious than 80-year-old men.

Sex differences in anxiety do vary across culture, but the variation is counterintuitive. The differences between the sexes tend to be smallest in the most patriarchal cultures, such as China, Korea, Pakistan, and Kenya, whereas the differences tend to be larger in nations that affirm gender equity, such as Sweden and the United States. In a more recent examination of these variations, one team of investigators concluded that "with improved national wealth and equality of the sexes, it seems differences between men and women in personality traits do not diminish. On the contrary, the differences become conspicuously larger" (David P. Schmitt and associates, "Why can't a man be more like a woman? Sex differences in big five personality traits across 55 cultures," *Journal of Personality and Social Psychology,* volume 94, number 1 (2008), pp. 168–182; the quotation is from page 169).

7. For example, the Hamilton Anxiety Rating Scale (HAM-A) was first published in 1959 and was in wide use by the mid-1960s. The HAM-A is still widely used by psychologists in assessing and quantifying anxiety.

8. Jean Twenge, "The age of anxiety? Birth cohort change in anxiety and neuroticism, 1952–1993," *Journal of Personality and Social Psychology,* volume 79, number 6 (2000), pp. 1007–1021. The two quotes are found on pp. 1008 and 1017, respectively.

9. See Robert D. Putnam, *Bowling Alone: The Collapse and Revival of American Community* (New York: Simon & Schuster, 2000). See especially chapter 8, "Reciprocity, Honesty, and Trust," pp. 134–147.

10. The quote from Madeline Levine is from her book *The Price of Privilege* (New York: Harper-Collins, 2006), p. 140. For more on the decline of informal social connections in the United States over the past 40 years, see Putnam, *Bowling Alone,* especially chapter 6, "Informal Social Connections," pp. 93–115.

11. Ichiro Kawachi and Lisa F. Berkman, "Social ties and mental health," *Journal of Urban Health,* volume 78, number 3 (2001), pp. 458–467.

12. Twenge, "The age of anxiety?" table 3, p. 1014.

13. I have also found evidence for a similar phenomenon in Europe, which I present in my book *Jungs im Abseits* (Munich: Koesel, 2009), www.koesel.de/Detail.asp?isbn=346630822. *Jungs im Abseits* began as a German translation of my book *Boys Adrift* but was extensively rewritten to include examples from continental (especially German-speaking) Europe.

CHAPTER 1

1. Ariel Levy, *Female Chauvinist Pigs: Women and the Rise of Raunch Culture* (New York: Free Press, 2005), p. 34.

2. These words are spoken by Pamela Josse, a precocious 12-year-old girl in Muriel Barbery's novel *The Elegance of the Hedgehog,* translated by Alison Anderson (New York: Europa Editions, 2008), p. 192.

3. Stephen Hinshaw and Rachel Kranz, *The Triple Bind: Saving Our Teenage Girls from Today's Pressures* (New York: Ballantine, 2009), p. 112.

4. American Psychological Association, Task Force on the Sexualization of Girls, *Report of the APA Task Force on the Sexualization of Girls* (Washington, D.C.: American Psychological Association, 2007). You can download the full text of the report at www.apa.org/pi/wpo/sexualization.html.

5. See previous reference, p. 3, emphasis added.

6. Margaret Mead's book *Coming of Age in Samoa* was a best seller when it was first published back in 1928, and it had tremendous influence on American popular culture for decades thereafter. Mead claimed to have found a society where uninhibited girls and boys engaged in unconstrained sexual intimacy beginning at the onset of puberty. Six decades later, a series of investigative reports demonstrated that Mead had gotten the story completely wrong. She had not lived with the islanders, but only interviewed a handful of them. Her primary informant, a 24-year-old woman named Fa'apua'a Fa'amu, invented an outrageous story about mixed-sex sleepovers and free sex among young teenagers. Fa'apua'a Fa'amu was a virgin at the time. Sixty years later, she recanted on camera and in a sworn legal affidavit, explaining that she had told the story to Mead as a joke, not dreaming that anyone would take it seriously. The reality turns out to be almost the opposite of what Mead reported: Samoan culture, like most other traditional cultures, has strict rules prohibiting sex until marriage, with severe punishments for transgressors. See, for example, Derek Freeman, *The Fateful Hoaxing of Margaret Mead: A Historical Analysis of Her Samoan Research* (New York: Basic Books, 1998).

7. Germaine Greer, *The Female Eunuch* (New York: McGraw-Hill, 1970), p. 4, emphasis in original.

8. Ariel Levy in her book *Female Chauvinist Pigs* (New York: Free Press, 2005), and Pamela Paul in her book *Pornified* (New York: Times Books, 2005) both call attention to the irony of these supposedly liberated 21st-century girls putting themselves on display for the boys and thinking that somehow this display is empowering and liberated.

9. For a book-length exploration of this point—that modesty can be sexual—see Wendy Shalit, *A Return to Modesty* (New York: Random House, 1999) and her follow-up, *Girls Gone Mild* (New York: Random House, 2007).

10. Gail Collins, "Bristol Palin's new gig," *New York Times*, May 6, 2009, available at www.nytimes.com/2009/05/07/opinion/07collins.html?_r=1&em.

11. "Playboy Enterprises shutting down *Playgirl* mag," August 4, 2008, www.cbsnews.com/stories/2008/08/04/paidcontent/main4320229.shtml.

12. See, for example, Heather A. Rupp and Kim Wallen, "Sex differences in response to visual sexual stimuli: a review," *Archives of Sexual Behavior*, volume 37 (2008), pp. 206–218; and Amy D. Lykins, Marta Meana, and Gregory P. Strauss, "Sex differences in visual attention to erotic and non-erotic stimuli," *Archives of Sexual Behavior*, volume 37 (2008), pp. 219–228.

13. See chapter 6 of my book *Why Gender Matters* (New York: Doubleday, 2005) for more evidence supporting this assertion.

14. Hinshaw and Kranz, *The Triple Bind*, p. 105.

15. For more about the popularity of suggestive T-shirts with messages such as "Your boyfriend is a good kisser," please see Ian Shapira's front-page article for the *Washington Post*, "Teens' T-shirts make educators squirm: suggestive messages challenge dress codes," September 27, 2006.

16. Marc Hollender, "The need or wish to be held," *Archives of General Psychiatry*, volume 22 (1970), pp. 445–453.

17. Courtney Martin, *Perfect Girls, Starving Daughters: The Frightening New Normalcy of Hating Your Body* (New York: Free Press, 2007), p. 54.

18. Jessica Bennett, "Generation diva: how our obsession with beauty is changing our kids," *Newsweek*, March 30, 2009, available online at www.newsweek.com/id/191247. The subtitle of Bennett's article, as just noted, is "how our obsession with beauty is changing our kids." I don't think that's quite right. Bennett mentions a few maniacal parents, such as some of the mothers on the TLC reality show *Toddlers & Tiaras*, who sit their young daughters down at the vanity and prod them to apply blush and lipstick. But in most families where a preteen girl is obsessed with beauty products, it's the girl, not the parents, who is pushing for it.

19. Pamela McClintock, "'Twilight' sequel goes worldwide," *Variety*, November 17, 2009, online at www.variety.com/article/VR1118011495.html?categoryid=13&cs=1.

20. According to *USA Today*, no previous author has ever captured the top four slots in their best-seller list for an entire year, as Stephenie Meyer's *Twilight* books did in 2008. See the article by Bob Minzesheimer and Anthony DeBarros, "Sellers basked in Stephenie Meyer's *Twilight* in 2008," January 16, 2009, available online at www.usatoday.com/life/books/news/2009–01–14-top-sellers-main_N.htm.

21. Carmen D. Siering and Katherine Spillar, "New Moon, Same Old Sexist Story," *Ms. Magazine*, November 17, 2009, available online at www.msmagazine.com/Fall2009/newmoon.asp.

22. See Mary Jo Murphy, "Nancy Drew and the Secret of the 3 Black Robes," *New York Times*, May 30, 2009, available online at www.nytimes.com/2009/05/31/weekinreview/31murphy.html.

23. Brooke Wells and Jean Twenge, "Changes in young people's sexual behavior and attitudes, 1943–1999: a cross-temporal meta-analysis," *Review of General Psychology,* volume 9 (2005), pp. 249–261.

24. See, for example, Jane Brown, Kelly Ladin L'Engle, and associates, "Sexy media matter: exposure to sexual content in music, movies, television, and magazines predicts black and white adolescents' sexual behavior," *Pediatrics,* volume 117 (2006), pp. 1018–1027; full text available online at http://pediatrics.aappublications.org/cgi/content/full/117/4/1018. These researchers interviewed girls as young as 12 and found that the more a girl is exposed to sexualized images in the media, the earlier she is to engage in sexual behavior.

25. I still find people who are not aware that Margaret Mead was the victim of a hoax when she wrote that girls in Samoa enjoy years of unconstrained sexual activity prior to marriage. See my note 6, above.

26. Wells and Twenge, "Changes in young people's sexual behavior and attitudes, 1943–1999," figure 1, p. 254.

27. For a thorough and scholarly reflection on the replacement of dating culture by hook-up culture, please see Kathleen Bogle, *Hooking Up: Sex, Dating, and Relationships on Campus* (New York: NYU Press, 2008). Bogle's book addresses only the college and university experience; we don't yet have a comparable scholarly book addressing the contemporary sexual experience of girls in middle school and high school.

28. Levy, *Female Chauvinist Pigs*, p. 93.

29. I'm referring to the November 2009 issue of *Cosmopolitan*.

30. Meg Meeker, *Strong Fathers, Strong Daughters: 10 Secrets Every Father Should Know* (New York: Ballantine, 2007), pp. 104–105.

31. Denise D. Hallfors and associates, "Which comes first in adolescence—sex and drugs or depression?" *American Journal of Preventive Medicine*, volume 29 (2005), pp. 163–170.

32. Laura Sessions Stepp, "Hot fun (or not fun) in the summertime," *Washington Post*, July 22, 2006, p. C1.

33. Stepp was quoted by Stephanie Rosenbloom, "A disconnect on hooking up," *New York Times*, March 1, 2007.

34. This episode of *The OC*, entitled "The Heartbreak," first aired on February 18, 2004. It's available for download on iTunes.

35. Although this blog is hosted by *Education Week*, the blog itself is anonymous. Here's the link, originally posted August 18, 2008: http://blogs.edweek.org/edweek/eduwonkette/2008/08/leonard_sax_girl_whisperer_or.html.

36. Barbara Fredrickson and associates, "That swimsuit becomes you: sex differences in self-objectification, restrained eating, and math performance," *Journal of Personality and Social Psychology*, volume 75 (1998), pp. 269–284. Fredrickson and her team replicated this finding in a more recent paper (lead author Diane Quinn, but only with women subjects), "The disruptive effect of self-objectification on performance," *Psychology of Women Quarterly*, volume 30 (2006), pp. 59–64. I do not attach much significance to the finding that boys did better while wearing swim trunks compared with boys wearing sweaters. In a more recent replication, the boys wearing swim trunks did less well than boys wearing sweaters; see Michelle Hebl, Eden King, and Jean Lin, "The swimsuit becomes us all: ethnicity, gender, and vulnerability to self-objectification," *Personality and Social Psychology Bulletin*, volume 30 (2004), pp. 1322–1331. Our culture does not expect boys to wear revealing clothes to school. Boys don't have to worry about whether their tummy is a "muffin top," and I haven't seen many boys wearing midriff shirts to school. So, even if boys and girls are equally vulnerable to

self-objectification while wearing swimsuits, it's still the girls who are at greater risk, because we don't expect boys to wear swimsuits (or their equivalent) to social gatherings or to school.

37. These figures are taken from http://katyperry.com, click on "who's that girl?" Downloaded November 27, 2009.

38. MTV's show was called *A Double Shot at Love.* If you feel a craving to watch full episodes of the show, you may do so at this link: www.mtv.com/ontv/dyn/a_double_shot_at_love/videos-full-episodes.jhtml.

39. Donn Teal, *The Gay Militants* (New York: Stein & Day), 1971.

40. You can read Megan Fox's June 2009 interview for *Esquire* magazine, in which she asserted that "everyone is born bisexual," at www.esquire.com/women/women-we-love/megan-fox-pics-0609?click=main_sr.

41. Researchers at Cornell University, examining data collected from a representative sampling of young Americans that included more than 20,000 individuals across the United States, found that 14.5 percent of the women were categorized as lesbian, bisexual, or "bisexual leaning heterosexual" (a category that reminds me of the Rikki/Vikki twins in the MTV show referenced above). Among young men, 5.6 percent were categorized as gay, bisexual, or "bisexual leaning heterosexual." See Ritch Savin-Williams and Geoffrey L. Ream, "Prevalence and stability of sexual orientation components during adolescence and young adulthood," *Archives of Sexual Behavior*, volume 36 (2007), pp. 385–394. The proportions in the United States might even be lower than in some European countries. For example, in Norway, more than 20 percent of girls and young women were categorized as lesbian or bisexual: see L. Wichstrøm and K. Hegna, "Sexual orientation and suicide attempt: a longitudinal study of the general Norwegian adolescent population," *Journal of Abnormal Psychology*, volume 112 (2003), pp. 144–151. In another study, 23 percent of girls and young women in New Zealand—nearly one in four—were sexually attracted to other girls and young women: see N. Dickson and colleagues, "Same-sex attraction in a birth cohort: prevalence and persistence in early adulthood," *Social Science and Medicine*, volume 56 (2003), pp. 1607–1615.

42. See, for example, Roy Baumeister, "Gender differences in erotic plasticity: the female sex drive as socially flexible and responsive," *Psychological Bulletin*, volume 126 (2000), pp. 347–374.

43. See, for example, Lisa Diamond, "The evolution of plasticity in female-female desire," *Journal of Psychology and Human Sexuality*, volume 18 (2006), pp. 245–274.

44. Levy, *Female Chauvinist Pigs*, p. 150.

45. Stephen Martino and associates, "Exposure to degrading versus nondegrading music lyrics and sexual behavior among youth," *Pediatrics*, volume 118 (2006), pp. e430–e441.

46. American Psychological Association, APA Task Force on the Sexualization of Girls, p. 7.

47. See, for example, the opening sequence in the popular teen movie *Superbad*, in which the two main characters debate the pros and cons of various online porn sites. This movie was among the top-grossing teen movies for 2007. Such a sequence—with characters casually discussing different genres of pornography—would have been unthinkable in a movie for teens 30 years ago.

48. Song of Songs, chapter 8, verse 4. The original reads:

הִשְׁבַּעְתִּי אֶתְכֶם בְּנוֹת יְרוּשָׁלָיִם׃ מַה-תָּעִירוּ וּמַה-תְּעֹרְרוּ אֶת-הָאַהֲבָה עַד שֶׁתֶּחְפָּץ׃

The literal translation would be: "I charge you, daughters of Jerusalem: Do not arouse and do not awaken love until she desires." The repetition of ideas—do not arouse, do not awaken—is a common usage in biblical Hebrew to express emphasis. The writer of this verse recognizes that while it is possible to arouse and awaken love before "she desires," it is not a good idea to do so: hence my translation, "Do not awaken love before its time." My translation is very similar to that found in the New American Bible: "Do not arouse, do not stir up love, before its own time."

CHAPTER 2

1. Author Jeffrey Eugenides made this comment in a commentary for National Public Radio, *All Things Considered,* "You must read this," May 18, 2009, www.npr.org/templates/story/story .php?storyId=103846270.

2. This quote was the lead heading in an article in *USA Today,* written by Maria Puente, entitled "Relationships in a twist over Twitter," April 15, 2009. The online version of the article, which does

not include the quote from Thich Nhat Hanh (although he is mentioned toward the end of the article), may be found at www.usatoday.com/printedition/life/20090415/twittertwaddle15_cv.art.htm.

3. Emily Nussbaum, "Say everything: kids, the Internet, and the end of privacy," *New York* magazine, February 12, 2007, http://nymag.com/news/features/27341/index2.html.

4. Sean Silverthorne, "Understanding users of social networks," *Harvard Business School Working Knowledge: A First Look at Faculty Research*, September 14, 2009, full text available online at http://hbswk.hbs.edu/item/6156.html.

5. Mark Bauerlein, *The Dumbest Generation: How the Digital Age Stupefies Young Americans and Jeopardizes Our Future* (New York: Tarcher, 2008), p. 132.

6. Thomas Fuchs and Ludger Woessman, "Computers and student learning: bivariate and multi-variate evidence on the availability and use of computers at home and at school," CESifo Working Paper #1321, available at http://ideas.repec.org/p/ces/ceswps/_1321.html. More information about the CESifo research network is available at www.cesifo-group.de/portal/page/portal/ifoHome/f-about.

7. Bauerlein, *The Dumbest Generation*, pp. 36, 42.

8. Bauerlein, p. 158.

9. Bauerlein, p. 136.

10. Quoted by Martha Irvine, "Are you a twit if you don't want to Twitter?" Originally published by the Associated Press on April 8, 2009, available at www.msnbc.msn.com/id/30111694/.

11. James S. Coleman, *The Adolescent Society: The Social Life of the Teenager and Its Impact on Education* (New York: Free Press, 1961), pp. 5–6.

12. Frederick Elkin and William Westley, "The myth of adolescent culture," *American Sociological Review*, volume 20 (1955), pp. 680–684.

13. Coleman, *The Adolescent Society*, p. 4.

14. The figure of 2,272 texts per month comes from Katie Hafner's article in the *New York Times*, "Texting may be taking a toll," May 25, 2009, online at www.nytimes.com/2009/05/26/health/26teen.html?_r=1&em.

15. See Katie Hafner's article (previous citation).

16. The Canadian government pulled Adderall off the Canadian market in February 2005. You can read the original announcement from Health Canada at www.hc-sc.gc.ca/dhp-mps/medeff/advisories-avis/prof/_2005/adderall_xr_hpc-cps-eng.php. In August 2005, Health Canada reversed its own decision and allowed the manufacturer to resume marketing Adderall in Canada. You can read discussion of this action in the *Canadian Medical Association Journal* (CMAJ) at www.cmaj.ca/cgi/eletters/173/8/858#3288.

17. Judith Rich Harris, *The Nurture Assumption: Why Children Turn Out the Way They Do*, revised and updated (New York: Free Press, 2009), p. 44.

18. See, for example, Rhoshel Lenroot and colleagues., "Sexual dimorphism of brain developmental trajectories during childhood and adolescence," *NeuroImage*, volume 36 (2007), pp. 1065–1073, available at www.pubmedcentral.nih.gov/articlerender.fcgi?tool=pubmed&pubmedid=17513132.

19. For more on the gendered nature of texting at the dinner table, see Sara Rimer, "Play with your food, just don't text!" *New York Times*, May 26, 2009, online at www.nytimes.com/2009/05/27/dining/27text.html.

20. Donna St. George and Daniel Devise, "Slur-filled web site hurtful but not illegal," *Washington Post*, May 17, 2009, online at www.washingtonpost.com/wp-dyn/content/article/2009/05/16/AR2009051602191.html?nav=hcmodule.

21. Nussbaum, "Say everything."

22. CBS News, "'Sexting' shockingly common among teens: latest case involves three teen girls in PA who sent nude pics to three boys," January 15, 2009, www.cbsnews.com/stories/2009/01/15/national/main4723161.shtml.

23. The latest survey on this topic is *Sex and Tech: Results from a Survey of Teens and Young Adults*, published in 2009 by the National Campaign to Prevent Teen and Unplanned Pregnancy, online at www.thenationalcampaign.org/sextech/PDF/SexTech_Summary.pdf. According to this survey, "39% of teens and 59% of young adults have sent or posted sexually suggestive emails or text messages—and 20% of teens and 33% of young adults have sent/posted nude or semi-nude images of themselves."

This survey included a roughly equal mix of females and males. Because girls and young women are much more likely than boys and young men to have nude or semi-nude photos taken of themselves, the figures for girls and young women may be higher than those reported here, because these figures include males.

24. CBS News, "Teen 'sexting' worries parents, schools: prosecutors have filed charges against kids who send out photos," February 4, 2009, www.cbsnews.com/stories/2009/02/04/tech/main 4776708.shtml.

25. Lisa Bloom, "Sexting: should teens be prosecuted?" April 2009, www.bettyconfidential .com/ar/ld/a/Should_teens_be_prosecuted_for_sexting.html.

26. Stephen Hinshaw and Rachel Kranz, *The Triple Bind: Saving Our Teenage Girls from Today's Pressures* (New York: Ballantine, 2009), pp. 130–131.

27. Nussbaum, "Say everything."

28. Clive Thompson, *Wired* magazine, "Clive Thompson on the age of microcelebrity: why everyone's a little Brad Pitt," November 27, 2007, www.wired.com/techbiz/people/magazine/15–12/ st_thompson.

29. See Clive Thompson's article (previous citation).

30. I am making an allusion here to Joshua Meyrowitz, *No Sense of Place: The Impact of Electronic Media on Social Behavior* (New York: Oxford University Press, 1985). Meyrowitz was writing primarily about the impact of television in the now-distant world at the very dawn of the Web. His comments apply with much greater force to the modern era.

CHAPTER 3

1. Courtney Martin, *Perfect Girls, Starving Daughters: The Frightening New Normalcy of Hating Your Body* (New York: Free Press, 2007), pp. 136, 192.

2. Martin, *Perfect Girls, Starving Daughters*, pp. 26, 30.

3. There are also "pro-mia" websites, i.e., sites that promote bulimia. But "pro-mia" sites appear to be less numerous than pro-ana websites. For more about the latter, see Sonya Lipczynska, "Discovering the cult of Ana and Mia: a review of pro-anorexia websites," *Journal of Mental Health*, volume 16 (2007), pp. 545–548; and Sarah Brotsky and David Giles, "Inside the 'pro-ana' community: a covert online participant observation," *Eating Disorders*, volume 15 (2007), pp. 93–109.

4. This photograph was taken by James Carver-Grenside, www.flickr.com/photos/jamescg/. The model is anonymous and the photograph is untitled. The photograph can be downloaded from Mr. Carver-Grenside's web page at this link: www.flickr.com/photos/jamescg/2109806408/.

5. http://mariamarchita.1hwy.com/whats_new.html.

6. www.pro-ana-nation.com/v1/index.php?option=content&task=view&id=9.

7. http://anasmartyr.piczo.com/aboutana?cr=5&linkvar=000044. This site is characteristic of some of the way-out pathological blogging that happens in the pro-ana community.

8. http://mariamarchita.1hwy.com/whats_new.html.

9. Kamryn Eddy, David Dorer, Debra Franko, and associates, "Diagnostic crossover in anorexia nervosa and bulimia nervosa: implications for DSM-V," *American Journal of Psychiatry*, volume 165 (2008), pp. 245–250, online at http://ajp.psychiatryonline.org/cgi/reprint/165/2/245.

10. Martin, *Perfect Girls, Starving Daughters*, p. 195.

11. Martin, p. 203.

12. Martin, p. 260.

13. For a useful introduction to this topic, see the review by Michelle Warren and Amanda Stiehl, "Exercise and female adolescents: effects on the reproductive and skeletal systems," *Journal of the American Medical Women's Association*, volume 54 (1999), pp. 115–120. Although the journal is unfortunately defunct, the full text of this article may be downloaded from http://jamwa.am wa-doc.org/index.cfm?objectid=28FE4035-D567-0B25-56C87A800800719C.

14. Anna Quindlen, *Being Perfect* (New York: Random House, 2005), pp. 47–48.

15. Madeline Levine, *The Price of Privilege: How Parental Pressure and Material Advantage Are Creating a Generation of Disconnected and Unhappy Kids* (New York: HarperCollins, 2006), p. 11.

16. Sara Rimer, "For girls, it's be yourself, and be perfect too," *New York Times,* April 1, 2007, online at www.nytimes.com/2007/04/01/us/01girls.html?_r=1&pagewanted=all.

17. Levine, *The Price of Privilege,* p. 180.

18. Levine, p. 134.

19. Liz Funk, *Supergirls Speak Out: Inside the Secret Crisis of Overachieving Girls* (New York: Simon & Schuster, 2009), p. 58.

20. Martin, *Perfect Girls, Starving Daughters,* p. 238.

21. National Center on Addiction and Substance Abuse, *Women Under the Influence* (Baltimore: Johns Hopkins University Press, 2006), p. 47.

22. National Center on Addiction and Substance Abuse, *The Formative Years: Pathways to Substance Abuse Among Girls and Young Women Ages 8–22* (New York: Columbia University, 2003), p. 24. The full text (242 pages) of this report may be downloaded in PDF format from www.casa columbia.org/ViewProduct.aspx?PRODUCTID=, click on "download for free."

23. National Center on Addiction and Substance Abuse, *Women Under the Influence,* p. 47.

24. John R. Knight, Henry Wechsler, and colleagues, "Alcohol abuse and dependence among U.S. college students," *Journal of Studies on Alcohol,* volume 63 (2002), pp. 263–270.

25. These figures are from the FBI's Uniform Crime Report, "Crime in the United States," published in September 2009. You can check these numbers yourself in the table "Ten-year arrest trends by sex," online at www.fbi.gov/ucr/cius2008/data/table_33.html.

26. Koren Zailckas, *Smashed: Story of a Drunken Girlhood* (New York: Penguin, 2005), p. 22.

27. Zailckas, *Smashed,* pp. 61, 62; emphasis added.

28. Zailckas, p. 64.

29. Zailckas, pp. 96, 224.

30. National Center on Addiction and Substance Abuse, "Big differences in why girls and boys use cigarettes, alcohol, and drugs," www.casacolumbia.org/absolutenm/templates/PressReleases .aspx?articleid=265&zoneid=46.

31. See, for example, National Institute on Alcohol Abuse and Alcoholism, "Are women more vulnerable to alcohol's effects?" *Alcohol Alert,* number 46 (1999), online at http://pubs.niaaa .nih.gov/publications/aa46.htm.

32. See, for example, Krista Medina and colleagues, "Prefrontal cortex volumes in adolescents with alcohol use disorders: unique gender effects," *Alcoholism: Clinical and Experimental Research,* volume 32 (2008), pp. 386–394.

33. Zailckas, *Smashed,* p. 235.

34. National Center on Addiction and Substance Abuse, *The Formative Years,* p. 25.

35. Stephen E. Gilman and Henry David Abraham, "A longitudinal study of the order of onset of alcohol dependence and major depression," *Drug and Alcohol Dependence,* volume 63 (2001), pp. 277–286.

36. See Beth Steger Moscato, Marcia Russell, Maria Zielezny, and colleagues, "Gender differences in the relation between depressive symptoms and alcohol problems: a longitudinal perspective," *American Journal of Epidemiology,* volume 148 (1977), pp. 966–974. See also J. Wang and S. Patten, "A prospective study of sex-specific effects of major depression on alcohol consumption," *Canadian Journal of Psychiatry,* volume 46 (2001), pp. 422–425; Andrea King, Nancy Bernardy, and Katherina Hauner, "Stressful events, personality, and mood disturbance: gender differences in alcoholics and problem drinkers," *Addictive Behaviors,* volume 28 (2003), pp. 171–187; and J. W. Maag and D. M. Irvin, "Alcohol use and depression among African-American and Caucasian adolescents," *Adolescence,* volume 40 (2005), pp. 87–101.These studies demonstrate that the association between depressed mood and subsequent alcohol abuse is much stronger in women than it is in men. However, this association appears to be much less strong, and the gender valence may be different, when one looks at children rather than teenagers or young adults. In a recent study of 9- to 13-year-olds, depressed mood at the first interview (when the subject was between 9 and 13 years of age) was associated with an increased risk of subsequent alcohol abuse only in boys, not in girls. See Rosa Crum and colleagues, "Is depressed mood in childhood associated with an increased risk for initiation of alcohol use during early adolescence?" *Addictive Behaviors,* volume 33 (2008), pp. 24–40.

37. Jennifer Ahern and colleagues, "'Culture of Drinking' and individual problems with alcohol use," *American Journal of Epidemiology,* volume 167 (2008), pp. 1041–1049.

38. National Household Survey on Drug Abuse, "Low rates of alcohol use among Asian youths," 2002, online at www.oas.samhsa.gov/2k2/AsianYouthAlc/AsianYouthAlc.htm.

39. Zailckas, *Smashed*, pp. 257–258.

40. National Center on Addiction and Substance Abuse, *Women Under the Influence*, p. 46. See also R. T. Rada, "Alcoholism and forcible rape," *American Journal of Psychiatry*, volume 132 (1975), pp. 444–446; and Vaughn Rickert, Roger Vaughan, and Constance Wiemann, "Adolescent dating violence and date rape," *Current Opinion in Obstetrics and Gynecology*, volume 14 (2002), pp. 495–500.

41. Zailckas, *Smashed*, p. 290.

42. Zailckas, p. 335.

43. See, for example, E. M. Pattison and J. Kahan, "The deliberate self-harm syndrome," *American Journal of Psychiatry*, volume 140 (1983), pp. 867–872; and E. M. Pattison and J. Kahan, "Proposal for a distinctive diagnosis: the deliberate self-harm syndrome, DSH," in *Suicide and Life-Threatening Behavior*, volume 14 (1984), pp. 17–35.

44. Patricia Adler and Peter Adler, "The demedicalization of self-injury," *Journal of Contemporary Ethnography*, volume 36 (2007), pp. 537–570.

45. Adler and Adler, "The demedicalization of self-injury," p. 538.

46. Karen Rodham and Keith Hawton, "Epidemiology and phenomenology of nonsuicidal self-injury," in Matthew Nock, ed., *Understanding Nonsuicidal Self-Injury* (Washington, DC: American Psychological Association, 2009), pp. 37–62. A recent survey of girls age 10 to 14 years of age, conducted by researchers at Yale University, found that 56 percent of girls had engaged in nonsuicidal self-injury at some point in their life; 36 percent of girls had engaged in nonsuicidal self-injury within the past year. See Lori Hilt, Christine Cha, and Susan Nolen-Hoeksema, *Journal of Consulting and Clinical Psychology*, volume 76 (2008), pp. 63–71.

47. Marina Khidekel, "The dark secret I could never tell anyone: *Seventeen* investigates the troubling cutting trend," *Seventeen* magazine, September 2009, pp. 194–197.

48. For a review of fourteen studies that examined gender differences in the propensity to nonsuicidal self-injury, see Rodham and Hawton, "Epidemiology and phenomenology of nonsuicidal self-injury," especially pp. 49–54 and table 3.4. For more information on the methodological complexities of estimating the true prevalence of non-suicidal self-injury, in girls *and* boys, please go to www.leonardsax.com, click on "Girls on the Edge" and follow the link to "chapter 3 notes."

49. For example, in a recent survey of Canadian youth 14 to 21 years of age, Mary Nixon and colleagues reported an overall prevalence of nonsuicidal self-injury of 17 percent. They didn't even mention, in their summary of their paper, that females were much more likely than males to hurt themselves this way. But their data show that 24 percent of females in their study were cutting themselves or otherwise deliberately harming themselves, compared with 8 percent of the males (there were also more females than males in the study overall, which is why the overall rate was closer to the female rate than a simple average of the two rates). The citation is Nixon and colleagues, "Nonsuicidal self-harm in youth: a population-based survey," *Canadian Medical Association Journal*, volume 178 (2008), pp. 306–312.

50. Levine, *The Price of Privilege*, p. 3.

51. For a recent review of the research linking child abuse to nonsuicidal self-injury, see Tuppett Yates, "Developmental pathways from child maltreatment to nonsuicidal self-injury," in Nock, *Understanding Nonsuicidal Self-Injury*, pp. 117–137.

52. This quote is from Favazza's introduction to Marilee Strong, *A Bright Red Scream: Self-mutilation and the Language of Pain* (New York: Penguin, 1998), p. xiv.

53. Favazza, p. xii.

54. For a recent review of this evidence, see Leo Sher and Barbara Stanley, "Biological models of nonsuicidal self-injury," in Nock, *Understanding Nonsuicidal Self-Injury*, especially the section entitled "Role of opioids in nonsuicidal self-injury," pp. 100–103. See Leo Sher and Barbara Stanley, "The role of endogenous opioids in the pathophysiology of self-injurious and suicidal behavior," *Archives of Suicide Research*, volume 12 (2008), pp. 299–308.

55. In his introduction in Strong, *A Bright Red Scream*, Dr. Favazza observes that "the normal course [of a girl cutting herself] is ten to fifteen years, during which the self-mutilation is interspersed with periods of total quiescence and with [other] impulsive behaviors such as eating disorders, alcohol and substance abuse, and kleptomania" (p. xii).

56. Shana Ross, Nancy Heath, and Jessica Toste, "Non-suicidal self-injury and eating pathology in high school students," *American Journal of Orthopsychiatry,* volume 79 (2009), pp. 83–92.

57. Mark Taylor, "End the university as we know it," *New York Times,* April 26, 2009, online at www.nytimes.com/2009/04/27/opinion/27taylor.html.

58. Quoted in Funk, *Supergirls Speak Out,* p. 44.

CHAPTER 4

1. Sandra Steingraber, *The Falling Age of Puberty in U. S. Girls: What We Know, What We Need to Know* (San Francisco: Breast Cancer Fund, 2007) p. 10; online at www.breastcancerfund .org/site/c.kwKXLdPaE/b.3291891/k.3AE5/Falling_Age_of_Puberty_PDF_Download.htm.

2. For the original article communicating the new guidelines, see Paul Kaplowitz and Sharon Oberfield, "Reexamination of the age limit for defining when puberty is precocious in girls in the United States," *Pediatrics,* volume 104 (1999), pp. 936–941. For an introduction to the controversy regarding this redefinition of precocious puberty, see Arnold Slyper, "The pubertal timing controversy in the USA, and a review of possible causative factors for the advance in timing of onset of puberty," *Clinical Endocrinology,* volume 65 (2006), pp. 1–8, online at www3.interscience.wiley.com/cgi-bin/fulltext/ 118581978/PDFSTART.

3. Steingraber, *The Falling Age of Puberty in U. S. Girls,* p. 10.

4. Steingraber, pp. 21, 22.

5. Dennis M. Styne and Melvin M. Grumbach, "Puberty: Ontogeny, Neuroendocrinology, Physiology, and Disorders," in Henry Kronenberg and colleagues, eds., *Williams Textbook of Endocrinology,* 11th ed. (Philadelphia: Saunders Elsevier, 2008), especially pp. 969–974.

6. See, for example, Jacqueline Johnson and Elissa Newport, "Critical period effects in second language learning: the influence of maturational state on the acquisition of English as a second language," *Cognitive Psychology,* volume 21 (1989), pp. 60–99.

7. See, for example, Eduardo Mercado, "Neural and cognitive plasticity: from maps to minds," *Psychological Bulletin,* volume 134 (2008), pp. 109–137; and C. S. Green and D. Bavelier, "Exercising your brain: a review of human brain plasticity and training-induced learning," *Psychology and Aging,* volume 23 (2008), pp. 692–701.

8. Steingraber, *The Falling Age of Puberty in U. S. Girls,* p. 16. For more on the trade-offs of puberty with regard to brain plasticity, see Cheryl Sisk and Julia Zehr, "Pubertal hormones organize the adolescent brain and behavior," *Frontiers in Neuroendocrinology,* volume 26 (2005), pp. 163–174; E. I. Ahmed, Julia Zehr, Cheryl Sisk, and colleagues, "Pubertal hormones modulate the addition of new cells to sexually dimorphic brain regions," *Nature Neuroscience,* volume 11 (2008), pp. 995–997; and A. Joon Yun, Kimberly A. Bazar, and Patrick Y. Lee, "Pineal attrition, loss of cognitive plasticity, and onset of puberty during the teen years: is it a modern maladaptation exposed by evolutionary displacement?" *Medical Hypotheses,* volume 63 (2004), pp. 939–950.

9. William Wordsworth, "Intimations of Immortality from Recollections of Early Childhood," written between 1802 and 1804.

10. Sarah Kate Bearman, Katherine Presnell, Erin Martinez, and Eric Stice, "The skinny on body dissatisfaction: a longitudinal study of adolescent girls and boys," *Journal of Youth and Adolescence,* volume 35 (2006), pp. 229–241.

11. Tamara Vallido, Debra Jackson, and Louise O'Brien, "Mad, sad, and hormonal: the gendered nature of adolescent sleep disturbance," *Journal of Child Health Care,* volume 13 (2009), pp. 7–18.

12. See, for example, Lars Wichstrom, "The emergence of gender differences in depressed mood during adolescence: the role of intensified gender socialization," *Developmental Psychology,* volume 35 (1999), pp. 232–245.

13. For more on this point, see chapter 5 of my book *Boys Adrift.* In particular, boys who are *later* to mature appear to be at greater risk, compared to boys who mature on time. See, for example, Julia Graber, John Seeley, Jeanne Brooks-Gunn, and Peter Lewinsohn, "Is pubertal timing associated with psychopathology in young adulthood?" *Journal of the American Academy of Child and Adolescent Psychiatry,* volume 43 (2004), pp. 718–726. In another report, investigators found that boys who reached puberty earlier than average were actually more likely to be successful in their careers as

adults and more likely to have satisfying marriages; the early-maturing boys were *not* more likely than other boys to smoke cigarettes or drink alcohol as adults. The study authors were Keiko Taga, Charlotte Markey, and Howard Friedman, "A longitudinal investigation of associations between boys' pubertal timing and adult behavioral health and well-being," *Journal of Youth and Adolescence*, volume 35 (2006), pp. 401–411.

14. Vaughn Rickert and Constance Wiemann, "Date rape among adolescents and young adults," *Journal of Pediatric and Adolescent Gynecology*, volume 11 (1998), pp. 167–175; Judith Vicary, Linda Klingaman, and William Harkness, "Risk factors associated with date rape and sexual assault of adolescent girls," *Journal of Adolescence*, volume 18 (1995), pp. 289–306.

15. Laurie Schwab Zabin, Mark Emerson, and David Rowland, "Childhood sexual abuse and early menarche: the direction of their relationship and its implications," *Journal of Adolescent Health*, volume 36 (2005), pp. 393–400.

16. The seminal study in this regard was published by researchers at Columbia University: Julia Graber and colleagues, "Prediction of eating problems: an 8-year study of adolescent girls," *Developmental Psychology*, volume 30 (1994), pp. 823–834. A similar pattern has been reported in Israel by Dorit Kaluski, Barnabas Natamba, Rebecca Goldsmith, and colleagues, "Determinants of disordered eating behaviors among Israeli adolescent girls," *Eating Disorders*, volume 16 (2008), pp. 146–159; and in Italy by Elena Tenconi, Noemi Lunardi, Tatiana Zanetti, and colleagues, "Predictors of binge eating in restrictive anorexia nervosa patients in Italy," *Journal of Nervous and Mental Disease*, volume 194 (2006), pp. 712–715. However, a study from the University of Texas failed to demonstrate an association between early menarche and increased risk of eating disorders. Erin Stice, Katherine Presnell, and Sarah Kate Bearman, "Relation of early menarche to depression, eating disorders, substance abuse, and comorbid psychopathology among adolescent girls," *Developmental Psychology*, volume 37 (2001), pp. 608–619, finds that though early menarche was associated with increased risk of depression and substance abuse, it was not associated with increased risk of eating disorders. These researchers conjecture that earlier studies from the United States showing such a relationship involved girls who were early maturers at a time when early puberty was a kind of "deviance" (p. 616). Now that so many girls are going through puberty early, it's no longer unusual, and hence no longer associated with an increased risk of eating disorders—or so these authors assert.

17. The association between early onset of puberty and subsequent risk of smoking and alcohol abuse, for girls, is strong. See, for example, (in chronological order, most recent first): Maria Jaszyna-Gasior, Jennifer Schroeder, Elissa Thorner, and colleagues, "Age at menarche and weight concerns in relation to smoking trajectory and dependence among adolescent girls," *Addictive Behaviors*, volume 34 (2009), pp. 92–95; Erika Westling, Judy Andrews, Sarah Hampson, and Missy Peterson, "Pubertal timing and substance use: the effects of gender, parental monitoring and deviant peers," *Journal of Adolescent Health*, volume 42 (2008), pp. 555–563; Grete Bratberg, Tom Nilsen, and colleagues, "Sexual maturation in early adolescence and alcohol drinking and cigarette smoking in late adolescence," *European Journal of Pediatrics*, volume 164 (2005), pp. 621–625; Stephanie Lanza and Linda Collins, "Pubertal timing and the onset of substance use in females during early adolescence," *Prevention Science*, volume 3 (2002), pp. 69–82; Margit Wiesner and Angela Ittel, "Relations of pubertal timing and depressive symptoms to substance use in early adolescence," *Journal of Early Adolescence*, volume 22 (2002), pp. 5–23; and Erin Stice, Katherine Presnell, and Sarah Kate Bearman, "Relation of early menarche to depression, eating disorders, substance abuse, and comorbid psychopathology among adolescent girls," *Developmental Psychology*, volume 37 (2001), pp. 608–619.

18. See, for example, Sarah Lynne, Julia Graber, Tracy Nichols, and colleagues, "Links between pubertal timing, peer influences, and externalizing behaviors among urban students followed through middle school," *Journal of Adolescent Health*, volume 40 (2007), pp. e7–e13; also Maria Celio, Niranjan Karnik, and Hans Steiner, "Early maturation as a risk factor for aggression and delinquency in adolescent girls: a review," *International Journal of Clinical Practice*, volume 60 (2006), pp. 1254–1262; and Andrea Waylen and Dieter Wolke, "Sex 'n' drugs 'n' rock 'n' roll: the meaning and social consequences of pubertal timing," *European Journal of Endocrinology*, volume 151 (2004), pp. 151–159.

19. Shannon Cavanagh, Catherine Riegle-Crumb, and Robert Crosnoe, "Puberty and the education of girls," *Social Psychology Quarterly*, volume 70 (2007), pp. 186–198.

20. Julia Graber, John Seeley, Jeanne Brooks-Gunn, and Peter Lewinsohn, "Is pubertal timing associated with psychopathology in young adulthood?" pp. 718–726. See also Riittakerttu Kaltiala-Heino and colleagues, "Early puberty is associated with mental health problems in middle adolescence," *Social Science and Medicine,* volume 57 (2003), pp. 1055–1064.

21. Karen Remsberg, Ellen Demerath, and colleagues, "Early menarche and the development of cardiovascular disease risk factors in adolescent girls: the Fels Longitudinal Study," *Journal of Clinical Endocrinology and Metabolism,* volume 90 (2005), pp. 2718–2724, online at http://jcem .endojournals.org/cgi/content/full/90/5/2718.

22. Many studies have demonstrated that an earlier onset of menarche is associated with an increased risk of breast cancer. See, for example, William Anderson and colleagues, "Estimating age-specific breast cancer risks: a descriptive tool to identify age interactions," *Cancer Causes and Control,* volume 18 (2007), pp. 439–447; Françoise Clavel-Chapelon and colleagues, "Differential effects of reproductive factors on the risk of pre- and postmenopausal breast cancer: results from a large cohort of French women," *British Journal of Cancer,* volume 86 (2002), pp. 723–727, online at www.pub medcentral.nih.gov/articlerender.fcgi?tool=pubmed&pubmedid=11875733; Motoki Iwasaki and colleagues, "Role and impact of menstrual and reproductive factors on breast cancer risk in Japan," *European Journal of Cancer Prevention,* volume 16 (2007), pp. 116–123; and Sumitra Shantakumar and colleagues, "Reproductive factors and breast cancer risk among older women," *Breast Cancer Research and Treatment,* volume 102 (2007), pp. 365–374. In addition, the tempo of puberty may be a factor. If a girl begins to develop breasts at age 8 but doesn't experience menarche until age 12, she has created a four-year-wide "estrogen window," which may predispose her to developing breast cancer as an adult. In one study of twin sisters, investigators found that the twin who began breast development first had a risk of developing breast cancer *five times higher* than the twin who began breast development later. The reference is Ann Hamilton and Thomas Mack, "Puberty and genetic susceptibility to breast cancer in a case-control study in twins," *New England Journal of Medicine,* volume 348 (2003), pp. 2313–2322, online at http://content.nejm.org/cgi/content/full/348/23/2313.

23. Chantal C. Orgéas and colleagues, "The influence of menstrual risk factors on tumor characteristics and survival in postmenopausal breast cancer," *Breast Cancer Research,* volume 10 (2008), online at www.pubmedcentral.nih.gov/articlerender.fcgi?tool=pubmed&pubmedid=19087323.

24. The prevalence of overweight among children roughly tripled between 1977 and 2007. See the CDC's article, "Childhood Overweight and Obesity," www.cdc.gov/obesity/childhood/index.html.

25. David Freedman, Laura Kettel Khan, Mary Serdula, and colleagues, "Relation of age at menarche to race, time period, and anthropometric dimensions: the Bogalusa heart study," *Pediatrics,* volume 110 (2002), p. e43.

26. Kirsten Krahnstoever Davison, Elizabeth Susman, and Leann Lipps Birch, "Percent body fat at age 5 predicts earlier pubertal development among girls at age 9," *Pediatrics,* volume 111 (2003), pp. 815–821.

27. Joyce Lee, Danielle Appugliese, Niko Kaciroti, and colleagues, "Weight status in young girls and the onset of puberty," *Pediatrics,* volume 119 (2007), pp. e624–e630.

28. Lise Aksglaede, Kaspar Sørensen, Jørgen H. Petersen, Niels E. Skakkebæk, and Anders Juul, "Recent decline in age at breast development: the Copenhagen puberty study," *Pediatrics,* volume 123 (2009), pp. e932–939. These researchers were careful to ensure that the girls studied in 2006–2008 had the same demographics—racial, ethnic, and socioeconomic status—as the girls in the early 1990s cohort. The quote comes from p. e935.

29. Arnold Slyper, "The pubertal timing controversy in the USA, and a review of possible causative factors for the advance in timing of onset of puberty," *Clinical Endocrinology,* volume 65 (2006), pp. 1–8.

30. Aksglaede and colleagues, "Recent decline in age at breast development: the Copenhagen puberty study," p. e935.

31. To be sure, there are occasional accounts of environmental toxins having masculinizing rather than feminizing effects. See, for example, L. G. Parks, C. S. Lambright, and colleagues, "Masculinization of female mosquitofish in Kraft mill effluent-contaminated Fenholloway River water is associated with androgen receptor agonist activity," *Toxicological Sciences,* volume 62 (2001), pp. 257–267, online at http://toxsci.oxfordjournals.org/cgi/content/full/62/2/257. As the authors of this

article observe, reports of masculinizing effects attributable to environmental toxins are much less common than reports of feminizing effects.

32. Miquel Porta, "Persistent organic pollutants and the burden of diabetes," *Lancet,* volume 368 (2006), pp. 558–599.

33. Felix Grün and Bruce Blumberg, "Endocrine disrupters as obesogens," *Molecular and Cellular Endocrinology,* volume 304 (2009), pp. 19–29.

34. Styne and Grumbach, "Puberty: Ontogeny, Neuroendocrinology, Physiology, and Disorders," p. 973.

35. Anne-Simone Parent, Grete Teilmann, and colleagues, "The timing of normal puberty and the age limits of sexual precocity: variations around the world, secular trends, and changes after migration," *Endocrine Reviews,* volume 24 (2003), pp. 668–693, online at http://edrv.endojournals.org/cgi/content/full/24/5/668. See also Anders Juul and colleagues, "Pubertal development in Danish children: comparison of recent European and U.S. data," *International Journal of Andrology,* volume 29 (2005), pp. 247–255.

36. Christine de Ridder and colleagues, "Dietary habits, sexual maturation, and plasma hormones in pubertal girls: a longitudinal study," *American Journal of Clinical Nutrition,* volume 54 (1991), pp. 805–813. See also Malcolm Koo and colleagues, "A cohort study of dietary fibre intake and menarche," *Public Health Nutrition,* volume 5 (2002), pp. 353–360.

37. See, for example, Rachel Tolbert Kimbro, Jeanne Brooks-Gunn, and Sara McLanahan, "Racial and ethnic differentials in overweight and obesity among 3-year-old children," *American Journal of Public Health,* volume 97 (2007), pp. 298–305, online at www.ajph.org/cgi/reprint/97/2/298. Curiously, these authors found that "having been breast-fed for at least 6 months significantly decreased the odds of overweight or obesity among children of obese mothers but did not significantly affect outcomes among children of nonobese mothers."

38. Sandra Steingraber, *The Falling Age of Puberty in U. S. Girls,* p. 47.

39. Elaine Burridge, "Bisphenol A: product profile," *European Chemical News,* April 14, 2003, p. 17.

40. Specifically, they found that though BPA can act like a female hormone in concentrations as low as 0.23 parts per *trillion,* it is commonly found in human tissues in concentrations of 0.3 to 4.4 parts per *billion.* See Frederick S. vom Saal and colleagues, "Chapel Hill bisphenol A expert panel consensus statement: integration of mechanisms, effects in animals and potential to impact human health at current levels of exposure," *Reproductive Toxicology,* volume 24 (2007), pp. 131–138.

41. Antonia Calafat and colleagues, "Exposure of the U.S. population to bisphenol A and 4-tertiary-octylphenol," *Environmental Health Perspectives,* volume 116 (2008), pp. 39–44.

42. Vom Saal and colleagues, "Chapel Hill bisphenol A expert panel consensus statement," p. 137.

43. Out of more than one hundred studies on the possible risks of BPA, the September 2008 FDA report (described in the next reference) cited only two studies—both funded by the plastics industry—that failed to demonstrate risk. These two industry-funded studies were subject to systemic bias. See John Peterson Myers and colleagues, "Why public health agencies cannot depend on good laboratory practices as a criterion for selecting data: the case of bisphenol A," *Environmental Health Perspectives,* volume 117 (2009), pp. 309–315, online at www.ehponline.org/members/2008/0800173/0800173.pdf.

44. For example, according to one industry website, www.bisphenol-a.org, "The weight of scientific evidence clearly supports the safety of BPA and provides strong reassurance that there is no basis for human health concerns from exposure to low doses of BPA." Industry websites defending the safety of BPA usually place great weight on a report published by the Food and Drug Administration (FDA) toward the very end of the Bush administration, in September 2008. However, that report received wide criticism for relying on just two industry-funded studies while ignoring more than a hundred studies published in peer-reviewed journals that demonstrated contrary findings. For more on efforts by the plastics industry to obstruct government action on BPA, see Lindsey Layton "Strategy being devised to protect use of BPA: groups hope to block ban of chemical," *Washington Post,* May 31, 2009, online at www.washingtonpost.com/wp-dyn/content/article/2009/05/30/AR2009053002121.html?hpid=topnews. In January 2010, the FDA officially changed its policy on BPA, stating that the agency now has "some concern about the potential effects of BPA on the brain, behavior and prostate gland of fetuses, infants and children," and announced $30 million in new research on the health effects of BPA. See Denise Grady, "F.D.A. concerned about substance in food

packaging," *New York Times*, January 15, 2010, www.nytimes.com/2010/01/16/health/16plastic .html?em.

45. Meg Kissinger, "Bill would ban BPA in baby products, [Wisconsin] would be third to prohibit chemical," *Wisconsin Journal-Sentinel*, June 14, 2009, online at www.jsonline.com/watchdog/watch dogreports/47482847.html.

46. Environmental Working Group, "Bisphenol A: Toxic plastics chemical in canned food," March 5, 2007, online at http://www.ewg.org/reports/bisphenola.

47. Edwin Aguirre, "Reports cite health risks from BPA exposure," University of Massachusetts Lowell eNews, December 12, 2008, www.uml.edu/Media/eNews/New_BPA_study.html.

48. See, for example, Ivelisse Colón and colleagues, "Identification of phthalate esters in the serum of young Puerto Rican girls with premature breast development," *Environmental Health Perspectives*, volume 108 (2000), pp. 895–900. See also Shanna Swan and colleagues, "Decrease in anogenital distance among male infants with prenatal phthalate exposure," *Environmental Health Perspectives*, volume 113 (2005), pp. 1056–1061; and Felix Grün and Bruce Blumberg, "Endocrine disruptors as obesogens," *Molecular and Cellular Endocrinology*, volume 304 (2009), pp. 19–29.

49. Sheela Sathyanarayana, Catherine J. Karr, Paula Lozano, and colleagues, "Baby care products: possible sources of infant phthalate exposure," *Pediatrics*, volume 121 (2008), pp. e260–e268. The quotations come from the "Conclusions" section on p. e266.

50. Elizabeth Weise, "California to ban phthalates in baby products," *USA Today*, October 16, 2007, www.usatoday.com/news/health/2007–10–15-toxic-toys_N.htm.

51. Please see my paper, "Polyethylene Terephthalate May Yield Endocrine Disruptors," *Environmental Health Perspectives*, full text online at www.leonardsax.com/PET.pdf.

52. P. Montuori and colleagues, "Assessing human exposure to phthalic acid and phthalate esters from mineral water stored in polyethylene terephthalate and glass bottles," *Food Additives and Contaminants, Part A: Chemistry, analysis, control, exposure, and risk assessment*, volume 25 (2008), pp. 511–518.

53. Again, please see my paper, "Polyethylene Terephthalate May Yield Endocrine Disruptors," *Environmental Health Perspectives*, for an overview of how temperature affects the leaching of phthalates from PET bottles. See also Mehdi Farhoodi and colleagues, "Effect of environmental conditions on the migration of di(2-ethylhexyl)phthalate from PET bottles into yogurt drinks: influence of time, temperature, and food simulant," *Arabian Journal for Science and Engineering*, volume 33 (2008), pp. 279–288.

54. Neil Osterwell, "Local and national legislation banning phthalates and bisphenol A considered," *Medscape Medical News*, July 7, 2008, www.medscape.com/viewarticle/577208_print.

55. Martin Wagner and Jörg Oehlmann, "Endocrine disruptors in bottled mineral water: total estrogenic burden and migration from plastic bottles," *Environmental Science and Pollution Research*, volume 16 (2009), pp. 278–286. The quotes (including the comment about "the tip of the iceberg") are from p. 284.

56. Michael Pollan, *In Defense of Food: An Eater's Manifesto* (New York: Penguin, 2008).

57. D. A. Pape-Zambito and colleagues, "Concentrations of 17-Estradiol in Holstein Whole Milk," *Journal of Dairy Science*, volume 90 (2007), pp. 3308–3313.

58. Shanthy Bowman, "Beverage choices of young females: changes and impact on nutrient intakes," *Journal of the American Dietetic Association*, volume 102 (2002), pp. 1234–1239.

59. For recent research and reviews on this topic, see Robert Matchock and Elizabeth Susman, "Family composition and menarcheal age: anti-inbreeding strategies," *American Journal of Human Biology*, volume 18 (2006), pp. 481–491; Jacqueline Tither and Bruce Ellis, "Impact of fathers on daughters' age at menarche: a genetically and environmentally controlled sibling study," *Developmental Psychology*, volume 44 (2008), pp. 1409–1420; and Jay Belsky and colleagues, "Family rearing antecedents of pubertal timing," *Child Development*, volume 78 (2007), pp. 1302–1321.

60. David Popenoe, *Life Without Father* (Cambridge, MA: Harvard University Press, 1996), p. 3.

61. Lawrence Berger and colleagues, "Parenting practices of resident fathers: the role of marital and biological ties," *Journal of Marriage and the Family*, volume 70 (2008), pp. 625–639.

62. The first report documenting earlier onset of menarche in girls who grew up without their father was reported by B. Jones and colleagues, "Factors influencing the age of menarche in a lower

socio-economic group in Melbourne," *Medical Journal of Australia,* volume 2 (1972), pp. 533–535. For an extensive review of this literature, see Bruce Ellis, "Timing of pubertal maturation in girls," *Psychological Bulletin,* volume 130 (2004), pp. 920–958.

63. See, for example, Bruce Ellis and colleagues, "Does father absence place daughters at special risk for early sexual activity and teenage pregnancy?" *Child Development,* volume 74 (2003), pp. 801–821.

64. See, for example, Bruce Ellis and Marilyn Essex, "Family environments, adrenarche, and sexual maturation: a longitudinal test of a life history model," *Child Development,* volume 78 (2007), pp. 1799–1817. However, Matchock and Susman found no effect of socioeconomic status in their retrospective study of roughly 2,000 young women, "Family composition and menarcheal age," pp. 481–491. Girls who grow up in low-income households in the United States typically are heavier than girls from more affluent households (see, e.g., Kimbro, Brooks-Gunn, and McLanahan, "Racial and ethnic differentials in overweight and obesity among 3-year-old children," pp. 298–305). As we have seen, girls who are overweight are also more likely to go through puberty earlier. So it's possible that the finding, reported only by some researchers, that girls from low-income families go through puberty earlier, may be confounded by the fact that girls from low-income families are more likely to be overweight.

65. See, for example, Jacqueline Tither and Bruce Ellis, "Impact of fathers on daughters' age at menarche: a genetically and environmentally controlled sibling study," pp. 1409–1420.

66. For example, Jay Belsky and colleagues, "Childhood experience, interpersonal development, and reproductive strategy," *Child Development,* volume 62 (1991), pp. 647–670, suggest that girls feel more insecure if they grow up without their fathers, and that insecurity leads them to eat more, which makes them get fat, and thereby accelerates puberty (p. 652).

67. For example, Matchock and Susman, "Family composition and menarcheal age," pp. 481–491, found that "10.3% of the father-absent girls described themselves as overweight while growing up, which was not significantly different from the 10.0% of father-present girls who described themselves as overweight" (p. 490).

68. See Bruce Ellis and colleagues, "Quality of early family relationships and individual differences in the timing of pubertal maturation in girls," *Journal of Personality and Social Psychology,* volume 77 (1999), pp. 387–401.

69. Laurie Schwab Zabin, Mark Emerson, and David Rowland, "Childhood sexual abuse and early menarche: the direction of their relationship and its implications," *Journal of Adolescent Health,* volume 36 (2005), pp. 393–400.

70. Jay Belsky and colleagues, "Family rearing antecedents of pubertal timing," *Child Development,* volume 78 (2007), pp. 1302–1321; see also Tither and Ellis, "Impact of fathers on daughters' age at menarche"; and also S. R. Jaffee, Avshalom Caspi, and colleagues, "Life with (or without) father: the benefits of living with two biological parents depend on the father's antisocial behavior," *Child Development,* volume 74 (2003), pp. 109–126.

71. Bruce Ellis and Judy Garber found that the presence of a stepfather was associated with *earlier* puberty in girls. See their paper "Psychosocial antecedents of variation in girls' pubertal timing: maternal depression, stepfather presence, and marital and family stress," *Child Development,* volume 71 (2003), pp. 485–501. However, Anthony Bogaert found no association between stepfather presence and early puberty in his sample of American girls, "Age at puberty and father absence in a national probability sample," *Journal of Adolescence,* volume 28 (2005), pp. 541–546. The lack of association in Bogaert's study still demonstrates that the presence of the stepfather is not able to compensate, on this parameter, for the absence of the biological father. Likewise, Matchock and Susman, "Family composition and menarcheal age," also found no association between early puberty in girls and the presence or absence of the stepfather; whereas girls raised without their *biological* father went through puberty earlier than girls raised with their *biological* father, regardless of whether a stepfather was present. Matchock and Susman were expecting to replicate the finding reported by Ellis and Garber; they admit that their actual finding, of no effect of stepfather presence on girls who were raised without a biological father, was "surprising" to them (p. 487).

72. For an entertaining introduction to this literature, see Douglas Field's article, "Sex and the secret nerve," *Scientific American Mind,* March 2007, pp. 21–27.

73. For a review of this research, see Mahmood Bhutta, "Sex and the nose: human pheromonal responses," *Journal of the Royal Society of Medicine,* volume 100 (2007), pp. 268–274.

74. John Vandenbergh and colleagues, "Partial isolation of a pheromone accelerating puberty in female mice," *Journal of Reproductive Fertility*, volume 43 (1975), pp. 515–523. See also J. R. Lombardi and John Vandenbergh, "Pheromonally induced sexual maturation in females: regulation by the social environment of the male," *Science*, volume 196 (1977), pp. 545–546.

75. See John Hoogland, "Prairie dogs avoid extreme inbreeding," *Science*, volume 215 (1982), pp. 1639–1641. A similar phenomenon was reported in marmoset monkeys; see S. Evans and J. Hodges, "Reproductive status of adult daughters in family groups of common marmosets," *Folia Primatologica*, volume 42 (1984), pp. 127–133.

76. Bhutta, "Sex and the nose," p. 271.

77. Matchock and Susman, "Family composition and menarcheal age."

78. Quoted in Mairi McLeod, "Her father's daughter," *New Scientist*, February 10, 2007.

79. Bettina Pause and colleagues, "The human brain is a detector of chemosensorily transmitted HLA-class I-similarity in same- and opposite-sex relations," *Proceedings of the Royal Society*, volume 273 (2006), pp. 471–478, online at http://rspb.royalsocietypublishing.org/content/273/1585/471.long.

80. Magda Vandeloo, Liesbeth Bruckers, and Jaak Janssens, "Effects of lifestyle on the onset of puberty as determinant for breast cancer," *European Journal of Cancer Prevention*, volume 16 (2007), pp. 17–25.

81. Steingraber, *The Falling Age of Puberty in U. S. Girls*, p. 48.

82. Styne and Grumbach, "Puberty: Ontogeny, Neuroendocrinology, Physiology, and Disorders," p. 1051.

83. Styne and Grumbach, p. 1030.

84. This was the conclusion of the 2009 consensus panel on the use of GnRH analogs. The panel based their conclusion primarily on two studies, one of which was authored by the lead author on the consensus panel, Jean-Claude Carel. See Liora Lazar, Anna Padoa, and Moshe Phillip, "Growth pattern and final height after cessation of gonadotropin-suppressive therapy in girls with central sexual precocity," *Journal of Clinical Endocrinology and Metabolism*, volume 92 (2007), pp. 3483–3489, online at http://jcem.endojournals.org/cgi/content/full/92/9/3483; and Jean-Claude Carel and colleagues, "Final height after long-term treatment with triptorelin slow-release for central precocious puberty: importance of statural growth after interruption of treatment," *Journal of Clinical Endocrinology and Metabolism*, volume 84 (1999), pp. 1973–1978. Similar findings were reported in a recent study of 87 girls who were treated for an average of four years, and then followed after treatment for an average of 10 years; see Anna Maria Pasquino and colleagues, "Long-term observation of 87 girls with idiopathic central precocious puberty treated with gonadotropin-releasing hormone analogs: impact on adult height, body mass index, bone mineral content, and reproductive function," *Journal of Clinical Endocrinology and Metabolism*, volume 93 (2008), pp. 190–195, online at http://jcem.endojournals.org/cgi/content/full/93/1/190.

85. Jean-Claude Carel and colleagues, "Consensus statement on the use of gonadotropin-releasing hormone analogs in children," *Pediatrics*, volume 123 (2009), pp. e752–e762, online at http://pediatrics.aappublications.org/cgi/content/full/123/4/e752.

CHAPTER 5

1. For an overview of some of the questions involved in any investigation of the efficacy of playing music to babies *in utero* see Robert Abrams and Kenneth Gerhardt, "The acoustic environment and physiological responses of the fetus," *Journal of Perinatalogy*, volume 20 (2000), pp. S30–S35, online at www.nature.com/jp/journal/v20/n1s/pdf/7200445a.pdf. There are a few anecdotal reports suggesting that babies whose mothers played music to them *in utero* enjoy some advantage compared with mothers who didn't play music to their babies *in utero*. But that doesn't tell us much. Mothers who play music to their babies *in utero* tend to be more educated and more affluent, compared with mothers who don't. Babies born to better-educated and more affluent mothers enjoy many advantages compared with babies born to less-educated, less affluent mothers. In order to settle this question, one would have to randomly assign pregnant mothers to play music to their babies in the womb, or not. Even if one could get permission from an Institutional Review Board to do such a study, it's hard to imagine how one would recruit mothers to participate. Mothers who believe in the benefits

of playing music wouldn't sign up, because they wouldn't want to risk being randomly assigned to the no-music group. Mothers who don't believe in the benefits wouldn't sign up either, because they wouldn't want to be bothered with playing music to their baby. And even if one managed to recruit a large cohort of scientifically-minded pregnant women willing to play music or not based on a random assignment, one would have to follow their babies for many years to establish whether a difference existed. In theory, such an experiment is possible, but I'm not holding my breath.

2. The program to which I am referring is "Your baby can read!" www.yourbabycan.com. The program was developed by Robert Craig Titzer, who earned his PhD at Indiana University in 1997 studying how well babies understand that a clear surface, such as plastic, can also be solid. This topic is not related to early reading. Dr. Titzer has published no scholarly research on any aspect of his reading program for infants. Instead, he cites his experience teaching his own baby daughter to read. In defense of the program, it should be noted that the company offers a 30-day money back guarantee.

3. For more on the acceleration of the early elementary curriculum between 1980 and 2000, especially with regard to kindergarten, see my article "Reclaiming Kindergarten," *Psychology of Men and Masculinity,* volume 2 (2001), pp. 3–12, available online at www.boysadrift.com/Sax_APA_2001.pdf.

4. See, for example, Ulla Leppanen and colleagues, "Letter knowledge predicts grade 4 reading fluency and reading comprehension," *Learning and Instruction,* volume 18 (2008), pp. 548–564.

5. For an overview of the trends in reading test scores, and a look at the controversy surrounding those trends, see Mary Ann Zehr, "H. S. reformers seize on NAEP scores to help make case," *Education Week,* May 13, 2009, online at www.edweek.org/ew/articles/2009/05/13/31naep-2.h28.html?r=69601591.

6. For more on this point, see Mark Bauerlein, *The Dumbest Generation: How the Digital Age Stupefies Young Americans and Jeopardizes Our Future* (New York: Tarcher, 2008), especially chapter 2.

7. For an introduction to this topic, including the source for the figure of nine minutes a day, see Sunil Iyengar and Mark Bauerlein, "It's not just the schools: leisure time, reading, and the competition for young minds," *Education Week,* April 18, 2007, online at www.edweek.org/ew/articles/2007/04/18/33iyengar.h26.html?r=113372547. Nine minutes a day does *not* include time spent online. As Bauerlein, *The Dumbest Generation,* shows, what teenagers are doing when they are looking at Web pages may be difficult to describe, but it is certainly not "reading" in the sense of reading a text sentence-by-sentence. See especially chapters 3 and 4.

8. I first quoted Rousseau in this context in my 2001 article "Reclaiming Kindergarten."

9. Again, much of the material in this section is taken from my 2001 article, "Reclaiming Kindergarten." For more about the history of Friedrich Froebel and his kindergarten, see Norman Brosterman, *Inventing Kindergarten* (New York: Harry Abrams, 1997).

10. Barbara Beatty, *Preschool Education in America: The Culture of Young Children from the Colonial Era to the Present* (New Haven, CT: Yale University Press, 1997), pp. 60–61.

11. For more evidence supporting this assertion—that children who have extensive outdoor experience early in life are more likely to be engaged and curious learners later on—see Richard Louv, *Last Child in the Woods: Saving Our Children from Nature-deficit Disorder* (Chapel Hill, NC: Algonquin Books, 2005).

12. Ellen Skinner and colleagues, "Individual differences and the development of perceived control," *Monographs of the Society for Research in Child Development,* volume 63 (1998), available for purchase online at www.jstor.org/pss/1166220.

13. See, for example, James Chapman, Robert Lambourne, and Phil Silva, "Some antecedents of academic self-concept: a longitudinal study," *British Journal of Educational Psychology,* volume 60 (1990), pp. 142–152.

14. Donalyn Miller is a sixth-grade teacher who believes strongly in the value of reading aloud to children in sixth grade. See her article "Never Too Old: Reading Aloud to Independent Readers," *Teacher Magazine,* March 10, 2009. Candy Blessing has made a case for reading aloud to high school students: see her article "Reading to kids who are old enough to shave," *School Library Journal,* April 2005, online at http://www.schoollibraryjournal.com/article/CA514023.html.

15. See, for example, Tricia Valeski and Deborah Stipek, "Young children's feelings about school," *Child Development,* volume 72 (2001), pp. 1198–1213.

16. See, for example, Joanna Uhry and Margaret Jo Shepherd, "Teaching phonological recoding to young children with phonological processing deficits," *Learning Disability Quarterly,* volume 20 (1997), pp. 104–125.

17. You can pull up these numbers at the *Education Week* website, www.edweek.org/media/29 nar-c1.pdf.

18. Starting school at age 7 rather than age 5 is certainly only one of several relevant factors that Finland has in place. Another factor no doubt would be the high prestige that public school teachers in Finland enjoy. Teachers in Finland are not paid a great deal more than American teachers are, but the profession of teaching is more highly regarded there than it is here, and teaching-training programs are often more selective in Finland than in North America. For more on this point, see Sandra Stotsky, "In reform, look to Finland, not 21st-century skills," *Education Week,* March 18, 2009, online at www.edweek.org/ew/articles/2009/03/18/25letter-2.h28.html?qs=Finland. See also Sean Cavanagh, "Top-scoring nations share strategies on teachers," *Education Week,* June 30, 2009. This article includes a statement from Timo Lankinen, director general of the Finnish National Board of Education, that fewer than 15 percent of applicants to schools of education in Finland are accepted. In Finland, according to Lankinen, "people dream to be teachers." Neither demographics nor climate appears to explain Finland's supremacy. In terms of the proportion of the population that is Caucasian, in terms of per capita income, and in terms of the climate and the amount of snowfall per year, Finland is a close match to the state of Utah, but Utah is nowhere close to Finland in terms of achievement on international tests. For more on this point, including the Utah-Finland comparison, see Kevin Carey, "Finlandia," December 15, 2008, on the *Education Week* website at www.quickanded.com/2008/12/lessons-from-finland.html.

19. For a review of this research, see Bauerlein, *The Dumbest Generation,* especially chapter 2.

20. To be sure, even a German *Waldkindergarten* (an outdoor kindergarten, with *all* activities taking place outdoors) usually has a run-in shelter for use during thunderstorms, to protect against lightning. But if it's just raining, with no lightning, the kids are outdoors in the rain—properly attired, one hopes. In her book *I Love Dirt!* (Boston: Trumpeter, 2008), author Jennifer Ward provides some great learning activities for kindergarten-age kids in the rain (pp. 36–40) and in the snow (pp. 122–142). The idea that kindergartners may benefit by spending hours outdoors, all year around, is perhaps starting to catch on in the United States. See Liz Leyden, *New York Times,* "For forest kindergartners, class is back to nature, rain, or shine," November 29, 2009, online at www.nytimes.com/2009/11/30/nyregion/30forest.html?_r=1&em.

21. Quoted in Debra Viadero, "New studies suggest why women avoid STEM fields," *Education Week,* June 17, 2009, p. 15.

22. In some cases—e.g., Berenbaum and Hines 1992 (full citation follows)—the researchers gave children a choice of just a few toys to play with. In other cases, investigators interviewed children and/or parents and asked them what kind of toys they prefer. See, for example (in chronological order), Brian Sutton-Smith and Benjamin Rosenberg, "Development of sex differences in play choices during preadolescence," *Child Development,* volume 34 (1963), pp. 119–126; Jane Connor and Lisa Serbin, "Behaviorally based masculine- and feminine-activity preference scales for preschoolers," *Child Development,* volume 48 (1977), pp. 1411–1416; Peter Smith and Linda Daglish, "Sex differences in parent and infant behavior in the home," *Child Development,* volume 48 (1977), pp. 1250–1254; David Perry, Adam White, and Louise Perry, "Does early sex typing result from children's attempts to match their behavior to sex role stereotypes?" *Child Development,* volume 55 (1984), pp. 2114–2121; D. Bruce Carter and Gary Levy, "Cognitive aspects of early sex-role development: the influence of gender schemas on preschoolers' memories and preferences for sex-typed toys and activities," *Child Development,* volume 59 (1988), pp. 782–792; and Sheri Berenbaum and Melissa Hines, "Early androgens are related to childhood sex-typed toy preferences," *Psychological Science,* volume 3 (1992), pp. 203–206.

23. Both figures here are taken from Janice Hassett, Erin Siebert, and Kim Wallen, "Sex differences in rhesus monkey toy preferences parallel those of children," *Hormones and Behavior,* volume 54 (2008), pp. 359–364. For the figure depicting toy preferences of children, Hassett and colleagues drew on data from Berenbaum and Hines, "Early androgens are related to childhood sex-typed toy preferences."

24. Hassett, Siebert, and Wallen, "Sex differences in rhesus monkey toy preferences parallel those of children."

25. There is a principle in logic known as "Occam's Razor," expressed this way by Isaac Newton in the *Principia Mathematica* (1687): "To the same natural effects we must, as far as possible, assign the same causes." Whatever explanation one invokes to explain the fact that male monkeys prefer trucks over dolls should logically be invoked to explain the same main effect in human children. Because the social construction of gender cannot be invoked to explain this finding in monkeys, it cannot (without violating Occam's Razor) be invoked as the primary explanation for this finding in humans.

26. I have borrowed the title of this section from Melissa Hines and Gerianne Alexander, "Monkeys, girls, boys and toys," *Hormones and Behavior,* volume 54 (2008), pp. 478–479.

27. Gerianne Alexander and Melissa Hines, "Sex differences in response to children's toys in non-human primates," *Evolution and Human Behavior,* volume 23 (2002), pp. 467–479.

28. Gerianne Alexander, "An evolutionary perspective of sex-typed toy preferences: pink, blue, and the brain," *Archives of Sexual Behavior,* volume 32 (2003), pp. 7–14.

29. Leslie Ungerleider and Mortimer Mishkin are the neuroscientists most often credited for being the first—in the early 1980s—to recognize explicitly the anatomical distinction between the "what" system and the "where" system. See, for example, their paper (co-written with Kathleen Macko) entitled "Object vision and spatial vision: two cortical pathways," *Trends in Neuroscience,* volume 6 (1983), pp. 414–417.

30. For a more recent review of this literature, see Melvyn Goodale and David Westwood, "An evolving view of duplex vision: separate but interacting cortical pathways for perception and action," *Current Opinion in Neurobiology,* volume 14 (2004), pp. 203–211.

31. Gerianne Alexander, Teresa Wilcox, and Rebecca Woods, "Sex differences in infants' visual interest in toys," *Archives of Sexual Behavior,* volume 38 (2009), pp. 427–433. For more information on sex differences in the vision of babies, see Anna Horwood and Patricia Riddell, "Gender differences in early accommodation and vergence development," *Ophthalmic and Physiological Optics,* volume 28 (2009), pp. 115–126.

32. Katrin Amunts and colleagues, "Gender-specific left-right asymmetries in human visual cortex," *Journal of Neuroscience,* volume 27 (2007), pp. 1356–1364, online at www.jneurosci.org/cgi/content/full/27/6/1356.

33. At most schools of education, it's politically incorrect even to suggest that best practice for teaching the subject areas might be different for girls compared with boys. Two notable exceptions to this unfortunate rule are Stetson University in Deland, Florida, and the University of Nevada at Reno.

34. Recent research suggests that whereas females reach full maturity, in terms of brain development, by about 22 years of age, males do not reach full maturity in terms of brain development until about 30 years of age. For more on this point, see my article "Gender differences in the sequence of brain development," www.education.com/reference/article/Ref_Boys_Girls/.

35. The principal investigator on this study was Professor Linda J. Sax—no relation to me! Emily Arms, Maria Woodruff, Tiffani Riggers, and Kevin Eagan were among the other investigators of the study, published in 2009, titled "Women graduates of single-sex and coeducational high schools," online at www.ncgs.org/researchshowsgirlsschoolgraduateshaveanedge/FINAL%20REPORT.pdf.

36. Joanna Sugden, "Girls get better results at single-sex state schools," *Times* (London), March 18, 2009, www.timesonline.co.uk/tol/news/uk/education/article5927472.ece.

37. James S. Coleman, *The Adolescent Society: The Social Life of the Teenager and Its Impact on Education* (New York: Free Press, 1961), p. 51, emphasis in original.

38. Coleman, *The Adolescent Society*, pp. 51, 52, emphasis in original.

39. Several studies have demonstrated that girls attending girls' schools are less likely to drink alcohol, compared with girls in the same community who attend comparable coed schools. It's hard to do such a study in the United States, because it is difficult to compare girls attending single-sex schools with comparable girls attending comparable coed schools when so few girls here attend single-sex schools. It is possible to do such studies in Ireland and in New Zealand, where single-sex public schools are widely available. See Avshalom Caspi and colleagues, "Unraveling girls' delinquency:

biological, dispositional, and contextual contributions to adolescent misbehavior," *Developmental Psychology,* volume 29 (1993), pp. 19–30. Dr. Caspi is a professor at the University of Wisconsin–Madison who traveled to Dunedin, New Zealand, because in New Zealand, unlike the United States, a large proportion of girls attend single-sex *public* schools, which makes it possible to compare girls attending girls' public schools with girls in the same neighborhood, same demographics, attending coed public schools. See also Joseph Barry, "Alcohol use in post-primary school children," *Irish Medical Journal,* volume 86 (1993), pp. 128–129; and Miriam Curtin, "Smoking and drinking among 15–16-year-old girls: do male peers have an influence?" *Irish Journal of Medical Science,* volume 173 (2004), pp. 191–192. If a single-sex school is not available, there is some evidence that an all-female residential community may confer similar benefits. For example, Carol Boyd and her seven colleagues found that women living in women's dormitories were less likely to engage in binge drinking compared to women at the same university living in coed dormitories. See Boyd and colleagues, "Heavy episodic drinking and its consequences: the protective effects of same-sex, residential living-learning communities for undergraduate women," *Addictive Behaviors,* volume 33 (2008), pp. 987–993. Based on questionnaires distributed in the early 1990s, Professor Henry Wechsler and his colleagues at the Harvard School of Public Health reported in 1998 that women attending women's colleges were much less likely to abuse alcohol, compared to women attending comparable coed colleges; see George Dowdall, Mary Crawford, and Henry Wechsler, "Binge drinking among American college women: a comparison of single-sex and coeducational institutions," *Psychology of Women Quarterly,* volume 22 (1998), pp. 705–715. Just a few years later, Wechsler and his colleagues reported that the difference in alcohol use between women at women's colleges and women at coed colleges practically evaporated during the mid- and late-1990s, ironically the same period during which colleges at least nominally increased their efforts to prevent binge drinking: the article is titled "Trends in college binge drinking during a period of increased prevention efforts," *Journal of American College Health,* volume 50 (2002), pp. 203–217. Wechsler concludes that women now begin their drinking careers much earlier, in high school or middle school rather than at college. Because most American women attend coed schools, and because girls are drinking earlier, most American women today have already established their habits of drinking (or nondrinking) prior to starting college. In other words, attending a women's college is not an effective way of *treating* alcohol abuse, but the all-female environment may be a way to *prevent* alcohol abuse in women who haven't yet begun to drink.

40. There are many anecdotal reports that girls who attend girls' schools are less likely to get pregnant compared with girls at coed schools. For example, at the Young Women's Leadership School in the Harlem neighborhood of New York City, school counselor Chris Farmer told me that only about one girl in 60 at his school has experienced a pregnancy. He estimated that at least one-third of girls at the neighboring coed schools have experienced a pregnancy. That public school in Harlem is a school of choice—girls *choose* to go there—so maybe it's just a selection effect: perhaps girls who opt for a girls' school wouldn't get pregnant even if they attended a coed school. That's a reasonable point, but consider stories like the one from the James Lyng High School in Montreal, 1998 through 2005. Lyng High is a public school serving a low-income neighborhood. Before 1998, roughly 15 to 20 girls at the school used to get pregnant each year; most of those pregnancies ended in abortion. Then the principal, Wayne Commeford, reinvented his school as a "dual academy," with girls on one floor and boys on another. The pregnancy rate dropped to just one or two a year—a factor-of-ten reduction—despite the fact that the same kids were attending the same school. After Commeford retired in 2006, the school reverted to the coeducational format. Grades and test scores at the school immediately plummeted: the school went from a respectable middle ranking of 297 in 2006—a very good ranking for a school serving an impoverished neighborhood—to 473rd (out of 474 total) by 2008. Peter Cowley, the Canadian researcher who documented the drop between 2006 and 2008, said that he went back and double-checked the numbers to make sure that he hadn't made a mistake. In 10 years of ranking Canadian schools in four different provinces, Cowley said he had never seen such an abrupt drop in any school's ranking. See Peggy Curran, "Rankings show troubling trends," *The Gazette* (Montreal), September 20, 2008, online at www2.canada.com/montrealgazette/news/story.html?id=8e767ef6-eb94-419e-9c05-8790569804c0. I wrote to Ms. Curran asking whether she knew whether the teen pregnancy rate likewise has returned to its previous pre-1998 rate of

about 20 pregnancies per year, but I haven't received any response (and the current principal, Craig Olenik, is refusing to speak with the press, according to Curran's article).

41. Jacqueline Granleese and Stephen Joseph, "Self-perception profile of adolescent girls at a single-sex and a mixed-sex school," *Journal of Genetic Psychology,* volume 154 (1993), pp. 525–530.

42. Education of adolescents throughout Europe, Asia, and Africa was single-sex until the mid-twentieth century; North America was unique in the late 19th and early 20th century in that coeducation was the norm rather than the exception in North American public schools. (Prior to 1860, essentially all high schools were single-sex, even in the United States.) For more on the history of coeducation in the United States as contrasted with other countries, see David Tyack and Elisabeth Hansot, *Learning Together: A History of Coeducation in American Public Schools* (New York: Russell Sage Foundation, 1992).

43. For more about best practice for engaging teenage girls in computer science, see the article by Caitlin Kelleher, professor of computer science at Washington University (St. Louis), entitled "Barriers to Programming Engagement," *Advances in Gender and Education,* volume 1 (2009), pp. 5–10, available online at www.mcrcad.org.

44. For more on this point, see Jan Van Hooff and Signe Presuchoft, "Laughter and Smiling," in Frans de Waal and Peter Tyack, eds., *Animal Social Complexity* (Cambridge, MA: Harvard University Press, 2003), pp. 260–287.

45. For more about primate hierarchies, including sex differences in how hierarchies are established and maintained, see Frans de Waal, *Chimpanzee Politics: Power and Sex Among Apes* (Baltimore: Johns Hopkins University Press, 2000).

46. I first wrote about this topic in an article entitled "The unspeakable pleasure: a study of human cruelty," for the magazine *The World & I,* volume 15 (2000), pp. 317–331.

47. For more on the greater concern of girls (on average) with pleasing the teacher, compared with boys, see Eva Pomerantz, Ellen Rydell Altermatt, and Jill Saxon, "Making the grade but feeling distressed: gender differences in academic performance and internal distress," *Journal of Educational Psychology,* volume 94 (2002), pp. 396–404.

CHAPTER 6

1. Quoted in Ying Wushanley, *Playing Nice and Losing: The Struggle for Control of Women's Intercollegiate Athletics, 1960–2000* (Syracuse, NY: Syracuse University Press, 2004), p. xiv.

2. See, for example, Jérôme Barral and colleagues, "Developmental changes in unimanual and bimanual aiming movements," *Developmental Neuropsychology,* volume 29 (2006), pp. 415–429. In 1974 Eleanor Maccoby and Carol Jacklin published an influential book entitled *The Psychology of Sex Differences* (Stanford University Press), in which they asserted that sex differences in spatial ability don't appear until after the onset of puberty. Maccoby and Jacklin suggested that these differences were merely a social construct, reflecting differences in how girls and boys are raised. By the late 1990s it was clear that the social constructionist theory of Maccoby and Jacklin did not fit the facts: sex differences in performance on spatial tasks are firmly in place by 5 years and do not appear to be a function of what kind of games kids are playing. Contrary to the predictions of Maccoby and Jacklin, differences in spatial performance between adult women and men are, if anything, less pronounced than the differences between 8-year-old girls and 8-year-old boys. For a review of the literature leading to our current understanding of the ontogeny of sex differences in spatial performance, see Susan Levine and colleagues, "Early sex differences in spatial skill," *Developmental Psychology,* volume 35 (1999), pp. 940–949.

3. Inger Holm and Nina Vøllestad, "Significant effect of gender on hamstring-to-quadriceps strength ratio and static balance in prepubescent children from 7 to 12 years of age," *American Journal of Sports Medicine,* volume 36 (2008), pp. 2007–2013.

4. See, for example, Jennifer Fredricks and Jacquelynne Eccles, "Children's competence and value beliefs from childhood through adolescence: growth trajectories in two male-sex-typed domains," *Developmental Psychology,* volume 38 (2002), pp. 519–533.

5. Tucker Center for Research on Girls & Women in Sport, *The 2007 Tucker Center Research Report: Developing Physically Active Girls* (Minneapolis: University of Minnesota, 2007), p. 19.

6. Michael Sokolove, *Warrior Girls: Protecting Our Daughters Against the Injury Epidemic in Women's Sports* (New York: Simon & Schuster, 2008), p. 57.

7. Sokolove, *Warrior Girls*, p. 57.

8. Tucker Center, *The 2007 Tucker Center Research Report*, p. 9.

9. Jennifer Fredricks and Jacquelynne Eccles, "Children's competence and value beliefs from childhood through adolescence: growth trajectories in two male-sex-typed domains," pp. 519–533.

10. Tucker Center, p. 10.

11. Stacey Smith, Mary Fry, and colleagues, "The effect of female athletes' perceptions of their coaches' behaviors on their perceptions of the motivational climate," *Journal of Applied Sport Psychology,* volume 17 (2005), pp. 170–177.

12. David Abel and Caroline Louise Cole, "Medford athlete dies at practice," *Boston Globe,* August 10, 2005, online at www.boston.com/news/local/articles/2005/08/10/medford_athlete_dies_at _practice.

13. According to a prepared statement from Ashley's cheerleading coaches, "At cheerleading camp, Ashley was selected a team all-star for consistently completing all the elite stunt sequences taught at the camp." See Megan Tench, "Ashley died in the pursuit of excellence," August 16, 2005, *Boston Globe,* online at www.boston.com/news/local/massachusetts/articles/2005/08/16/ashley_died _in_the_pursuit_of_excellence/.

14. See Megan Tench's article (previous citation).

15. Kathleen Burge, "After cheerleader's death, a closer look at the sport," *Boston Globe,* April 18, 2009, online at www.boston.com/yourtown/news/newton/2009/04/by_kathleen_burge_globe _staff.html. Incidentally, the cheerleader whose death is referred to in the headline of this story was Lauren Chang, who died in 2008, not Ashley Burns.

16. Frederick Mueller and Robert Cantu, *Catastrophic Sports Injury Research: Twenty-sixth Annual Report* (Chapel Hill: University of North Carolina, 2008), available online at www.unc.edu/ depts/nccsi.

17. Burge, "After cheerleader's death, a closer look at the sport."

18. Both quotes in this paragraph come from Burge's article (previous citation).

19. Committee on Sports Medicine and Fitness, American Academy of Pediatrics, "Intensive training and sports specialization in young athletes," *Pediatrics,* volume 106 (2000), pp. 154–157 (emphasis added), online at www.pediatrics.org/cgi/content/full/106/1/154.

20. Council on Sports Medicine and Fitness, American Academy of Pediatrics, "Overuse injuries, overtraining, and burnout in child and adolescent athletes," *Pediatrics,* volume 119 (2007), pp. 1242–1245, online at www.pediatrics.org/cgi/content/full/119/6/1242.

21. Sokolove, *Warrior Girls,* p. 277.

22. Sokolove, p. 281. Emphasis in original.

23. Sokolove, p. 234.

24. Sokolove, p. 211.

25. Tucker Center, *The 2007 Tucker Center Research Report,* p. 12.

26. Likewise, Sokolove, *Warrior Girls* (p. 84), observes that it appears to take a more serious injury to drive women out of military service, compared with men.

27. Holm and Vøllestad, "Significant effect of gender on hamstring-to-quadriceps strength ratio."

28. Thomas Kernozek and colleagues, "Gender differences in lower extremity landing mechanics caused by neuromuscular fatigue," *American Journal of Sports Medicine,* volume 36 (2008), pp. 554–565.

29. Scott Landry, Kelly McKean, and colleagues, "Neuromuscular and lower limb biomechanical differences exist between male and female elite adolescent soccer players during an unanticipated run and crosscut maneuver," *American Journal of Sports Medicine,* volume 35 (2007), pp. 1901–1911.

30. Sally Mountcastle and colleagues, "Gender differences in anterior cruciate ligament injury vary with activity: epidemiology of anterior cruciate ligament injuries in a young, athletic population," *American Journal of Sports Medicine,* volume 35 (2007), pp. 1635–1642.

31. Julie Agel, Elizabeth Arendt, and Boris Bershadsky, "Anterior cruciate ligament injury in National Collegiate Athletic Association basketball and soccer," *American Journal of Sports Medicine,* volume 33 (2005), pp. 524–531.

32. Philippe Neyret and colleagues, "Partial meniscectomy and anterior cruciate ligament rupture in soccer players: a study with a minimum 20-year followup," *American Journal of Sports Medicine*, volume 21 (1993), pp. 455–460.

33. David Swenson and colleagues, "Patterns of recurrent injuries among U.S. high school athletes, 2005–2008," *American Journal of Sports Medicine*, volume 37 (2009), pp. 1586–1593.

34. Running backward is just one part of the complete program. See www.aclprevent.com/pep_replacement.htm for more information.

35. Bert Mandelbaum, Holly Silvers, and colleagues, "Effectiveness of a neuromuscular and proprioceptive training program in preventing anterior cruciate ligament injuries in female athletes: 2-year follow-up," *American Journal of Sports Medicine*, volume 33 (2005), pp. 1003–1010.

36. I first learned of Samantha's story in Michael Sokolove's book *Warrior Girls*, which tells her story through December 2007. I am grateful to Samantha and her mother, Suzanne, for updating me through December 2009.

37. Dan Cohen, "Area girls' lacrosse coaches mostly opposed to helmets," *News-Times* (Danbury, CT), July 18, 2009, online at www.newstimes.com/ci_12868222.

38. Specifically, these investigators found that the overall rate of concussion per 1,000 athlete-exposures was 0.36 in girls' soccer, compared with 0.22 in boys' soccer (0.36 is 60 percent greater than 0.22); the risk was 0.21 in girls' basketball, compared with 0.07 in boys' basketball (0.21 is 300 percent greater than 0.07). See Luke Gessel, Sarah Fields, and colleagues, "Concussions among United States high school and collegiate athletes," *Journal of Athletic Training*, volume 42 (2007), pp. 495–503, available online at www.pubmedcentral.nih.gov/articlerender.fcgi?artid=2140075.

39. Sokolove, *Warrior Girls*, p. 254.

40. See, for example, Rhoshel Lenroot and colleagues, "Sexual dimorphism of brain developmental trajectories during childhood and adolescence," *NeuroImage*, volume 36 (2007), pp. 1065–1073, especially figure 2(d) on page 1068. The lateral ventricles are significantly larger in boys than girls at every age, even at ages 10 through 13—ages at which these authors note the average girl is actually taller than the average boy (see their comment on page 1070).

41. According to the NCAA/Ohio State University study cited above, contact between the head and the soccer ball was associated with concussion in 5,350 girls and in 1,716 boys; see Luke Gessel, Sarah Fields, and colleagues, "Concussions among United States high school and collegiate athletes," pp. 495–503; these specific figures will be found on page 497. Of course, another explanation for this finding might simply be that girls are three times more likely than boys to hit the ball with their heads, but that explanation seems implausible.

42. See, for example, Alexis Colvin and colleagues, "The role of concussion history and gender in recovery from soccer-related concussion," *American Journal of Sports Medicine*, volume 37 (2009), pp. 1699–1704. Her team found that "these differences do not appear to reflect differences in mass between genders" and that "gender appears to be more important than the mass of the player in post-concussive testing."

43. Sokolove, *Warrior Girls*, p. 256.

44. Tucker Center, *The 2007 Tucker Center Research Report*, p. 55.

45. Katherine Gunter and colleagues, "Impact exercise increases BMC [bone mineral content] during growth: an 8-year longitudinal study," *Journal of Bone and Mineral Research*, volume 23 (2008), pp. 986–993.

46. Kerry McKelvie and colleagues, "A school-based exercise intervention elicits substantial bone health benefits: a 2-year randomized controlled trial in girls," *Pediatrics*, volume 112 (2003), pp. e447–e452, available online at http://pediatrics.aappublications.org/cgi/reprint/112/6/e447.

47. Kathleen Janz and colleagues, "Physical activity and femoral neck bone strength during child-hood: the Iowa bone development study," *Bone*, volume 41 (2007), pp. 216–222.

48. Keith Loud, Catherine Gordon, and colleagues, "Correlates of stress fractures among pre-adolescent and adolescent girls," *Pediatrics*, volume 115 (2005), pp. e399–e406, available online at http://pediatrics.aappublications.org/cgi/content/full/115/4/e399.

49. For example, in one recent study, 29 percent of girls who had broken a bone had a history of not drinking any milk, compared with 12 percent of girls who had never broken a bone; but among boys, there was no significant difference in the likelihood of drinking milk, or not drinking milk,

when comparing boys who had broken a bone with boys who had never broken a bone. The reference is "Fractures during growth: potential role of a milk-free diet," *Osteoporosis International,* volume 18 (2007), pp. 1601–1607. In addition, C. McGartland and colleagues found that drinking soda was associated with brittle bones in girls but not in boys; see their article "Carbonated soft drink consumption and bone mineral density in adolescence," *Journal of Bone and Mineral Research,* volume 18 (2003), pp. 1563–1569. In boys, activity seems to be even more important in determining bone density than it is in girls; see, for example, Susi Kriemler and colleagues, "Weight-bearing bones are more sensitive to physical exercise in boys than in girls during pre- and early puberty: a cross-sectional study," *Osteoporosis International,* volume 19 (2008), pp. 1749–1758. For more evidence that diet is the primary determinant of bone density in females, whereas activity is the primary determinant of bone density in males, see my chapter entitled "Dietary Phosphorus as a Nutritional Toxin: The Influence of Age and Sex," pp. 158–168 in Victor Preedy and Ronald Watson, eds., *Reviews in Food and Nutrition Toxicity* (New York: CRC Press, 2003).

50. D. Ma and G. Jones, "Soft drink and milk consumption, physical activity, bone mass, and upper limb fractures in children: a population-based case-control study," *Calcified Tissues International,* volume 75 (2004), pp. 286–291.

51. Katherine Tucker and colleagues, "Colas, but not other carbonated beverages, are associated with low bone mineral density in older women: the Framingham Osteoporosis Study," *American Journal of Clinical Nutrition,* volume 84 (2006), pp. 936–942.

52. C. McGartland and colleagues, "Carbonated soft drink consumption and bone mineral density in adolescence" (see earlier reference).

53. L. Esterle and colleagues, "Milk, rather than other foods, is associated with vertebral bone mass and circulating IGF-1 in female adolescents," *Osteoporosis International,* volume 20 (2009), pp. 567–575. See also Leann Matlik and colleagues, "Perceived milk intolerance is related to bone mineral content in 10- to 13-year-old female adolescents," *Pediatrics,* volume 120 (2007), pp. e669–e677, available online at http://pediatrics.aappublications.org/cgi/content/full/120/3/e669. The role of milk in building strong bones seems to be especially important in Caucasian girls; see, for example, another recent report from Esterle's group, "Higher milk requirements for bone mineral accrual in adolescent girls bearing specific Caucasian genotypes in the VDR promoter," *Journal of Bone and Mineral Research,* volume 24 (2009), pp. 1389–1397.

54. A. Z. Budek and colleagues, "Dietary protein intake and bone mineral content in adolescents," *Osteoporosis International,* volume 18 (2007), pp. 1661–1667.

55. See, for example, the paper by Norman Carvalho and colleagues, "Severe nutritional deficiencies in toddlers resulting from health food milk alternatives," *Pediatrics,* volume 107 (2001), pp. e46–e53, available online at http://pediatrics.aappublications.org/cgi/reprint/107/4/e46.

56. Mary Murphy and colleagues, "Drinking flavored or plain milk is positively associated with nutrient intake and is not associated with adverse effects on weight status in U.S. children and adolescents," *Journal of the American Dietetic Association,* volume 108 (2008), pp. 631–639.

57. In my experience, lactose intolerance is over-diagnosed among children. Before assuming that your child is lactose-intolerant, ask: can she eat a bowl of regular ice cream without getting severe GI symptoms? If she can, then she is not lactose-intolerant. Lactose intolerance means that a child does not have enough of the enzyme *lactase,* which breaks down milk sugar (lactose) into its component sugars, glucose and galactose. Buy pre-digested milk such as Lactaid milk, and mix in some lactase enzymes (available at most grocery stores) into the Lactaid milk. Those simple measures will be sufficient for most children who truly have mild-to-moderate lactose intolerance. If in doubt about the diagnosis, ask your doctor to request a *hydrogen breath test.* As the AAP Committee on Nutrition observed in its review article on this topic, "some patients think they are lactose intolerant when they prove not to be . . . ." The hydrogen breath test is a simple, non-invasive test that can resolve the confusion. You can read the full text of the AAP's Committee on Nutrition at http://pediatrics.aappublications.org/cgi/content/full/118/3/1279. The reference is "Lactose intolerance in infants, children, and adolescents," *Pediatrics,* volume 118 (2006), pp. 1279–1286.

58. Jennifer Flynn, Stella Foley, and Graeme Jones, "Can BMD assessed by DXA at age 8 predict fracture risk in boys and girls during puberty? An eight-year prospective study," *Journal of Bone and Mineral Research,* volume 22 (2007), pp. 1463–1467.

59. Karin Allor Pfeiffer and colleagues, "Sport participation and physical activity in adolescent females across a four-year period," *Journal of Adolescent Health,* volume 39 (2006), pp. 523–529.

60. Rod Dishman and colleagues, "Physical self-concept and self-esteem mediate cross-sectional relations of physical activity and sport participation with depression symptoms among adolescent girls," *Health Psychology,* volume 25 (2006), pp. 396–407.

61. Maike ter Wolbeek and colleagues, "Predictors of persistent and new-onset fatigue in adolescent girls," *Pediatrics,* volume 121 (2008), pp. e449-e457, available online at http://pediatrics.aappublications.org/cgi/content/full/121/3/e449.

62. Elsie Taveras and colleagues, "The influence of wanting to look like media figures on adolescent physical activity," *Journal of Adolescent Health,* volume 35 (2004), pp. 41–50.

63. Tucker Center, *The 2007 Tucker Center Research Report,* p. 21.

64. Jeanne Nichols and colleagues, "Prevalence of the female athlete triad syndrome among high school athletes," *Archives of Pediatrics and Adolescent Medicine,* volume 160 (2006), pp. 137–142, available online at http://archpedi.ama-assn.org/cgi/content/full/160/2/137.

65. M. K. Torstveit and J. Sundgot-Borgen, "Participation in leanness sports but not training volume is associated with menstrual dysfunction," *British Journal of Sports Medicine,* volume 39 (2005), pp. 141–147.

66. If you're not familiar with group contrast effects, you will find a good introduction to the topic in Judith Rich Harris, *The Nurture Assumption: Why Children Turn Out the Way They Do,* 2nd ed. (New York: Simon & Schuster, 2009), chapter 7, pp. 115–135.

67. See, for example, the closing paragraphs in Kelly Holleran, "Educators report benefits from gender-segregated teaching," *Charleston Daily Mail* (West Virginia), November 7, 2007.

68. Carol Cronin Weisfeld and colleagues, "Female inhibition in mixed-sex competition among young adolescents," *Ethology and Sociobiology,* volume 3 (1982), pp. 29–42.

69. Kandy James, "'You can feel them looking at you': the experiences of adolescent girls at swimming pools," *Journal of Leisure Research,* volume 32 (2000), pp. 262–280. Although this report describes girls' experience at swimming pools, I've heard similar comments made by girls in almost every other kind of physical activity when boys are present.

70. See, for example, Anna Engel, "Sex roles and gender stereotyping in young women's participation in sport," *Feminism and Psychology,* volume 4 (1994), pp. 439–448. A number of schools that have adopted the single-sex format for physical education have found that the all-girls format results in more girls participating. For example, teacher Janet Fendley says that she was "astounded" by the increase in girls' participation in physical education after her school (Smith Elementary in Martinsville, Indiana) adopted the single-sex format for physical education. See Hannah Lodge, "Some gain advantage from single-sex education," *Reporter-Times* (Martinsville, IN), August 21, 2006. Likewise, physical education instructors noticed a big jump in participation at Andersen Junior High School in Chandler, Arizona, after that school adopted the single-sex format for physical education. See Mike Burkett, "Teachers like same-sex classes," *Mesa Independent* (Chandler, AZ), August 22, 2006.

71. Fabienne d'Arripe-Longueville and Christophe Gernigon have published several articles on this topic: see, for example, "Peer-assisted learning in the physical activity domain: dyad type and gender differences," *Journal of Sport and Exercise Psychology,* volume 24 (2002), pp. 219–238.

72. Tucker Center, *The 2007 Tucker Center Research Report,* p. 18.

73. Richard Ryckman and Jane Hamel, "Male and female adolescents' motives related to involvement in organized team sports," *International Journal of Sport Psychology,* volume 26 (1995), pp. 383–397.

74. Kandy James, "What designers should know about how adolescent girls use space," *Implications* (a newsletter from the University of Minnesota), volume 4, number 9 (2006), online at http://www.informedesign.umn.edu/_news/sept_v04r-p.pdf.

75. Courtney Martin, *Perfect Girls, Starving Daughters: The Frightening New Normalcy of Hating Your Body* (New York: Free Press, 2007), p. 256.

76. Madeline Levine, *The Price of Privilege: How Parental Pressure and Material Advantage Are Creating a Generation of Disconnected and Unhappy Kids* (New York: HarperCollins, 2006), p. 183.

CHAPTER 7

1. T. S. Eliot, *The Four Quartets,* section II.

2. For a scholarly review of the evidence that girls on average are more concerned with pleasing their parents than boys are—not only in our species, but also among juvenile chimpanzees—see my book *Boys Adrift,* chapter 2, especially the section "What Are Little Girls Made Of?" pp. 22–27.

3. Benedict Groeschel describes the years of puberty as the years of spiritual awakening in *Spiritual Passages: The Psychology of Spiritual Development* (New York: Crossroads, 1983), especially in the sections "Stages of Human Development," pp. 43–53, and "Religion of Adolescence," pp. 68–69.

4. All quotes in this paragraph are from Christian Smith and Melinda Lundquist Denton, *Soul Searching* (New York: Oxford University Press, 2005), p. 261.

5. The story of Deborah Norris, and the quotes from Stephanie Berry and William Pollack, are found in Elizabeth Olson, "A rise in efforts to spot abuse in youth dating," *New York Times,* January 3, 2009, online at www.nytimes.com/2009/01/04/us/04abuse.html.

6. From *Jenseits von Gut und Böse,* chapter 4, section 75. Nietzsche's original reads, "*Grad und Art der Geschlechtlichkeit eines Menschen reicht bis in den letzten Gipfel seines Geistes hinauf.*" The translation is my own.

7. Robert Bly and Marion Woodman, *The Maiden King: The Reunion of Masculine and Feminine* (New York: Holt, 1998), p. xvii.

8. For more on this point, see Anne Constantinople, "'Masculinity–Femininity': an exception to a famous dictum?" *Feminism and Psychology,* volume 15 (2005), pp. 385–407.

9. The breakthrough publication in this regard—the article that really changed the way scholars thought about gender, crystallizing the then-emerging understanding of gender as being two-dimensional rather than one-dimensional—was Alfred Heilbrun, "Measurement of masculine and feminine sex identities as independent dimensions," *Journal of Consulting and Clinical Psychology,* volume 44 (1976), pp. 183–190.

10. In book 3, §270 of *Die Fröhliche Wissenschaft* (*The Gay Science*), Nietzsche writes, "*Du sollst der werden, der du bist*": you should become what you are. Nietzsche understood that becoming who you are is not an easy task: the subtitle of his final book, *Ecco Homo,* was "*Wie man wird, was man ist*": how one becomes what one is. Nietzsche himself cited the Greek poet/philosopher Pindar as his inspiration for this idea.

11. Bly and Woodman, *The Maiden King,* p. 173.

12. Bly and Woodman, p. 22. "Disappointment" is capitalized in the original.

13. Bly and Woodman, pp. 22, 23.

14. Courtney Martin, *Perfect Girls, Starving Daughters: The Frightening New Normalcy of Hating Your Body* (New York: Free Press, 2007), p. 251.

15. For more about the negative consequences of the hook-up culture for women in college and beyond, see Kathleen Bogle, *Hooking Up: Sex, Dating, and Relationships on Campus* (New York: NYU Press, 2008), especially chapters 6 and 7.

16. Bly and Woodman, *The Maiden King,* p. 20, cite Joseph Chilton Pearce, *Evolution's End: Claiming the Potential of Our Intelligence* (New York: HarperCollins, 1992) as the source of this idea: see chapter 22 in Pearce's book, especially p. 190.

17. For more on this point, see Kathleen Kovner Kline, ed., *Authoritative Communities: The Scientific Case for Nurturing the Whole Child* (New York: Springer, 2008), especially pp. 17–18.

18. Tom Slater, "Call of Duty: Modern Warfare 2 smashes industry records," *GamesBeat,* November 27, 2009, online at http://games.venturebeat.com/2009/11/27/call-of-duty-modern-warfare-2-smashes-industry-records/.

19. Smith and Denton, *Soul Searching,* p. 221.

20. Smith and Denton, table 34, p. 222.

21. Smith and Denton, table 36, p. 224.

22. Smith and Denton, p. 225.

23. Smith and Denton, table 37, p. 225.

24. Smith and Denton, p. 194.

25. Smith and Denton, p. 246.

26. Lisa Miller and Merav Gur, "Religiosity, depression, and physical maturation in adolescent girls," *Journal of the American Academy of Child and Adolescent Psychiatry,* volume 41 (2002), pp. 206–214.

27. W. A. Mirola, "A refuge for some: gender differences in the relationship between religious involvement and depression," *Sociology of Religion,* volume 60 (1999), pp. 419–437.

28. Shirley Feldman and colleagues, "Is 'what is good for the goose good for the gander'? Sex differences in relations between adolescent coping and adult adaptation," *Journal of Research on Adolescence,* volume 5 (1995), pp. 333–359.

29. Alethea Desrosiers and Lisa Miller, "Relational spirituality and depression in adolescent girls," *Journal of Clinical Psychology,* volume 63 (2007), pp. 1021–1037.

30. Desrosiers and Miller, "Relational spirituality and depression in adolescent girls," p. 1032.

31. Rabbi Sasso made these remarks to Christa Tippett on the public radio program *Speaking of Faith,* May 7, 2008, available online at http://speakingoffaith.publicradio.org/programs/spirituality ofparenting/index.shtml.

32. T. S. Eliot, *The Four Quartets,* section II.

33. This is a quotation from a teenager interviewed by Smith and Denton, *Soul Searching,* p. 133.

34. Smith and Denton, p. 133. Italics in original.

35. Smith and Denton, p. 135.

36. Smith and Denton, p. 179.

37. The passage I have in mind is from T. S. Eliot's *Ash Wednesday,* section V: "Where shall the word be found, where shall the word / Resound? Not here, there is not enough silence."

38. The first three sentences of this paragraph are my paraphrase of Smith and Denton, *Soul Searching,* p. 267.

39. Carole Townsend, "Amigos for Christ helps hurricane victims in Nicaragua," *Gwinnett Daily Post* (Georgia), November 7, 2006.

40. Smith and Denton, *Soul Searching,* make this comment (p. 247): "Most American adolescents live the vast majority of their extrafamilial lives in age-stratified institutions and consuming age-targeted products and services. American youth spend about 35 to 40 waking hours per week from between 12 and 17 years in mass-education schools that sort them into classes by single-year age differences. Teens spend the greater part of their weekdays with and being socialized by their age-identical peers. In off-school hours, they often spend many hours watching television programs that are also targeted to their specific age groups. Another major use of time by young people is in sports, hobbies, and play, also spent with other youth of similar age. Structurally, therefore, the schedules and institutions that organize youths' lives tend to isolate and limit their contacts, exposures, and ideas to those available from others their own age. In such situations, trends in and pressures from peer groups become highly influential and narrow."

41. Quoted in Sarah Kershaw, "How much Girl Talk is too much?" *New York Times,* September 11, 2008, online at www.nytimes.com/2008/09/11/health/11iht-11talk.16078388.html.

42. Quoted in Sarah Kershaw's article (see previous reference).

43. For an encyclopedic exposition of the decline in such groups—after a peak in the mid-20th century—see Robert D. Putnam, *Bowling Alone: The Collapse and Revival of American Community* (New York, Simon & Schuster, 2000).

44. Bly and Woodman, *The Maiden King,* p. 22.

45. Bly and Woodman, p. 138.

46. Bly and Woodman, p. 180.

permission credits

The following images have been reproduced with permission of the copyright holder:

Pg. 25: Figure 1 is reprinted with permission of the American Psychological Association from the article by Brooke E. Wells and Jean M. Twenge, "Changes in young people's sexual behavior and attitudes, 1943–1999: a cross-temporal meta-analysis," *Review of General Psychology,* volume 9, number 3 (2005), p. 254.

Pg. 29: Figure 2 is reprinted with permission of the American Psychological Association from the article by Barbara L. Fredrickson, Tomi-Ann Roberts, Stephanie M. Noll, Diane M. Quinn, and Jean M. Twenge, "That swimsuit becomes you: sex differences in self-objectification, restrained eating, and math performance," *Journal of Personality and Social Psychology,* volume 75, number 1 (1998), p. 279.

Pg. 69: Photograph is by James Carver-Grenside, www.flickr.com/photos/jamescg/.

Pg. 90: Figure 3 is reprinted by permission of Oxford University Press from the article by Jennifer Ahern, Sandro Galea, Alan Hubbard, Lorraine Midanik, and S. Leonard Syme, entitled "'Culture of Drinking' and Individual Problems with Alcohol Use," *American Journal of Epidemiology,* volume 167, number 9 (2008), p. 1046.

Pg. 108: Figure 4 is in the public domain.

Pg. 110: Figure 5 is a registered trademark of the Playtex Marketing Corporation.

Pp. 134, 135: Figures 6 and 7 are reprinted with permission from Elsevier from the journal *Hormones and Behavior,* volume 54, Janice M.

index